RAY ARCEL

RAY ARCEL
A Boxing Biography

Donald Dewey

McFarland & Company, Inc., Publishers

Jefferson, North Carolina, and London

Unless otherwise indicated within the text or in the endnotes, the quotations appearing in this book come from an unpublished memoir Ray Arcel wrote with his wife Stephanie in his last years and to which she gave the author total access.

All photographs courtesy Stephanie Arcel.

Frontispiece: A dandyish Arcel during one of his frequent road trips with fighters, this time in Portland, Oregon, in the late twenties.

LIBRARY OF CONGRESS CATALOGUING-IN-PUBLICATION DATA

Dewey, Donald, 1940–
    Ray Arcel : a boxing biography / Donald Dewey.
      p.   cm.
    Includes bibliographical references and index.

    ISBN 978-0-7864-6968-0
    softcover : acid free paper ∞

    1. Arcel, Ray.   2. Boxers (Sports) — United States — Biography.
I. Title.
GV1132.A675D48 2012
796.83092 — dc23
[B]   2012014489

BRITISH LIBRARY CATALOGUING DATA ARE AVAILABLE

Front cover: Ray Arcel in a Philadelphia gym in the early thirties with Barney Ross (photograph courtesy Stephanie Arcel)

Manufactured in the United States of America

McFarland & Company, Inc., Publishers
  Box 611, Jefferson, North Carolina 28640
  www.mcfarlandpub.com

For Stephanie Arcel
The Muse of Muses

Table of Contents

Acknowledgments

In addition to Stephanie Arcel, the author is indebted to numerous people for the time they gave him to answer often irritating questions and to point him in the right direction to annoy other people. I would particularly mention in this regard Ray Arcel's granddaughters, niece, and several in-laws; Jerry Izenberg; the late Bill Gallo and Gil Clancy; Fran Kessler; David Smith of the New York Public Library; Steve Siegel; and Roy Singh.

Introduction

If Ray Arcel had been in politics, he would have been a key advisor to every president from Woodrow Wilson to Bill Clinton. If he had been in the motion picture industry, he would have been responsible for putting both Rudolph Valentino and Denzel Washington on their feet in front of the camera. As an exercise guru, he was active before Jack LaLanne was born. He was associated with more championships than the New York Yankees, more crash diets than Jenny Craig, and more conmen than P.T. Barnum. One of his most conspicuous rewards for his Zelig-like ubiquity was a Mob-ordered murder attempt that left him barely clinging to life.

Arcel's realm was the theater of physical prowess and organizational savagery known as professional boxing. Without his prominence for much of the 20th century, backers of the sport would have had considerably less to back, opponents of the sport would have had markedly less to rail against, and the very notion of professional boxing as a sport would have lost much of the credibility it has sweated to retain. His prominence was all the more startling insofar as he himself was not a fighter, a promoter, or a manager, but a trainer — a role the popular imagination has usually configured as a sweater, a peak-cap, and a towel that jump up into the ring with a stool whenever the bell announces the end of a boxing round. Arcel didn't disdain such stereotypes; he just made sure they remained irrelevant.

Arcel's journey through prizefighting crossed all the ethnic timelines and tested all the structural power lines. When he started out, professional boxing was an Irish and Jewish escape hatch from slums; before he was finished, he had guided Italians, African Americans, and Latinos toward ghetto exits. The promoters who benefited from his skills ran the gamut from neighborhood gym satraps to shadowy underworld bosses to the glitzy overworld dream guys of casino hotel arenas. Long before

1

HBO and ESPN were putting their call letters into the ring, he was going through boxing's ABCs as the front man for a national television network. He shook hands with mayors and governors, defied congressmen, and received the rarest of honors from presidents. Ray Arcel was always a main event.

He was also an anomaly in a game that was never play. His austere persona and laconic pronouncements constantly drew comparisons with Talmudic scholars and others who were attributed with more intellectual than physical priorities. He was fluent at turning questions back on the questioner, whether those doing the asking were government bodies or newspapermen. The former fumed and threatened retaliation, the latter welcomed him to their club of visceral skepticism. It was the least of the paradoxes of Arcel's career that someone so unassuming when he wasn't directly involved in training should have been able to reduce the most critical sportswriters of his age (Damon Runyon, Red Smith, Bill Heinz, etc.) to a fan club. "Don't be a district attorney" was a phrase attached to him for decades — both as a warning that he had said as much as he intended saying on a given topic and as a lament that there were too many accusations to go around to be smug about landing on some specific one. Inevitably, this produced some boilerplate tales about him that contained everything except fact and some defenses of his own that contained everything except candor.

Statistically, Arcel's record of training champions, from Benny Leonard to Roberto Duran and Larry Holmes, set precedents; in absolutely every one of the classic boxing weight categories at least one charge ended up wearing a jeweled belt. But from the very start, Arcel's career raised questions, not least why a teenager said to be intellectually gifted enough to be accepted by New York's prestigious Stuyvesant High School and encouraged at home to become a doctor would end up as a boxing trainer. The choice was not some lazy development of circumstance, either; before he was out of his teens, when others his age were contemplating romantic lives, including that of being a boxer, he let it be known that training was for him. Within the boxing world there was similar wonder about why, despite regular opportunities, he generally eschewed the more lucrative role of being a manager. To these and similar questions his admirers in and out of the media were usually content replying with some variation on "he worries about fighters, not the fights." Arcel's own response? "Don't be a district attorney."

For someone so heavily identified with New York, Boston, London, and other metropolitan boxing centers throughout his long life (he died at the age of 94 in 1994), Arcel, in fact, saw the light of day in Terre Haute, Indiana. It wasn't a turn-of-the-century Terre Haute of straw hats and ice cream parlors, but of the Socialist firebrand and union organizer Eugene V. Debs, an early political acquaintance of Arcel's father. When the family was forced to move to New York City because Arcel's fatally ill mother wanted to be near her parents for the end, the daily reality became that of the scuffling Jewish neighborhoods portrayed by Sergio Leone's *Once Upon a Time in America* where the brutality of violence was inseparable from the brutality of poverty. It was in this ambience that Arcel discovered what would be the economic, political, and social center of his life — the gymnasium. Over the years that followed, the gyms would have many names and locations (some would have the same name in different locations), but always they would serve as Arcel's canvas, both literally and figuratively.

1

The Spare Man

One of baseball's oldest clichés is that the sign of a good umpire is his consistency. By that criterion Ray Arcel would have made a phenomenal umpire over decades of replies to questions about his ring experiences, his impressions of given fighters and promoters, and his views on the techniques and cultural impact of professional boxing. So consistent was he in his responses that sifting through volumes of newspaper columns and magazine articles about him leaves the suspicion that, much more than in the cases of other sports figures, writers took to lifting quotes from each other, commas and colons included. Recordings of interviews with sports and non-sports questioners alike also replay the exact same anecdotes and reminiscences, the principal additions being the subject's adenoidal New York tones and intermittent dry laugh. What undercuts the suspicion of mass plagiarism, however, is that even an extensive memoir he compiled with his second wife Stephanie at her request resounds with tales, turns of phrase, and a narrative arc identical to those scattered throughout hundreds of periodicals from Boston and New York to Los Angeles and Seattle. What Ray Arcel said once, he said a thousand times, and mostly without contradicting himself.

The uniformity of his reflections at least metaphorically suggested another kind of trainer — this was the way things were tracked, there were narrow rules governing it, no veering left or right if you expected to get anywhere. For all his insistence that every fighter had to be handled differently, that no two boxers were the same, all his perceptions came from within the Ray Arcel universe that answered to very fixed laws. And the first of these laws, inscribed more deeply the longer his career stretched, was that he simply didn't want to be surprised by anything that happened. The issue wasn't mere commotion. If a fighter had a reputation as a carouser, Arcel prepared himself for that, even if it meant having to pull his charge out of bars or away from the cops in the wee hours. If the fighter never saw a bed he didn't want to keep warm until noon, Arcel prepared himself for that, too, even if it meant having to keep a bucket of cold water at the ready. If the fighter had a tendency to sit down for a meal and confuse the platters for the plates, Arcel was equally prepared, right down to imposing a diet of chewing without swallowing. Character couldn't — or shouldn't — have caught him unawares; that was the essence of his training approach. But his confidence in having read the character of his fighters also described the contours of his own character, and that wasn't a particularly liberal exercise. Once he had formulated his approach, further reviews weren't contemplated. It was hardly coincidental that most of those around him singled out Roberto Duran's infamous *"no mas"* withdrawal against Sugar Ray Leonard in November 1980 as Arcel's most discombobulating moment as a trainer. Whatever he had assured himself of with Duran over years of professional collaboration and friendship, *"no mas"* had never been an ingredient of it. There had been no preparation for such a Roberto Duran character.

Although he trained champions in every classification that existed in his time, Arcel himself maintained a life-long image of all that was spare — physically so, emotionally so, gentlemanly so. Physically, he indulged no extras; the years brought graying, hollows, and wrinkles but no constitutional changes in his slight frame. At the table he was even more Spartan than spare, indulging no potatoes, bread, or other starches, eating meat economically, outlawing desserts altogether. A preoccupation with weight (for himself as much as for his fighters) made water a prime nemesis: "When you swallow it, it stays in the body." Emotionally, what couldn't be dealt with philosophically was consigned to memory, from where even resentments and hilarities could be evoked at leisure. Courtesy wasn't optional, it was the premise for everything from conversing to going through a door (women first). Surviving pictures suggest a man who went with his family to the beach because that was expected of him but never thought it necessary to strip down further than a sports shirt and slacks. If there was a characteristic photo of Ray Arcel, its center wasn't the Benny Leonard or Larry Holmes pictured next to him, or even his own particular level of tight grin for the occasion, it was his white dress shirt closed to the wrists. Sometimes he wore a tie visibly, but always he wore a tie.

It was A. J. Liebling in *The Sweet Science* (1956) who supplied scores of writers with figurative access to Arcel by saying he was "severe and decisive, like a teacher in a Hebrew school."[1] There had been comparable impressions in print before, but any subsequent profile that did not lean heavily on images of the learned and the scholarly (Torah references didn't hurt) has been lost to the ages. Most of these evaluations did double duty: establishing even his blandest observation as a Chauncey Gardiner kind of laconic wisdom and reassuring that, exceptional or not, Arcel was evidence that professional boxing had more colors than black and blue. His most extravagant supporters in the press could go so far as to claim that none — repeat, none — of the fighters under his tutelage had ever been hurt in the ring. More routinely, there were such aphorisms as "to rest is to rust," "never overestimate yourself and never underestimate the other guy," and "a quitter never wins and a winner never quits," cited as being thrown out offhandedly and as being critical keys to his personality. Whatever else emerged from such media celebration, a very civil Ray Arcel did.

Being civil, of course, frequently has a backspin: What you see is all you're entitled to get. Asked if he could recall a single remark from Arcel that had surprised him in all their years of friendship, veteran sportswriter Jerry Izenberg admitted having to think for some time before falling back on the trainer's response to the Duran fiasco.[2] Arcel's second wife of some four decades learned of the existence of his step-mother only when they were doing the memoir she had requested.[3] What she didn't learn about even then was the existence of extra in-laws — a half-sister and a step-brother Arcel had never bothered to mention to her.[4] At the core of these befuddlements of people who might have been expected to know more was another Arcel maxim, honored as a given in his relationships rather than as an explicit instruction: "Don't be a district attorney." A variation on this, offered whenever questioned about his relationship to somebody caught up in some personal drama or even criminal scandal, however long ago it might have been, was simply, "That was none of my business." Long before don't-ask-don't-tell, there was the Arcel generation's why-even-think-about-asking — an assumption so recessive that violating it bewildered its carriers. This didn't make all the anecdotes and reminiscences genteel; after all, they were mostly culled from the boxing world. Nor did it make them the truth and the whole truth; when all was said and done, forgetting about a sister took some doing. So did a conspicuous pattern of avoiding questions about the worst moments of his life — the death of a wife, the attempted suicide of a daughter — by quickly turning the conversation back to the significance of the fights he was working on at the time or retreating to some version of a baffled "Who can explain that kind of thing?" But it did make their narrator as instinctively economical and single-minded as he had trained the best part of a century of professional boxers to be.

2

The Boy from Indiana

In 1883, poet Emma Lazarus penned the words "Give me your tired, your poor, your huddled masses yearning to breathe free, the wretched refuse of your teeming shore" that would soon afterward end up inscribed on the Statue of Liberty. It was also in that year that Adelia Arcel and her three teenage sons, Ramil, Solomon, and David, were among the thousands of Russian Jews then streaming into New York to escape their homeland's latest pogrom in retaliation for the shooting of Czar Alexander II. Not with them was Adelia's husband Ramil, killed by Czarist troops back in Odessa.

What the widow found in the city after an arduous Atlantic crossing was a metropolis boiling over with social tensions. In addition to the nativist hostility of long-established residents of other ethnic backgrounds, she came up quickly enough against the snobbism of Central European Jews toward Russian émigrés — a separation that cut through religion and economics as much as through general cultural outlooks, and that for generations would abet the Eastern Europeans being squeezed into the scruffy tenements of Manhattan's Lower East Side. Already hampered by her primitive English, Adelia decided New York was not the best setting for gaining an economic foothold for her sons, who themselves were divided between remaining together as a family and ceding to restlessness about going off to start their own lives. The family bonds prevailed, and not for the last time. Probably not familiar with the quote itself, Adelia nevertheless embraced the often-heard advice from the late *New York Tribune* publisher Horace Greeley to "Go west, young man." Although her grandson would later say his forebears were "just put on a train that stopped in Terre Haute, Indiana, and they got off," family stories suggest that fellow immigrants from Russia named Levine had acquaintances already established there, and Adelia followed their lead.

While considerably less volatile than New York, the Terre Haute of the time was hardly Eden. Although its population of some 26,000 could have fit into a Manhattan neighborhood, the city had its own urban disorders brought on by recently ravaging floods that residents would need long months to overcome. It didn't exactly fit the profile as the ideal place for observant Jews, either, with one of its chief commercial claims being that it ranked among the country's most important whiskey distillers, and its religious institutions not including a single synagogue until eight years later, in 1891.[1] This was of no little importance to Adelia, who kept a Kosher home and insisted on strict adherence to Sabbath abstentions. But the woman who had emigrated all the way from Russia wasn't about to be sidetracked by relatively minor inconveniences. Within a few short months, while their friends the Levines began selling handkerchiefs and other dry goods, she and her sons established themselves as peddlers in dried fruits, candy, and nuts both within the city and in the surrounding area. On lean days they had to tote their wares beyond the city limits on foot, in better days they were able to reach their customers in a horse-drawn cart. Eventually they were successful enough to get off the road and establish a wholesale business in which others came to them for product. The step after that was the opening of a store called Addie's Confectionary in honor of the family matriarch.

But business success proved a costly tradeoff for the family. Within six years of each other, Ramil (in June 1891, at the age of 27) and Solomon (in December 1897, at the age of 31) died of respiratory ailments. That left David to manage the store with his mother. The shop's prominence boosted David's social standing, and he was soon hobnobbing with local politicians, most conspicuously with Eugene V. Debs, who would later go on to establish the Socialist Party and run five times for president. When David Arcel knew him, Debs was a militant in the railway workers union, but had also already served as Terre Haute's city clerk twice and been an Indiana state assemblyman. It didn't hurt Arcel's relations with him that Debs had a long family history in the grocery store business.[2]

In September 1898, at the age of 38, David married Rose Wachsman, who as a child had emigrated with her family from Rumania to Brooklyn. How he met the appreciably younger Wachsman (she was only 22) never became family knowledge, with descendants converging only on the view that he was "very closed-mouthed about personal things" — a description that would also be applied generations later to another member of the family. Their first-born, named after the grandfather who was killed in Russia and the uncle who died in Terre Haute, was Ramil (Ray) Arcel, who came into the world on August 30, 1899, at 812 South Fourth Street — a neighborhood of mostly modest clapboard houses intersected by small commercial streets. With Terre Haute's first synagogue only a few blocks away at 418 South Fourth Street, it came as close as anywhere else to being the city's Jewish area. But beyond that, it was also a district that, for both good and bad, was staking a claim to historical footnotes. Within sight of the Arcel living room window was the home of Russell Benjamin Harrison, the only son of the 23rd president of the United States and the operator of the city's trams. Then there were the Keatons, the grandparents of silent screen star Buster Keaton. A few houses closer lived the Goldmans with their sons Mayer, who would become synonymous with the right of every accused person to have a public defender, and Edwin, who would lend his name to one of New York City's most emblematic bands. Also nearby were Max and Theresa Blumberg, who rented a room to teacher Ida Finkelstein. When the African American George Ward confessed to stabbing and shooting Finkelstein to death in 1901, he was dragged from his jail cell by a mob, sledge-hammered to death, then had his body mutilated, burned, and lynched. According to official local documents, Ward has been Terre Haute's only lynching victim.[3]

The Arcels had their own reasons for remembering 1901. After months of failing health, Rose was diagnosed as having diabetes, then an incurable disease. Pregnant with her second child, she asked her husband to move back near her parental home in Brooklyn so she could be there for both the birth and what she had come to accept as the end. After liquidating his store, David Arcel did just that, also bringing his mother along to the kind of Lower East Side flat that Adelia had shunned upon first arriving in America and that his older son would remember only as "cold and dark." Shortly after the move back east, the second son, Solomon, named after the younger deceased uncle, was born. That was also the beginning of a years-long game of tag with record bureaus, since the teenage Solomon, in the name of qualifying for the draft during World War I, would add four years to his age, making him not only older than Ray but born out of wedlock.[4] Neither was true.

David hardly found the same business situation in New York that he had left with Addie's Confectionary in Terre Haute. Initially he tried to go into the dairy business, wholesaling cheeses and creams. But, as his older son acknowledged years later, "that was a mistake. He knew nothing about dairy." When that business failed, the family was forced to fall back on the little that was left from the proceeds from the liquidated store in Indiana for getting along. But with David unable to find a niche for his familiar candy and nuts trade for months, the most modest daily expenses became extravagant. As "cold and dark" as the Lower East Side flat was, its rent was also more than other places were demanding uptown. Thus, after only a few months of living at the southern tip of Manhattan, the family moved first to East 93rd Street, then further up to the dowdy East Harlem neighborhood of 106th Street between Second and Third avenues. The latter apartment might not have had much glamour, but it did have the cachet of five rooms. Depending on which block you called home, the area was either heavily Jewish or something of a "Little Italy"; the block the Arcels moved into was considered part of the latter. Moreover, within its concentration of Italian-American families, East Harlem was notorious as a Petri dish for the Black Hand forerunners to the Mafia. If David and Rose Arcel weren't enthusiastic about their move, their boys proved to be even less so, and for a slew of daily reasons on the street.

Not long after moving uptown, Rose succumbed to her diabetes, leaving Ray and Solomon largely in the care of their grandmother while David tried to maintain his footing as a candy agent. The boys went to a public elementary school on 105th Street between First and Second avenues, and, for the religious training insisted upon by their grandmother, to the Talmud Torah at Lexington and 11th Street. In one of the few glimpses given of David's sense of humor, Ray said his father had a habit of wondering aloud "What language could these two be speaking?" whenever his two sons conversed between themselves in the Hebrew they had picked up during their religious lessons. It didn't take the sons long, either, to realize that thanks to Hebrew they could sneak through the stray thought in their father's presence that probably wouldn't have been appreciated in English.

Between one formal learning setting and another, both boys were expected to help out not just with errands, but with fixed jobs. While Solomon worked in a series of garages and machine shops, Ray found work as a delivery boy for groceries in the area. Seventy years after the fact, he told on interviewer:

I'll never forget carrying these huge paper bags of groceries and going down through one staircase after another marked DELIVERY. The only thing that kept my mind off how heavy the bags were was the darkness of those cellar places. I knew if I fell and broke anything, it wasn't the customer who was going to pay for it and it certainly wasn't going to be the store. Dumbwaiters were the only way you delivered in those days, and sometimes you'd pull at the ropes in the cellar until you had your hands full of splinters and little cuts. After I hoisted it all upstairs, I'd wait until the customer took the package and then pull the rope down again, hoping there would be a tip. Sometimes there was, sometimes there wasn't.[5]

Dank cellars on delivery runs weren't the only times Ray had to worry about the darkness of East Harlem. "My father never drank or smoked. His only real vice was this mania he had for fresh baked rolls in the morning. And by the morning I mean five A.M., before the baker started his deliveries to the stores around the neighborhood. So every day before dawn, Sol and I would take turns. We'd have a nickel and we had to go down to get a dozen rolls right out of the oven. Maybe the best thing we got out of it was it helped us overcome any fears we might have had about darkness. The halls in the house were unlit, and the streets, no matter the time of year, were semi-dark. Sometimes you couldn't see your hand in front of your face."

What the boys could see on occasion, they would have preferred not to have seen. "You could never forget you were in a Black Hand neighborhood. They terrorized the local merchants and shook them down for money. More than once, Sol and I had to step over dead bodies in the hallway. We always assumed they were people who hadn't paid up. And for sure, there were a lot of those bodies we were the first ones to discover being up so early in the morning for my father's rolls. It never surprised us when some squad car would come pulling up in front of the house a few hours later."

What squad cars ignored totally were the social relations between the Italian and Jewish kids. Arcel was given to painting a grim picture of Solomon and him being practically the only Jews within miles of their daily tussles with Italian kids, though, in fact, from the point of view of sheer numbers, the Jews outnumbered the Italians in East Harlem. Asked point-blank once "there were no other Jewish families around the neighborhood?" he insisted: "There was none whatsoever."[6] At best, he could have only been recalling the 106th Street block between First and Second avenues where he lived. Stated Arcel:

You can imagine what it was like. If we got to school or home from school without getting into a fight, it was a small miracle. The Italian kids would use that word *mazzacristo* (Christ killer) like it was the most normal thing in the world. All the usual city stuff. *Kike* this, *Kike* that. "You Jews ain't got any guts. You won't fight." Of course, then you *had* to fight. If I got killed, I still had to do it. One thing you had to do was make the other guy respect you. It was really a very rough neighborhood, especially when we first moved there and the other kids didn't know us. Little by little, though, things thawed out. When there was a ball game to be played on the street, usually sewer stickball, suddenly all the ethnic insults stopped.[7]

Arcel also admitted to looking forward to Christmas. "You weren't Christian, Jew, or anything else when you helped to distribute food baskets to the poor families at Christmas. Jimmy Hines*, a big Democratic Party boss, made sure every merchant in his district contributed something to the baskets. Race, color — none of it meant anything at the end of the year. If you were poor, you got your basket. The gratitude of those people was incredibly touching. And speaking personally, no matter how much they weighed and how high up the people lived in those tenements, those baskets never seemed heavy to me and those stairs never seemed steep."

If the Arcels weren't poor enough to rate the baskets, they weren't far from it. Each of the boys had only one pair of shoes for going to school, but otherwise had to go around barefoot, even when playing in the street. "We really didn't think of it as anything special," Ray's second wife Stephanie remembers him telling her. "All the kids went around like that. You came home from school, you took your shoes off, you did any homework you had to do, and if you didn't have a job to go to, you went out and played until it was time for supper."[8]

Which itself wasn't exactly gourmet class:

We managed. That I recall, we never really missed any meals. Sometimes I'd go to the butcher with my father and he'd ask the butcher if there were any liver scraps around for our cat. The butcher never believed we had a cat, but he didn't make a thing out of it. The main thing was we always had this big pot of barley soup in the kitchen, and you'd keep adding to it with this and that as the week went along. After we were there for awhile and got to know some of the kids, we'd have them in for some of the soup. They were mostly Italians, and they'd never had barley soup before. I always thought I made out

*Jimmy Hines was the epitome of the Tammany Hall political boss whose public largesse was sponsored by his private graft. For many years he was considered particularly useful to mobster Dutch Schultz.

pretty good on that because they in turn would invite me to their homes on Sunday nights and I'd get all this great spaghetti. For them it was every day stuff, but for me it was a great treat.

To supplement the food around the kitchen table, there were always petty thefts. "Everybody did it. You'd swipe a potato or two from the grocery stand and make some 'roast mickeys' right there on the street. If a cop came along, he didn't say anything. He knew where you got the potato, but he wasn't going to start hauling kids down to the station house for that. Even better were the weddings on Sunday nights. There was always great food at those receptions, and we'd break in and eat as much as we could before somebody spotted us and chased us out."

Not too long after the death of Rosa, in 1904, David Arcel married the widow Rebecca Turtletaub, who had a nine-year-old son, Sydney, from a first marriage. An emigree with her family from Austria, Rebecca was five years younger than David. Their only child, Mollie, named after her mother, was born in 1906. According to Ray, his step-mother, known familiarly as Becky, was "our mother in every way. She never objected to having our grandmother live with us. She went into the situation with her eyes open, and really never made it feel like she was suffering any hardship. For my grandmother, it was enough that she kept a Kosher home. She was a lovely woman." Other testimony, however, suggests that relations between Ray and Solomon and their step-mother weren't quite so harmonious.[9] In any case, it was Rebecca and her family who supplied most of the guests for Ray's *bar mitzvah.* "My uncles died when they were young, and I didn't really have any family other than Rebecca's. But she went out of her way to make sure it wasn't anything I should have felt shortchanged about."

As for David, his older son depicted him as a somewhat remote figure who mainly made his presence felt when he wasn't satisfied with something. "He was a real disciplinarian. You didn't fall down on the job. He also had this way of saying things so they sounded like those sayings you saw on the schoolroom walls. One was 'Always leave a little something for the next person.' Another was 'Watch your step and never try to get even because you'll never get even.' I never forgot those sayings of his."

David Arcel's ambition for his first-born was that he become a doctor. To this end he made sure Ray stayed at the top of his class in grammar school and was more than receptive when the boy announced one night

Rebecca with Ray and his brother Solomon.

that he wanted to go to the prestigious Peter Stuyvesant High School downtown on 15th Street. Although Ray's interest in Stuyvesant had largely stemmed from the fact that a friend from elementary school was going there, his father seized on it as an occasion for making sure his son profited from the Latin being offered — what he considered a helpful step toward medicine. One of Ray's favorite tales was how he pocketed the nickel he was given for carfare to roller skate the four miles — plus back and forth between his home and school, using the money instead for lunch. But how often he actually did that remains obscure. Widely published stories that he graduated from Stuyvesant find no confirmation in the school's remaining records. Although most administrative materials dating back before 1930 were disposed of years ago, Stuyvesant has maintained what it terms a "discharge" file for monitoring how students left, and Arcel's name does not appear in it. Moreover, his frequently cited assertion that he was a member of the school's cross-country track team finds no endorsement in any yearbook published between 1914 and 1918, the years in which he would have matriculated.[10] At best, Arcel appears to have exaggerated his time at Stuyvesant to one reporter, and, in line with so many of his other statements, this was picked up by subsequent writers until it became part of the boilerplate arguing the trainer's intellectual acuity compared to colleagues. In any case, by his teens he had already set his sights on a goal that didn't require good grades in Latin.

3

Settling In

If Ray Arcel had a center to his life outside school in his early teens, it was at the Union Settlement Hall on East 104th Street between Second and Third avenues. Inspired by Hull House in Chicago, the Settlements (there were dozens of them scattered around the city) represented an initiative by members of the Union Theological Seminary to live in poorer neighborhoods for a closeup appreciation of the daily problems of residents. It was one part getting kids off the street, one part keeping them close to Christian moral principles, and one part setting the groundwork for some viable trade in later years. Given the Protestant sponsorship of the houses, a whiff of the popular "muscular Christianity" of the time could always be detected, but the immediate objective, especially after early missteps toward proselytizing, was what one spokesman characterized as "community, not personal, salvation ... by acting as a clearing house of social needs."[1] The better equipped settlements, such as that on 104th Street, included libraries, penny banks, and gymnasiums, and accommodated hundreds of youths a week. In line with the uptown hall's location in a heavily Jewish neighborhood, Yiddish-language signs were often posted outside for special events. It was at the Settlement that at the age of 15 Ray Arcel had his first direct experience with the world he would make his own for the rest of his life:

> They had all kinds of athletic programs there. Boxing was number one with me, and a lot of my friends were as interested in it as I was. That kept us in shape for what seemed like serious money at the time. In those days there were a lot of small clubs within the settlements, and you could book yourself into them by buying a number of tickets that cost anywhere from a quarter to a dollar. For appearing in a four-round fight, you got 50 percent of the amount of the tickets you sold. The whole purse usually amounted to two or three bucks. You never knew who you were fighting. There were no boxing commission rules or regulations. They didn't weigh you in, they just measured you to make sure you didn't have some giant going in against a runt. The kids

fighting were all from the neighborhood, and one week's opponent could be your second the next week and vice versa. It was really all about challenging one another. Altogether I was in about 12 fights. If they'd had divisions, I would have been a lightweight. After the fights were over, we'd all go to a place called Joe's for coffee and cake. Before we were through, we usually spent most of the dollar or two we'd earned.

Among those Arcel knew through his ring experiences at the Urban Settlement was Benny Valgar. A bantamweight dubbed the "French Flash," Valgar and his widowed mother had fled Czarist Russia under much the same circumstances as Arcel's grandmother and father, but had settled in Paris instead of the United States. When Valgar crossed the Atlantic shortly before the outbreak of World War I, he won the United States amateur championship, then immediately embarked on a professional career. More important for Arcel was that it was Valgar who drew him to Grupps Gymnasium across town at 116th Street near Eighth Avenue — a significant walk for most people from the East Side but not for a teenager gradually clarifying his career intentions. (The trek also turned out to be a short hop compared to the distances Arcel would soon be asked to walk around the city.) Valgar wasn't the only attraction on the West Side; in fact, Grupps Gymnasium was where most of the East Coast–based professional fighters of the day trained. Making Arcel feel immediately at home were the wannabes, almost all of them Jews and Italians from either his East Harlem streets or from his original neighborhood on the Lower East Side. It was there that he met Dai Dollings and Frank "Doc" Bagley, the two trainers who would give him his biggest push toward his career.

Dollings was a Welshman who had moved into boxing after training marathon runners in his home country. In 1914 he had crossed the Atlantic at the request of welterweight Ted "Kid" Lewis (Gershon Mendeloff), who had his eyes on the division championship practically since having his first professional fight at the age of 15, and who counted on Dollings' austere training methods to give him a conditioning edge. A strict vegetarian with a spare body, the Welshman would continue to walk at least 10 miles a day well into his eighties. Lewis, for one, acknowledged being cowed by him. "He was a very strict, conscientious trainer and, much as we all admired him, he had us all scared. He never spared himself when he was training a boxer and was a great believer in hard work. After meals he would take me on the road to cover an average of

12 to 16 miles a day, walking and running. It was stiff work and the call
to bed was the sweetest music of the day for me."[2]

When Arcel first met him at Grupps Gymnasium, Dollings was
merely in his late fifties and thought nothing of dragging teenagers from
one end of Manhattan Island to the other:

> He was a funny sort of guy. He lived on 15th Street and he was so frugal he
> wouldn't spend the nickel to get on a streetcar to get to the gym. He'd walk
> from 15th Street to 116th Street where the gym was. That was about five miles,
> a hundred blocks. Rain, snow, hail, he'd walk. He'd come up to the gym and
> he'd say: "You bloody Americans, you're made of tissue paper." The truth was,
> he wasn't a particularly pleasant guy. He always seemed to be angry. When he
> talked to you, he'd always point his fist at you. I don't think he meant anything
> special by it, but you could see even fighters like Lewis being intimidated by
> it. But I didn't let that bother me. I was so interested in asking him questions,
> I'd walk down to his house with him, and since I didn't have the nickel carfare
> to come back uptown, I'd walk all the way back home.

It took Dollings a little time to acknowledge that the boy was serious
about wanting to become a trainer. Zen masters never probed more for
making a student really think about what he was asking. "Over and over
he kept asking why I wanted to be a trainer. When I told him that was
my ambition, he'd let it go for awhile, as if that was an answer, then
come right back later on with the same question. At first the most I got
out of him was along the lines of 'If you're going to be a trainer, be the
best one or don't bother with it at all.' Maybe I just wore him down,
and I don't think all those marathon walks down to 15th Street with him
hurt. Anyway, I knew I'd made a breakthrough of some kind one day
when he told me I didn't really want to be a trainer, I wanted to be what
he called an analyst."[3]

As Arcel recalled the distinction made by Dollings, "He'd tell me,
'See what the other guy has. See what his strengths are, see what his
weaknesses are. See how you can overcome anything he has to offer. Just
to train your fighters, have them hit the bag and skip rope and develop
stamina, that doesn't mean anything. Get it out of your head this is just
some blooming gymnasium. This is a school where these guys come to
learn their lessons and where you should be learning them, too.'"

And one other thing: "Patience. I didn't realize it at first, but it was
there in just the way he'd listen to my questions hour after hour. Then
he told me the same thing about analyzing fighters. I shouldn't jump to
conclusions too fast, I should have the patience to see if my first impres-

sions were right. If I wasn't going to be patient, I wasn't going to be a trainer *or* an analyst, at least not a very good one."

It was upon this early counsel that the disciple would base his approach to every fighter he handled for most of the 20th century. "Every young man that came to me, I remembered what Dollings had told me. I made a complete study of his personal habits, his temperament, because there are some people you can scold and some people you have to be careful with. No two people are alike. And unless the kid was obviously not cut out for the ring, I always took my time figuring him out."

There were also smaller tips picked up from Dollings that remained in Arcel's head. "One thing you see far too often," he told one interviewer in the 1980s, "is a fighter coming back to his corner after a round and immediately being manhandled by everybody there. This one has this to say, that one has that to say. What I always kept in my mind from watching Dollings was that the fighter came back to *rest*, to *relax*. The last thing he needed was all that screaming at him. A little water, and that should have been it. I think the middleweight Mickey Walker put it best when he said that that minute's rest between rounds was like a week's vacation. I never understood why trainers and managers didn't get that."[4]

If Dai Dollings came with the somewhat exotic background of training marathon runners in Wales, Doc Bagley had a solid ring reputation as the fastest cut man in the business, not to mention a past that included studying medicine, probably the first in his trade to do so. Also in his fifties at the time, he would give Arcel his first practical experiences dealing with professional fighters. "He'd take me in the corner with him to swing the towel on the fighter. Some of those fight clubs were little more than cigar boxes, and not just because of their size. Everybody smoked. If you stood at the back of the arena, you couldn't see the fight because the smoke was so thick. I used to swing the towel to get the fighter a little air.... If I do say so myself, I became a crackerjack towel swinger. I could do all kinds of fancy tricks using that towel on a fighter."

But Bagley had even more tricks between rounds. "In those days you didn't have coagulants to stop bleeding. Bagley was an expert in that situation. What he'd do was chew tobacco, then take some of it out of his mouth and press it on the cut. He called it painting the cut with new skin, and my job was to wave the towel even harder to dry up the skin before the bell rang. It was really effective at stopping the bleeding."

The good news was that Bagley was impressed enough by his towel waver to give him a bigger assignment. The bad news was that Arcel couldn't wait to imitate Bagley down to the grittiest detail:

> One day he called me and told me he had a young man boxing over in New Jersey and wanted me to go over with him. I was thrilled. He couldn't have told me anything that would've excited me more. I had one thought in my head: I was going to be Doc Bagley! I was going to be in charge! I was going to be the one bandaging the boxer's hands! Naturally, the first thing I did was buy a plug of chewing tobacco. I was so excited taking the fighter over to Jersey. So the fight starts, and I'm in the corner, and what I'm secretly hoping is that my fighter gets cut so I can apply the skills I learned from Bagley. Then there was this little flurry in the ring, and I was sure I saw a flow of blood, so I bit down hard into the chewing tobacco. From that moment I didn't know what happened. Suddenly I was underneath the ring, and there was an ambulance there with a doctor examining me. When he asked me what happened and I told him, he was the first of a long line to laugh at me. The next day, after I told Bagley what had happened, I became the laughing stock of the gym.

And that wasn't the only fallout. "I never knew what happened to my fighter. I didn't even know if he collected the money due him. Sometimes I think it was that incident that kept me away from all kinds of tobacco for the rest of my life."

His Jersey debacle aside, though, neither Dollings nor Bagley hesitated to entrust him with duties that might have seemed insignificant to outsiders but that were regarded as crucial to boxing denizens. Through Dollings, for instance, he became close to Kid Lewis, so much so that he ended up being the boxer's Guardian of the Shields. Until 1902, when a London dentist named Jack Marles came up with a special gum shield, fighters wanting to protect their teeth in the ring usually had to resort to orange rinds. That wasn't good enough for Lewis, and, according to Arcel, for a special reason. "[Lewis] had crooked teeth, and the fruit peel thing didn't help him very much. So he had a friend who worked in a dental clinic in London make a sort of gum rubber that could be put in his mouth to prevent him from biting into his lip while he was in the ring. He had four or five of those pieces, and he elected me Guardian of the Gum Shields! I used to keep them in a soap box until he needed them. And it was no small thing when he needed them, either. We're not talking about the slip-in mouthpieces that came along later. Lewis's teeth were so crooked it usually took about 15 minutes to get one of the shields in his mouth properly. Practically speaking, though, that was the beginning of the mouthpiece."

The mouthpieces didn't always go unnoticed by adversaries.

There was a period there when Lewis and Jack Britton faced each other a good twenty times. They fought everywhere, from New York to New Orleans, from Boston to Toronto. Between them they ruled the welterweight division for about seven years. The last time they faced each other was at Madison Square Garden in 1921, when Britton held the title. Everybody's in the center of the ring before the fight — Lewis, Britton, Britton's manager Dumb Dan Morgan, and Ted's manager Jimmy Johnston. Dollings tells me to go out and see what they're talking about for so long. The holdup is Morgan, who might have been called Dumb Dan, but who wasn't at all dumb. He's pointing to the mouthpiece in Lewis's mouth and protesting to the referee that it's a foreign substance and shouldn't be allowed. Johnson starts screaming. "You son of a bitch, this is the twentieth time these two have fought, and you never said anything about it before!" I thought Morgan and Johnson were going to have their own fight right then and there. Finally, they go over to the chief inspector for the bout, and he rules that Morgan is right, that the shield is a foreign substance. Britton won a unanimous 15-round decision. I never had any doubt that fight was decided with all the squabbling before it even started. Without his shield, Lewis was uncomfortable the whole way.

It was also Dollings and Lewis who taught Arcel the right way to bandage a fighter's hands before a bout:

Ideally, a fighter does his own wrapping because nobody knows better than he does how the bandages feel. But not too many of them have ever done it. Dollings would always have me watch how he wrapped Lewis, how he applied the bandage so the Kid would have a good grip. He taught me that putting the bandage on too tight would hurt a fighter. First you wrapped the wrist, then you crisscrossed it right on top of the hand. Then you brought the bandage over on the thumb. At that point you have the fighter make a fist to see if he's comfortable. It's only when you've bandaged the thumb that you have a real idea about how tight the bandage should be. Then you crisscross it again on top of the hand, going round and round. You overlap layers over the knuckles, then finally bring the bandage around and cross it over one final time. In those days you could use any amount of bandage you wanted. Some boxers would wrap their hands with black electrical tape, and that could be very dangerous. Even that wasn't the worst of it. Some guys would sprinkle plaster of Paris over the bandages, then wet it all. Then you had others who packed tea between the bandages. There was no law against any of it. You had no commissions or rules and regulations.[5]

Yet another valuable tip picked up from Dollings was the art of massage. "He was absolutely adamant about how you never let a fighter go from a workout and straight out the door. The same thing after a fight. The key, he'd always say, was to have your fighter perfectly relaxed after everything was over, and the key to that was a massage. Nobody was better at that than Dollings, and he made sure I learned how to do it, too, by massaging him so he could tell me where I was going right and wrong."

Even as he was learning the subtleties of his trade, however, Arcel was also busy dodging moments of truth at home, where his father had never given up hope of having a doctor in the family. "We had this neighbor who saw me leaving the house with a black gym bag, and she told my father and step-mother about it. When they asked me what I was doing with the bag, I told them I was a traveling salesman. 'What are you selling?' they asked. 'Hooks, jabs, and uppercuts,' I said like a smart guy. I got away with that once or twice before I told them the truth. By then they'd figured it out on their own, anyway. I don't think there was any one definite moment when we came clean with one another. It was all very gradual."

The same was true of his move into full-time training. And he didn't think of it as an especially humbling career choice, either. Few connected to the sport did. As Doc Kearns, manager of Jack Dempsey and Mickey Walker, once put it: "The trainer is the guy who knows the fighter best — if he knows his business. He eats and sleeps with the boy, takes walks with him, plays cards with him, finds out whether he's a guy that has to be needled or let alone. By the time they get into the ring, a good trainer knows exactly what's in the fighter, and how and when it can be best brought out. A smart manager will let him run the corner."[6]

As Arcel himself would tell Dave Anderson years later in *In the Corner*: "The story of boxing is the story of the trainer. Because the trainer is the boss, the trainer is the pillar of hope for every fighter."[7] That attitude firm in his mind from the very beginning, Arcel never found it necessary to make himself the center of attention. Those who didn't understand his role weren't important to him, anyway.

4

Jungle Gyms

However decided he was about being a trainer by his late teens, Arcel also found that age within the crosshairs of the military draft introduced for raising an army for World War I. Like thousands of others, he took the preemptive step of getting a job at a war plant. It was almost a fatal choice.

The plant that hired him in 1918 was run by the T.A Gillespie Company in the Morgan district of Sayreville, New Jersey, in Middlesex County. Commonly referred to at the time as the Morgan Depot, it furnished an estimated 10 percent of the arms used by American forces in Europe. On the evening of October 4, shortly after Arcel and other day-shift workers had gone home, the factory exploded in what turned out to be a disaster whose effects weren't tallied for months. The blast itself caused a fire and a chain reaction of blazes that raged on for three days, destroyed some 300 buildings, took at least 64 lives, and ultimately required the full-scale reconstruction of Sayreville and nearby South Amboy. Because so many people were left homeless, however, they also became vulnerable to the 1918 flu epidemic that was sweeping through the United States (and just about everywhere else in the world) at the time, leading researchers to attribute some of these casualties to the blast for a full appreciation of its impact.

Almost a century later the causes of the Morgan Depot explosion remain debatable. In its immediate aftermath, there were stories about an errant spark and charges about company carelessness. Most of all, there were suspicions of yet another successful sabotage operation by German agents who practically frolicked through war plants in New Jersey during World War I, causing major damage everywhere from the Hudson River to Trenton. Ordnance from the blast was still being recovered from near a grammar school in the area as late as 1997.[1] Arcel, who commuted to his job from his parents' home in Manhattan, barely mentioned the episode in the oceans of interviews he gave over the years, most typically saying, "There was a big explosion one day where I was working so that put an end to that [job]."[2]

As might have been expected, the daily commute across the river hardly stilled his long-range ambitions. The magnet for his earliest professional activities, Grupp's Gymnasium, was run by ex-boxer Billy Grupp, who had led with his chin in the ring and with his mouth out of it. Thanks to his connections, Grupp had little trouble turning his Harlem location into the first word for fighters in the New York area to keep in shape and make the hookups that would get them on commercial cards. He wasn't shy about attracting attention to his enterprise. On one occasion, in 1916, he got aspiring actress Hildreth Whitehouse to climb in against one Young Atkinson. Whitehouse handled herself well enough to get through the first round but never got to start the second because of the intervention of alerted police. The proprietor said he didn't know what all the commotion was about: Atkinson had sent more than one man to the canvas in the first round and nobody had complained then.[3]

It was at Grupp's that Arcel drew close to Benny Leonard, who won the world lightweight championship in 1917 and who had the kind of popular following usually associated with heavyweights. "Leonard was one of the many Jewish fighters around then. You had Abe Goldstein, Willie Jackson, Benny Valgar, Lave Cross, and on and on. Most of them had changed their names because they didn't want to bring shame on their families for what they were doing. Leonard's real name, for example, was Benjamin Leiner."

While fighters of Irish and Italian backgrounds went through similar dilemmas when it came to their families, Leonard's case was accentuated because of his strict Orthodox upbringing. According to Arcel, the problem came to a head when his parents could no longer ignore his mysterious popularity. "Leonard had a following, right from the start. One day, there was this little bus in front of his house down on the Lower East Side, and all these guys were climbing in to go see him fight. 'What's going on here?' Leonard's mother asks, and when she finds out they're all going to see her son fight, she goes running upstairs, all upset. When Leonard comes home later that night, his father is waiting for him. The father worked as a presser, earned about eight dollars a week. He demands to know what Leonard has been up to. Benny reaches into his pocket and hands his father the thirty-five dollars he's made fighting in a preliminary. When the father sees this, he says to his son, 'When are you going to fight again?'"

It was no surprise to Arcel that Leonard was the unofficial leader of the Jewish fighters at Grupp's. And not just the Jewish fighters, either. "You have to remember there were no radios or TVs or any other kind of distraction like that in those days. Even if you had some spending money, and I can't remember any who did, where would you go to spend it? A ballgame once or twice in the summer? There was certainly nothing like basketball or hockey in the winter. You'd spend 10 to 12 hours a day in a gym, and that meant a lot of sitting around when you just absorbed what guys like Leonard could teach you. They all respected him, revered him, really."

That also applied to fighters who had their own following. In 1922, for instance, Gene Tunney became obsessed with the fact that he had dropped the heavyweight title to Harry Greb on a series of unobserved fouls and other tricks more artful than artistic. In the aftermath of the bout, Tunney simplified his day into two tasks — going to the gym and pounding the bag, and calling up his manager Billy Gibson to find out if a rematch had been scheduled. Exhausted by the constant calls and even by loud invasions of his restaurant on 149th Street and Third Avenue by his manic boxer, Gibson asked Leonard, one of his other fighters, to drop down at the gym and talk to Tunney. Arcel, who was there when Leonard showed up, recalled what happened next:

> As soon as people saw it was Leonard, they all became a little quiet. Leonard goes over to where Tunney is working on the bag furiously, watches for a few seconds, and then says hello. Tunney knows he's there, but doesn't stop punching. Finally, he says he's going to beat Greb as soon as he gets the guy in the ring. Leonard says, "How, throwing your right hand? Where you going to hit him with your right hand? On the chin? The only place you hit Harry Greb with a right is in the body, right under the heart. Try working on that if you have to keep at it like you are. But remember: the longer it takes for a rematch, the better for you." What he was reminding Tunney of, and what Tunney had lost sight of, was that nobody had more bouts than Harry Greb. He'd have twenty or twenty-five fights a year. And fight or no fight, he went from woman to booze to woman. Nobody could keep up that pace for too long, and for three or four days in a row Leonard dropped by the gym to remind Tunney of that. And when Tunney finally did meet Greb again, he kept pounding him under the heart like Leonard told him. He destroyed the guy![4]

In Arcel's estimation, Leonard's main asset was his ability to think, the personification of his mantra — repeated to columnists throughout his career as the secret to successful boxing — of "brains over brawn." "He had the sharpest mind of anyone I'd met. Nothing *just happened* with him. He saw other fighters with cauliflower ears? Well, he made sure to wear headgear. He was the one fighter I saw who could make you do things *he* wanted you to do. He could feint you into knots. He was the master of the feint. With me he was just as great as he could be. I used to ask him a million dumb questions and he was never in too much of a hurry to show me the answers. I like to think I absorbed all he told me."

Leonard proved to be a little less patient with Grupp, and few were surprised. For all his flamboyance, the gym owner was far more conspicuous for his alcoholism. And he wasn't a pretty drunk, on more than one occasion staggering around his own premises and denouncing Jews. As Arcel would recall it, "He's out there one day and he's hollering: 'If it wasn't for the Jews there woulda been no war.' He was referring to World War I. Over and over again, 'If it wasn't for the Jews there woulda been no war. And they're responsible for everything else, too!'"

Grupp might have chosen a worse audience than Leonard, Valgar, and the other Jewish fighters for these outbursts, but it is hard to imagine what it might have been. Finally, one day they had had enough of all the anti–Semitic ranting and, at Leonard's urging, decided to investigate another recently opened space on 125th Street and Seventh Avenue that might serve their training needs. The formal name of the place was the Marshall Stillman Athletic Club — a source of endless confusion. The proprietors were millionaires Alpheus Geer and Hiram Mallison, whose charity work focused on rehabilitating prison inmates. In honor of a mutual relative, they named their enterprise the Marshall Stillman Movement and saw boxing as one of many activities useful for rebuilding the bodies and psyches of the released convicts. But since neither Geer nor Mallison had any desire to manage the place on a day-to-day basis, they brought in one Louis Ingber for the task. Depending on the source, Ingber at the time was either a policeman, a private detective, or a streetcar conductor. More definitely, he was someone who had never needed counseling for low self-esteem and who never met a man he couldn't treat worse than the previous one he had encountered. Within a couple of years, even before Geer and Mallison decided to get out of the gymnasium business, Ingber became so synonymous with Stillman's that most people meeting him for the first time simply assumed his name was Lou Stillman — an error he ultimately stopped correcting.

Arcel had many first impressions of Ingber and his premises, most of them falling within the stunned-to-astonished range. "To begin with, he didn't know who Benny Leonard was, didn't know any of the fighters, didn't know much about professional boxing at all. The place itself was no bigger than a living room. You couldn't move in the joint. The best thing they had was a ring, that was nice. And they had a punching bag. There was a toilet in the back, and they put sort of a fence around it to give Leonard what was supposed to be his dressing room."

It took only a couple of exhibitions by Leonard for Ingber to realize he might have a going concern. Arcel: "When Leonard went up there to train, the place was mobbed with people to watch him. Or at least as mobbed as such a small place could be. But Ingber sees what a great attraction Leonard is. He really doesn't know what the hell is going on, but he figures he'll charge 15 cents admission for what all these people seem to want."

If Ingber needed any further incentive for the gymnasium business, he got it in 1920 when New York's Walker Law legalized 15-round bouts that were determined by the decisions of a qualified judge. At that point he took on a partner to help finance the establishment of a bigger place downtown on Eighth Avenue between 54th and 55th streets. This was to prove to be the first of several moves, most of them in and around Eighth Avenue and culminating in the most famous of the establishments at 919 Eighth, until final closure in 1959. Along the way he built up the kind of outsized character that Billy Grupp had aspired to, making him the darling of sportswriters and the fuel for anecdotes generations later. He proved particularly quotable on the seediness of his clientele and of the gymnasium itself, never apologizing for having "a joint so thick with fighters they used to knock each other down shadow boxing." He would have been the last one to object to the description of the gym offered by Budd Schulberg in *The Harder They Fall*: "The smells of this world are sour and pungent, a stale gamy odor blended of sweat and liniment, worn fight gear, cheap cigars, and too many bodies, clothed and unclothed, packed into a room with no noticeable means of ventilation."[5] Once pointing out an area where managers and matchmakers gathered for making deals, Ingber was heard to gripe: "A million dollars worth of business goes on there, and most of those guys look like they can't buy a nickel cigar."[6] Asked why the gym itself looked so decrepit, with cigarette butts littering the floor, tobacco smoke thickening the air, the windows fogged over, and plaster falling regularly from the ceiling, he usually made sure the questioner wasn't permitted back in to ask a second time. As for his management philosophy, he summed that up simply: "Big or small, champ or bum, I treated 'em all the same way — bad. If you treat them like humans, they'll eat you alive."[7]

Ingber didn't back off from fighters, either, and there was more than one scene of him decking a boxer, usually over unpaid dues. Jackie Graham, brother of welterweight contender Billy Graham in the 1950s, was quoted by Ronald K. Fried in *Corner Men* as saying: "Cantankerous is too kind a word [for him]. Obnoxious is a more accurate word. He was an obnoxious man. I mean, he would scream obscenities across the room.... If you owed gym dues — a lot of those guys, they were hurtin,' they didn't have money — he'd scream across 'You fuckin' nigger, you owe me dues from last month' — that kind of stuff.... That's not nice now. It wasn't nice then. It will never be nice. But it didn't bother him."[8]

Asked once how he had the gall to challenge men whose livelihood was knocking others to the canvas, Ingber replied: "I can lick most guys with bluff, so I haven't gotten into a fight since I was a kid. I've carried a gun all my life, used to carry two of them."

One of the more vivid descriptions of Stillman's was offered by trainer-manager Lou Duva to Dave Anderson:

> I used to ... watch the great trainers like Ray Arcel, Whitey Bimstein, Mannie Seamon ... watch them handle their fighters in the three rings. Then watch the managers maneuvering on the pay phones in the back. There must've been a dozen phone booths, but no doors on the booths. That was their office. Phony calls and all that there stuff. They'd be on the phone pretending to be working on a match. But it was all bullshit. Stealing phone calls. If a promoter wanted to talk to a certain manager about getting a fighter to fill in a show at the last minute, the manager who answered the phone would tell him the other manager wasn't around but he had a fighter who would fill in. The managers were always maneuvering.[9]

If Arcel ever needed to demonstrate his diplomatic talents, Ingber was Exhibit A. As fellow trainer Angelo Dundee said, "I think Ray and I were the only guys who never got into it with him. We just didn't seem to bother him."[10]

One Arcel credit with Ingber was that he brought to the gymnasium two cronies from the streets of the city who were among the most prominent fighters of the 1920s — Abe Goldstein and Charlie "Phil" Rosenberg. Both of them ended up wearing championship belts.

5

Training Wheels

Arcel always called Abe Goldstein, a bantamweight who grew up in a city orphanage, "my first and favorite world champion."

Standing at 5'5" and at an average 112–115 pounds, Goldstein's relations with the trainer preceded his professional status. "He was still just an amateur bantamweight when he asked me to help in his corner when he was boxing a lad with a reputation named Jack Eile.... I expect I was more trouble than help on that occasion, but, anyway, Abe won, and when he said, 'You did pretty good tonight, Ray,' I knew my career had started.... When Abe turned professional a little later in 1916 — he was only 17 at the time — I went with him."

Goldstein's rise through the bantam ranks was hardly an instant success story. On the up side, he lost only once in his first 40 fights, 16 of his wins by knockout. This put him in position for a title fight in 1921 against flyweight champion Johnny Buff, but he was on the canvas for keeps by the second round. There followed another string of 19 victories before coming up against Johnny Sheppard in April 1922 and going down in a 10-round decision. According to Arcel, the Sheppard loss might have spelled the end for Goldstein's serious ambitions if not for somebody else's eleventh-hour injury.

He got his chance at the title in 1924 by luck and a good deal of courage on his part. Joe Lynch was bantamweight champion at the time, and he agreed to box Joe Burman for the laurels. But two days before the fight, Lynch says he tripped over his dog, of all things, and hurt himself so he can't make the match. I never really believed that story. Who could? I always thought he just couldn't make the weight and backed out. But one way or another, the bout was going to have to be cancelled. That afternoon, though, one of the promoters came around to Stillman's and asked me if Goldstein would be willing to substitute for Lynch. It wouldn't be a title fight without Lynch, but it would still be a big fight because of Burman's ranking as the leading contender in the division. Abe was somewhere near Reading, Pennsylvania, with his brother, a traveling

31

salesman. It took me almost 12 hours, but I finally tracked him down. When I told him what had happened, he said he'd be right back to the city.

Being back in the city was one thing; not having been near a ring or even a punching bag since his last fight five weeks earlier was another:

> The one thing we had on our side was that Abe could eat a ton of bricks and never weigh more than 116 pounds. Plus, he might have been a bantamweight, but he could punch like a flyweight. Anyway, he gets on the scale, and there he is at the perfect 116 again. Then the promoter Willie Lewis pulls the commissioner aside and says, "You know, Commissioner, this Goldstein is doing everybody a big favor by being here even though he hasn't been working out. Couldn't we cut it from a 15-round bout to a 12-rounder? Just to make it a little more even?" Burman and his handlers say they don't care one way or the other. They're figuring on sending Abe to the canvas long before twelve *or* fifteen rounds! And the commissioner agrees. All that's nice, but there was still the fight itself. When Abe asked me what I thought his chances were, I had to tell him the truth. "I'm going to throw you to the lions, kid," I said. "It's a chance in a thousand, but we'll do it together." Twenty-four hours later, he was standing in his corner at Madison Square Garden with Burman glaring across the ring at him. I never felt closer to any fighter than I did that night to Abe.

In the opening rounds, Goldstein showed the effects of not having trained for the bout, mistiming punches and falling into awkward crouches. Arcel admitted to the whitest of lies when the fighter would return to his corner at the end of a round and ask how he was doing. "Like a champion, I kept telling him because in my mind that was exactly how he was behaving. He had enough heart for a dozen fighters."

Midway through the 12-round bout, Burman was appreciably ahead on points, but Goldstein was not only still on his feet, he had begun to settle in, his blows starting to rattle his opponent. Arcel described what happened next:

> By the end of the tenth round I reckoned it even. When we started the eleventh round, the fans were on their feet and they didn't sit down again. With his head ducked down between his shoulders, Abe moved in, hitting with both hands. Burman came back at him and the two of them stood flat-footed smashing at one another. It wasn't boxing, it was a fight. The twelfth round was the same, but Burman began to give ground. Abe thudded a couple on the bridge of his nose, and he went into the ropes. Abe was after him like a tiger, and when the final gong came, he was still beating a tattoo on him. The referee came across to Abe and lifted his hand. Our one chance in a thousand had come off!

Goldstein's exhibition meant more than a victory over Burman, it also set up a championship fight with the clumsy dog owner Joe Lynch five months later. In addition, according to Arcel, it gave him standing as a trainer. "I owed it to him the way he always went around saying he owed his success to me. The bottom line is that we made each other."

In the bout against Lynch, Goldstein prevailed for the championship on a 15-round decision that said little about the systematic beating that he gave Lynch but that somehow didn't put the reigning title-holder down for good. A few months after that, Goldstein again walked out of the ring a winner in defending his title against Charles Ledoux, the bantamweight champion of Europe and almost a decade older. By this time, periodicals were referring to Goldstein with such sobriquets as "the Harlem Assassin." But the ride didn't last long. After another title defense win against Tommy Ryan, Goldstein was matched against Eddie Martin, a Brooklyn native who had his own sobriquet of "Cannonball" for the way he charged out of his corner into his adversary. Recalled Arcel, "It was a bout that packed them in like sardines [in the old Madison Square Garden]. In the third round Martin made a miraculous comeback from the slugging Abe had been giving him. At one point he looked like he was out cold, but at the count of eight he was suddenly up on his feet again, as clever a feint as you might see. They went on from there pretty even, but I figured the opening rounds had to add up to a decision for Abe. I told him that, too, at the end of the fight when we were all waiting for the cards to come in."

Arcel was wrong. The judges made Martin Brooklyn's first champion in any division in a quarter-century. There was considerable grumbling about the verdict, not least from Goldstein's trainer, but even those who had scored in favor of the reigning champion had not given him so great an edge as to claim robbery. Goldstein never fought for the bantamweight title again, but Arcel did, and he didn't waste too much time predicting when he would, either. "After the fight," he recalled, "I walked into Martin's dressing room to congratulate him. 'You took the title from me tonight, Eddie,' I said, 'but I'll win it back with Rosenberg.'"

6

Travels with Charlie

Abe Goldstein was only one of several bantamweights and flyweights handled by Arcel at the dawn of his career. ("They started me at the low end of the weight divisions," he laughed more than once. "Maybe they figured I'd cause less harm that way.") The most prominent of the others were Charlie Phil Rosenberg and Frankie Genaro.

Although Arcel was always quick to emphasize that Genaro (real name: Frank DiGennaro or DiGennara, depending on the source) never claimed a world championship but only an American championship under his tutelage, the flyweight (5'2" and 112 pounds) affected the trainer's career in more ways than one. After a childhood ambition to become a jockey got him little further than cleaning up stables, the Bronx native turned to amateur boxing — and to the first of his aliases. At his baptismal bout in 1919 against Sammy Nable, he fought under the name of A.J. DeVito. As he explained it later, "It was my first fight, and I wanted to try out before applying for my AAU card so I borrowed my cousin's."[1] More confident after his win over Nable, he received his own certification and went on to take the New York State and National flyweight championships. Even that turned out to be only the prelude, however, to the gold medal he won in Antwerp at the 1920 Olympic Games by defeating two Frenchmen, a Dane, and a Norwegian. It was then that Genaro decided to turn professional.

DiGennaro-DeVito-Genaro's rise through the pro ranks was aided not a little by a Filipino who billed himself as Pancho Villa (real name: Francisco Guilledo). After two earlier victories over Villa in Jersey City and Brooklyn, Genaro met him for a third encounter at Madison Square Garden* with the American flyweight title on the line and with Arcel in

---

*There have been four Madison Square Gardens in New York City history. The first one, opened in May 1879 at Madison Avenue and 26th Street, and associated with P.T. Barnum

his corner. Once again Genaro came out on top, qualifying him as an opponent for world champion Jimmy Wilde. A Welshman who had retired after a record 88 straight wins, 75 of them by knockout, Wilde was talked back into the ring by promoter Tex Rickard. But the Genaro challenge never came off. In negotiations with Rickard, Genaro's manager demanded more money than the promoter was ready to yield, so that when the championship bout finally took place, it was between Wilde and, instead of Genaro, the thrice-beaten Villa.

Genaro would go on to defend his American title a couple of times and even win a version of the world championship, though without Arcel. But all was not lost as far as the trainer was concerned when it came to the Villa-Wilde match-up. In attending the fight as a spectator, he said he picked up another valuable lesson about the role of seconds:

> Up to the sixth round Wilde was holding his own. Then when the bell rang, he dropped his hands to return to his corner. At that very second Villa slammed him with a right hand to the jaw. Wilde's eyes glazed over, he fell against the ropes, and then face down on the canvas. His seconds jumped in and got him over to his stool, but you could see he was gone. And I blamed the seconds. They made only the feeblest kind of protests to the ref about Villa's punch. If they had squawked loud enough, the ref would have been forced to do something, maybe even disqualify Villa. At the very least the commotion would have given Wilde the rest he obviously needed. But no, they let their fighter come out for the next round in regular time, and Villa almost immediately knocked him cold. I vowed I'd never let a fighter of mine ever be caught that way.

Genaro also played an ultimately beneficial role in Arcel's training of his second world champion, Charlie Phil Rosenberg. Rosenberg's real name was Charlie Green, one of nine children of a widow who made her living with a pushcart on the Lower East Side and who often had the responsibility of stealing rolls from bakeries so his siblings could have something to eat. Unlike Genaro, Villa, and numerous others, Green actually knew a person with the name he took for his first bout — an authentic Phil Rosenberg who couldn't make a scheduled fight and who told Green to go ahead and collect the $15 on the table in his name. Green didn't win the fight under either name, but he kept at it — until

(continued from page 34) productions, was razed to the ground a decade later for a Stanford White creation that seated 8,000 and was for a long time the second tallest building in the city. It was the scene of prize fights (among other things) incessantly until being replaced by a third Garden at 50th Street and Eighth Avenue in November 1925. The present Garden at 34th Street and Eighth Avenue was opened in February 1968.

he had lost four more of his first five. That might have done it for another ring career except for two things — the solid coterie of Green's Lower East Side friends who nagged at him to keep fighting and a flamboyant manager with a lengthy underworld history named Harry (Champ) Segal.

One of the immediate problems posed by Green's enthusiastic friends was their habit of showing up for fights and spurring him on to victory with cries of "Charlie! Charlie!" At one bout a boxing official heard the cries and thought he was being helpful by advising the cheering section the fighter's name was Phil. The most quick-witted of the friends explained that the fighter's full name was actually Phil Charles Rosenberg, but the friends only used the middle one. From that point on, Charlie Green was identified in print and just about everywhere else with the double Rosenberg name.

As for Segal, he got into managing after a lengthy ring career of 118 bouts spanning bantamweight to welterweight divisions. Some records have him winning 78 of those fights by knockout, with no fewer than 50 of those victories coming in the first round. His background had more than one point in common with Arcel's — Russian immigrant parents, his earliest years on the Lower East Side before his family moved north in Manhattan (in his case to Harlem), initial training at a Union Settlement House. By the age of 17, however, he also had narrowly escaped conviction on a drug possession rap, and that record would fill out in the years to come, including a brief jailing on suspicion of homicide and numerous arrests for running a book. One of his closest friends for years was the mobster Bugsy Siegel. Segal was said to have prevailed on Al Capone more than once to have payment on a gambling debt postponed, and the same gambling habit forced him to go several times to bootlegger, gunman, and Cotton Club proprietor Owney Madden to take on a financial interest in one of his fighters. One of those fighters was Rosenberg.[2]

As for Segal's own relationship with Rosenberg, it was a many-tortured thing. At first he wanted nothing more than to sever his ties with the fighter, having come to hurried second thoughts that Charlie Green under any name had a lot of fortitude but not very much talent. On one occasion he had been forced to come to Rosenberg's physical rescue against lightweight Benny Valgar. After reluctantly giving Valgar permission to mix it up with Rosenberg at Stillman's behind the heavier fighter's promise just to do some boxing, he watched in fury as his fighter started being belted around. Calling a halt to the proceedings, he jumped into the ring and challenged Valgar to take him on instead. When the boxer, known as the "French Flash," agreed, Segal got himself trunks and gloves, then returned to the ring and battered Valgar so badly that Stillman himself had to intercede to end matters. (Valgar was so impressed that he announced to one and all that Segal would be his manager one day, and indeed the two did later work together.)

But that still left the Rosenberg situation. With the fighter showing no inclination to find another line of work, Segal decided to send the message through an opponent who would — it was hoped — slap the Lower East Side product around without hurting him much. The adversary chosen for the task was Genaro, then working his way toward his duels with Villa and known more for the rapid-fire delivery of his blows than for their thunder. The only trouble with that strategy was that when the two met at Madison Square Garden in May 1922, Rosenberg gave Genaro enough of a fight to barely lose. It was after that tussle that Arcel introduced himself to Rosenberg and, saying how impressed he was, offered to be his trainer.

Following Cannonball Martin's defeat of Goldstein, the winner's camp singled out Rosenberg as its next opponent. Segal was so anxious to get the title shot that he not only agreed to demands from Martin's handlers for 50 percent of the gate but also posted a $10,000 forfeit fee as a hedge against Rosenberg not making the 118-pound limit. And just in case that wasn't clear enough, Martin's manager Charley Cook stalled and stalled for a good three months before signing an agreement, the hope (and fact) being that Rosenberg would use the time to drop into a few more bakeries. Called in to supervise the training program, Arcel was appalled by the hole Segal had gotten himself into. "I laid it out for him. 'Are you crazy? I just put the guy on the scales, and he's 155 pounds. How we going to get any further than the weigh-in?' One thing about Segal: He didn't panic easily. We still had three months for training, he said, so that's plenty of time to get off all that extra weight. Since there was no way of talking him out of calling everything off, I suggested we go down to Hot Springs, Arkansas, for the baths. Benny Leonard and Kid Lewis had both gone there and had nothing but good things to say about the place. So Segal said okay, go to Arkansas."

For Arcel, his first training trip outside the State of New York in December 1924 was a sightseeing tour of torment:

We started serious training the moment we arrived. He was on a strict diet, we had long walks up and down the hills, and of course the mineral baths. The first walk was before breakfast — up and down the hills, up and down, and he wasn't shouting his thanks to me as we went along. Then he had a small breakfast — juice, eggs, a cup of tea, and toast. Then he was allowed to rest for a little bit before we went down to the baths. There were attendants there, but I made sure I did all the massaging tricks I'd learned from Dollings. The only other meal he was allowed during the day — and not just meal, the only other time he was allowed to put something in his mouth — was dinner, and that was steak, vegetables, a cup of tea, and nothing else. Then it was off to bed. He fought me, he fought his weight, he wanted to fight the world. Living with him was the worst kind of curse. It was absolutely awful. He hated me like nobody had ever hated me before. But after two weeks he had lost 20 pounds, and I knew it was time to get back to New York and the next phase.

The next phase were three tune-up bouts that Segal objected to initially for fear of Rosenberg becoming too worn down, but which he finally acceded to under Arcel's nagging. Within the five weeks leading up to the title fight, Rosenberg won a 10-round decision over Buck Josephs, did the same against Harry Gordon, and knocked out Nat Pincus in the eleventh round of a 12-round contest. "For each of those fights," Arcel told Elli Wohlgelernter, "I made him wear a pair of thick woolen trunks under his silk ones. It was his stomach and thighs that carried most of the surplus weight. When he came back to his corner, I wrapped a thick Turkish towel all around him, and allowed no water to fall on him at all. As the sweat poured from him, it was soaked up in the trunks and the towel."[3]

Two weeks before the scheduled meeting with Martin, Rosenberg was down to 120 pounds, a loss of 35 pounds since Arcel had taken him in hand. It was at this point, according to some sources, that Rosenberg received some impromptu — but arguably decisive — instruction from Abe Attell, who never forgot to remind listeners that he had reigned over the featherweight division from 1901 to 1912. According to a story ultimately traced back to Segal,[4] the manager and the two fighters were sharing a cab in New York when Attell told Rosenberg that the key to beating Martin was an "inside cuff" punch that he had used successfully during his career. After demonstrating the punch in the back of the cab, Attell then monitored Rosenberg's drills with it in the gym until he was telling everybody, "The kid does it better than I ever did!"

Arcel never addressed the importance of Attell's advice or how it affected his own program with the fighter. What was clearer was that the approaching deadline for the title bout didn't ease relations between trainer and fighter; on the contrary, it made Arcel even more vigilant.

> He was proud of himself for having lost so much, but also in the mood to celebrate it. I told him the only celebrating would be for him to relax a little more, but he'd have to keep up the walking every day. We'd run in Central Park in the morning, then we'd walk down 65 blocks from 118th Street and Fifth Avenue where we were living down to Stillman's over on Eighth Avenue. After he did some boxing, we'd go back over the same route. It was an ordeal for both of us. I had to live with him and endure all the insults and screaming and cursing. There was no question I became his whipping boy. He couldn't have cared less that everything I was putting him through, I was doing, too. What he ate, I ate. We never deviated. He was in jail, and I was in jail with him.

Not even going to bed at night brought much relief:

> I always had to sleep with one eye open. He'd get up in the middle of the night to go to the bathroom, and I would stand there with the door open. He kept cursing me. "I just want to gargle," he'd say, and I'd tell him, "I'm watching your Adam's apple, Charlie. Don't swallow that water. You can gargle, but spit it out." When he went back to bed, I'd give him a tablespoon of Calf's Foot Jelly, which usually soothed him. But he didn't let it go at that even then. He'd start talking to himself, but just loud enough so I could hear him. "What did I ever do to deserve this? How did I ever wind up with this rotten son of a bitch with me? What did I do?" It became such a routine, these mutterings of his in bed, that they actually put me to sleep.

The day before the March 28th fight, Rosenberg registered 118 pounds, 37 less than when his training had started. To celebrate, Segal took his fighter and trainer to dinner where Rosenberg was restricted to a small filet mignon, lettuce, and celery. But later that afternoon Arcel caught him in their kitchen about to drink a glass of milk. When the trainer exploded, the fighter's meek response was that "my mother told me to do it." Reminded that his mother wasn't fighting the next day, Rosenberg put aside the milk but also the meekness. "After this fight is over," he warned, "I'm going to kill you. And then I'm going to throw myself into a tub of ice water."[5]

That night Arcel had a moment when he thought Rosenberg wasn't going to wait for the fight to make good on his threat. "I was fast asleep. Suddenly I get this terrific clout on the side of the ear. As soon as I shoot up in bed, I get a smash on the nose. 'Come on and fight, you bum,' Charlie is snarling, and starts hitting me again. I'm just about to grab him when I see he's fast asleep! He's already fighting Martin in his dreams!

I was pretty beat up that night, and just to make sure he didn't come in after me again, I took my pillow and slept on the floor until morning."

As a final hedge against any unpleasant surprises at the weigh-in, Arcel had the fighter skip breakfast altogether. The precaution proved unnecessary when Rosenberg weighed in at 116 pounds. What that mainly netted Arcel was another death threat, this one from Segal, who revealed that he had indeed bet heavily on Rosenberg. "When he told me he'd kill me if we lost, I told him to do it right then and there because I was too exhausted to have to go through the rest of the day to the fight worrying about him, too!"

By the time Rosenberg climbed into the ring that night, Segal had picked up the intelligence that the fighter's drastic weight loss would be the key to Martin's strategy — just charge in on the assumption that Rosenberg would be too weak from his diet. In turn, Rosenberg was instructed not to waste any energy, to stay rooted to one spot if necessary, but not go running around after Martin. The theory was good, the results were better. After several rounds of deftly holding off Martin with his boxing ability, a surprisingly energetic Rosenberg indeed began chasing his opponent, and his momentum never palled until the final bell. He took the decision by a comfortable margin and displaced Martin as champion.

After the fight, Segal hosted a big party for Rosenberg and his friends. Arcel didn't tag along. "I was tired and feeling pretty bruised for a lot of reasons. I changed my clothes and went home." What he missed, among other things, was the start of a 20-year boast by Attell that the "inside cuff" demonstrated in the taxi had been responsible for Rosenberg's victory. On the other hand, he also missed the chance to point out that while he had brought Rosenberg's weight down by 39 pounds, he had lost 49 pounds of his own!

Over the next few years Rosenberg's defense of the title proved to be Arcel's ticket to seeing a lot of the United States, as far as Los Angeles. With the slippery Segal calling the tune, however, it was seldom a matter of boarding a train to a fight site, working out for a few weeks, and then climbing into the ring for the bout. More than once the fight itself turned out to be almost incidental to Segal's stormy relations with local characters and his sudden need to leave Rosenberg in Arcel's care while he scooted off elsewhere. The most Byzantine affair, though, occurred in New York in July 1927, when Rosenberg was scheduled to meet Bushy Graham for the title.

In the weeks leading up to the fight, Segal became convinced that there could be no second miracle weight loss regimen for qualifying Rosenberg as a genuine bantamweight. Instead of another trip to Hot Springs, his genial solution was to approach Bill Parr, Graham's manager, with an offer to buy up 50 percent of the boxer, thereby assuring himself of a win no matter whose arm was raised in the air at the end of the evening. Rosenberg himself assented to the deal, though it was never ascertained how profoundly he grasped its implications. But though Parr quickly went along with the idea of a secret partner, there was still the question of the scales. This Segal resolved by telling Rosenberg and Arcel to get down to 122 pounds (four over the maximum) and then stop worrying, contending that no boxing commissioner would call off a championship fight at Madison Square Garden just because of a little bulge. He proved to be one-fourth right.

When Rosenberg came in at 122½ against Graham's 117½, Commissioner Bill Muldoon ruled that this disqualified the champion and that the title automatically passed to Graham. But before he could declare the fight was off, Segal got into his ear to remind him of the crowd massing at Madison Square Garden and how weigh-ins were hardly the appropriate site for deciding champions merely for a couple of pounds. Muldoon bought a piece of the argument — he allowed the bout to go on but without the title being at stake. When the Madison Square Garden crowd was informed of the change, it came close to rioting in the arena, settling back to moderate fury only when it was distracted by the pummeling Rosenberg gave Graham over 15 rounds. Rosenberg needed the distraction, too, since he was slamming Graham around while teetering under what was later analyzed as a narcotic dropped into his pre-fight tea.

And then things *really* got messy.

When Segal and Rosenberg went down to Muldoon's office the next day to collect their purse, what they got was a handshake for a battle well fought and a suspension for not meeting the weight requirement. The initial suspensions of a few weeks had hardly begun when Muldoon also learned of the ownership conniving between Segal and Parr. This led to another meeting in the Commissioner's office where both fighters and both managers, as well as promoter Jess McMahon, were suspended for a full year. Before the dust had settled, all the concerned parties were also sued by fans for overcharging for a fight falsely advertised as a title bout. Arcel was able to demonstrate that he knew nothing of all the finagling, so he wasn't among those suspended.[6]

But he *was* almost taken for a ride.

Up to the Graham fight, the trainer hadn't taken the threats from both Segal and Rosenberg to kill him all that seriously, thinking they were just exasperated bluster. But that changed a couple of days before the bout when Madden called Arcel to ask whether Rosenberg would make the weight. Arcel told him he wouldn't, and the fighter, eavesdropping on the conversation, exploded and ran to Segal. By his own testimony in a series of interviews with the American Jewish Congress in 1983, Arcel knew he was in trouble. "They weren't kidding around. They had some tough characters always hanging around them. I didn't know what they did, and didn't want to know. But then one day outside Stillman's, there's Charlie and Segal and two of these tough guys, and they tell me to get into a car. I tell them no, thanks, get out of there, and call Madden. He can't believe it's because of what I'd told him on the phone, but he doesn't waste any time. He gets Segal and Charlie over to his office and lays it out for them: Nothing better happen to Ray Arcel because I'm his friend. That was the end of the threat."[7]

But, oddly, it was not the end of Arcel's working relationship with either Segal or Rosenberg. Asked how he could have possibly continued working with people who had threatened his life, the trainer could say only that he "had lost respect for them, but it was work and they didn't do it anymore."

New Rules

The most influential development in Arcel's early career had nothing to do with his meeting Dai Dollings and Doc Bagley, or with his training of champions like Abe Goldstein and Charlie Phil Rosenberg. For him, as for innumerable other trainers (not to mention managers, promoters, and the fighters themselves), boxing's most significant date in the early 20th century was March 25, 1920, when the Walker Law for sanctioning the sport was passed in Albany by the New York State Legislature. Sponsored by future New York City Mayor James (Jimmy) Walker, the legislation effectively ended decades of back-and-forth government attitudes toward professional boxing east of the Mississippi and proved vital to the sport's development because of the tendency of other states in the region to emulate New York's lead on any and all sides of the legality question. Without the Walker Law, Arcel would have had plenty of reason to regret not having studied medicine, as his father had desired.

By and large, boxing's status in the East was determined by the dominating party in the state government, with Democrats promoting it and Republicans preferring tennis. The first official notice of the sport in New York dated back to 1859, when it was specifically outlawed. The ban remained on the books (if not always enforced) until 1896, when the Horton Law decriminalized ring activity. This still permitted overzealous county and municipal police forces to bar fights and even arrest participants, but there was little enthusiasm for prosecuting cases that would ultimately be thrown out of court. On the other hand, the zealots made their propaganda point through relentlessness, so that only four years later, in 1900, the Lewis Law overthrew the Horton Law, and boxing was back to being banned except as an amateur activity for the members of private clubs.

The next turn came in 1911, when another piece of legislation from

Albany — the Frawley Act — deposed the Lewis Law. Under the Frawley Act, boxing was again permitted but within very strict guidelines. The chief thrust of the guidelines was to guard against gambling corruption by declaring that bouts could go only 10 rounds, and that if neither fighter had been knocked out in that time, the fight would end in a no-decision. The law also established a three-man State Athletic Commission, claimed the power to license both clubs and fighters, and collected a five percent tax on the gate of every bout. Within the first year of the legislation, New York State opened 89 clubs, more than half of them in New York City. Almost as fast, the holes in the law became apparent. The no-decision crux of the legislation, for instance, was practically superseded by the practice of daily newspapers and the periodical *The Police Gazette* to weigh in with their own verdicts, and before long the ND stood for Newspaper Decision rather than No Decision, thus enabling gamblers to step up their action. Then, in 1917, the monitoring claims of the law were ridiculed twice over — first when boxer Stephen "Young" McDonald was killed in the ring and then when a promoter accused the chairman of the Athletic Commission of extorting payoffs from him.[1] With the Republicans back in charge in Albany, the Frawley Law joined the Horton Law as another once-upon-a-time bright idea.

Boxing's return to illegality came as an unpleasant surprise to William Gavin, an Englishman who dreamed of establishing in New York a private club patterned after his National Sporting Club in London. He had planned on financing his venture with the stock he had sold in the London club to a group of American millionaires. Instead, he had to focus his energies initially on winning over state politicians, and he had some strong arguments on his side, not least the fact that the Armed Forces had made frequent use of boxing for training soldiers during World War I and that the official ban had done little to curb boxing activities around the United States at underground venues. The most receptive to Gavin's blandishments turned out to be Senator James Walker, who secured enough votes on March 25, 1920 (30 to 19), to once again make boxing legal. Key provisions of the Walker Act, drawn all but verbatim from the rules Gavin had projected for his club, included matches lasting 15 rounds, bouts fought to official decisions, and the assignment of referees and judges (as well as a physician) to every fight. Past distinctions between what constituted boxing as opposed to prizefighting were rendered irrelevant under the overriding consideration that legality was defined by the auspices under which the bout was held, and that ring tussles of any kind not supervised by the state-controlled commission were illegal. Governor Al Smith sought to hold up the enactment of the law for some months but was eventually talked into signing it by pressures brought to bear by, among others, clergymen in his own Catholic Church and American Legion posts whose members had boxed while in the service. Other states quickly followed New York's lead and repealed their own bans. With tweaks here and there every so often, the Walker Act has remained the constitution of professional boxing ever since.

In New York, Gavin followed up his successful lobbying by hiring Tex Rickard, a ballyhoo artist in the P.T. Barnum mold who had promoted the racism-imbued 1910 Jack Johnson–Jim Jeffries championship fight in Reno, not only to arrange the first matches under the new law but also to find a suitable site for a sport that figured to draw thousands of fans. That turned out to be the second version of Madison Square Garden. But by the time the first bout was held under the new rules in September 1920, Rickard had picked up new partners in mining millionaire Frank Armstrong and circus impresario John Ringling, and Gavin was on a ship back to England, cleaned out by his spending for getting the Walker Law on the books, never to see his original club dreams for America realized. Rickard would soon do without Armstrong as well, and made it something of a trifecta when his ties with Tammany Hall secured the decisive support of the previously cautious Governor Smith against opposition to using Madison Square Garden for boxing.

Less than a year after enactment of the Walker Law, 80,000 fans, spending close to two million dollars, descended on Boyle's Thirty Acres in New Jersey to see Jack Dempsey batter around Georges Carpentier for the heavyweight championship. More important, the fight was carried by the WJZ affiliate of RCA, making it the first radio network bout.[2] By 1927, when Gene Tunney benefited from the infamous "long count" against Dempsey in Chicago's Soldier Field before 104,000 fans to take the heavyweight title, the national radio audience was estimated at topping 50 million.[3]

8

Valgarisms

Although he admired no one more than Abe Goldstein and had more of a tumultuous relationship with Charlie Phil Rosenberg than with anyone, Arcel's closest friend in the early years was undoubtedly Benny Valgar, the Russia-born "French Flash." After winning the title as the best amateur bantamweight in the United States, Valgar entered the professional ranks as a featherweight, and then in later years fought as a lightweight. If he had one distinction, he had several, not least being the only boxer recorded as having fought 200 or more fights without being knocked out or even TKOed. In the Arcel lexicon, he attained even higher prominence by being the one fighter the trainer didn't hesitate to compare to Benny Leonard: "When it came to all-around ring generalship, Benny Valgar was on a par with Leonard, though Leonard was the better puncher. From 1915 I saw them all, and I don't hesitate to say Leonard was the fastest-thinking fighter. But for cleverness Valgar was right there in his class." Leonard himself was also quoted as calling the Frenchman "the fastest boxer I ever knew."[1]

For all his gifts, Valgar never fought a title fight when his boxing prowess might have earned him the crown. The closest he came was in 1920 in Newark during an eight-round bout against featherweight champion Johnny Kilbane, when anything short of a knockout still meant a no decision. (Arcel: "Kilbane was scared of Valgar. He refused to fight him anywhere to a decision.") Five of the six New York dailies covering the fight gave the decision to the Flash; the *New York Times* went so far as to plaster the "win" over all eight columns of its sports page.[2] But this wasn't good enough to take the title, since Kilbane was never floored. Valgar never met Kilbane again, at least in part because he put on the pounds of a lightweight.

It didn't help Valgar's title opportunities that he was managed by the same Billy Gibson who managed Leonard. Although the two boxers often sparred in the gym, Gibson never lost sight of who was the head of his stable. Why Valgar never sought out another manager has been lost to the ages, but Gibson's concentration on Leonard gave Arcel more opportunities to hover over the Frenchman, including taking several trips out of New York. One trip was to Toledo for a match against one KO Jaekle:

> We got to town a few days before the fight, which gave us time to do some workouts at the local gym and also for me to get a look at Jaekle. He was a very strong fighter, somebody who wasn't going to want to box too much, so I told Valgar to keep him in the center of the ring, keep slapping at him, make him miss, then counter. I stressed the same thing the night of the fight. "Stay away from the ropes," I reminded him. "He's going to come out ripping and try to knock you out in the first round. Just keep him in the middle of the ring." Sure enough, as soon as the bell rings, Jaekle goes charging out and before I know it, he's got Benny on the ropes, pounding away. Benny's completely stuck. When the round ends and he comes back to the corner, I fly into him. "You did just the opposite of what I told you to do! He hit you with punches you never get hit with. You don't stay in the center of the ring, he's going to hurt you and you're going to go down."

Valgar's reaction?

> Not a word. Maybe a nod just to shut me up, but not a word. The bell rings for the second round, and again it's only seconds before Jaekle has him against the ropes. I'm thinking there's no way he's not going to go down. Same scene when he comes back to his corner after the round. I start berating him again, he starts nodding again. But then he looks up at me and in this English with the thick French accent he had, he says, "Don't worry, Ray. From now on it will be Arcel and vulgar, painters and decorators." And that's exactly what happened. For the rest of the fight he painted and decorated Jaekle — jabs here, hooks there, Jaekle swinging wildly and hitting nothing. He won easily. And from that day on he never stopped talking about the painters and decorators.

Arcel also liked recounting another trip to Ohio with Valgar, this time to Springfield, where he came up against the racial and ethnic prejudice that would prove to be one of the sub-themes of his travels. "We were there for a fight against a guy called K.O. Mars. At the time, Springfield was notorious for the big Ku Klux Klan chapter it had. One day we're walking along the street, and there's this guy sitting outside a dry goods store. He says hello, we stop and talk, and while we're talking I notice that his name on the window is a very Jewish name. So I ask him how he got along in a town with the KKK. And he says, 'Not bad, I sell them their sheets.'"

Arcel seldom had to be pressed to praise Valgar. "He was the first guy who taught me, back when we were walking over to Grupps from the East Side, that boxing was brain over brawn. His one drawback was that he didn't have much power. Otherwise, as a boxer, he was right there with Benny Leonard. But it was that power that cost him, and why he never got to fight for the title."[3]

According to the trainer, Valgar also had what he called a "peculiarity" that led to more than one misunderstanding with impatient officials:

Benny was a very high-strung guy, and like clockwork before his fights, his temperature would shoot up and he'd start saying he was sick to his stomach. One night we were waiting to go on against a featherweight named Joe Fox, and Benny has about the worst attack of nerves I'd ever seen. He actually starting writhing on the floor. The promoter comes in and sees him like that and starts tearing into me. How could I have let a fighter in that condition ruin his big boxing show? I didn't bother arguing with him. I just picked Benny up in my arms and marched him out of the dressing room toward the ring. You can imagine the sight. The trainer carrying his boxer. Fox sees all this and couldn't be happier. The bell rings and he rips out of his corner ready to set some world record for first-round knockouts. Benny hits him with a left hook that wiped the grin off his face. They ended up going ten rounds before Benny won. The bettors were furious. The only ones who weren't amazed were me and Benny. As soon as his feet touched the canvas, he wasn't sick anymore.

Most of the stories about Valgar, from Arcel and others, portray him as a sweet man who just happened to communicate his sweetness most effectively through his fists (though rarely to any murderous degree). One tale that never failed to delight at Stillman's was about the evening he went to watch two other fighters and, only minutes before the bout, was approached by the promoter to substitute for one of the boxers who had suddenly taken ill. Valgar said fine and was quickly fitted out in trunks and gloves. But because there were no shoes for him, the story went, he had to decision his opponent while dancing around in the ring in wing tips and garters.

Another tale revolved around another fight threatened with cancellation because of a missing fighter, but this time it was Valgar who was on the verge of being stood up. The solution was to draft as his opponent Arcel's predecessor as his trainer, Mannie Seamon. As Seamon recalled it:

I told him it was crazy, that I was no fighter, that at most I could get through a couple of rounds. To make things worse they slapped this name of Frankie Wilson on me, and this with almost the whole arena Jews there for seeing their French Jew Valgar flatten his opponent. Valgar was clever, though. He started jabbing me with lefts, and that annoyed the crowd. They went from cheering on Benny to yelling for both of us to be thrown out of the ring. I don't know what I was thinking, but I get into a clinch to catch my wind and I yell out, "Come on, you French bum, fight!" Why do we do the things we do? Anyway, that gets Benny mad and he starts pounding away at me. Somebody told me Jack Dempsey was sitting ringside and couldn't stop laughing.

True to his word, Seamon lasted into the second round. "I don't know how many times they threw the towel in for me, but every time the referee threw it right back out again. The only reason that fight ever ended was because he got tired counting up to eight and nine."[4]

Never much of a slugger, and, outside a few seconds in the first round, mainly carrying the trainer, Valgar managed to get Seamon out of the ring with little physical damage to show for it. But decades later the fighter's legend also included his lack of a punch. Arcel:

He was already on his way down when we were making a trip around the country. One night Benny looked around the arena and saw only a handful of customers. Benny looked at me and said, "Ray, what's the matter? Why aren't we drawing?" I said, "Benny, the fans want action. They don't want to see any of that fancy jab and run stuff. Get out there and slug." Benny said he would do that. The round started. Benny went out with a rush, but did nothing but box. When the round was over, I said to him, "Why didn't you go out there and slug?" He looked at me and said, "I tried, Ray, honestly I did. My arms were willing, but my brain wouldn't let me do anything wrong!"

9

Partners

By the middle of the Twenties, Arcel had consolidated his reputation to the point that he was overwhelmed with offers for taking on fighters. He wasn't the only one. Equally in demand was Morris "Whitey" Bimstein, yet another product of the Lower East Side whose family got him out of the neighborhood to move north — in his case to the Bronx rather than to East Harlem. Like Arcel, Bimstein had Doc Bagley to thank for his expertise in dealing with cuts during a bout; unlike him, he had a substantial boxing career of his own, having fought some 70 times under the name of Johnny White (among other aliases) before joining the Navy in World War I and being assigned duty as a boxing instructor. This established a life-long pattern: When he died in 1969 at the age of 72, Bimstein could say he had never earned a dollar that wasn't somehow connected to boxing. Along the way, his fighters included the biggest names in the sport — Jack Dempsey, Gene Tunney, Benny Leonard, Georges Carpentier, James Braddock, Rocky Graziano, and Rocky Marciano, to name merely a handful.

One of Bimstein's most repeated tales was how he went from fighting to training. In a version published by a Cleveland newspaper in 1939, he said:

> I'm one of those boxers who never trained, and I [was] lucky to make three bucks a night. Well, one night I make six bucks by fighting two places. But what really turns me into a second is one night when I get murdered over in Queens. I used to get a little cut on tickets I could sell before the fight, but this night some politician is having a clambake and I only sell six tickets to my own fight. My end is half a buck. The other guy gives me a great going-over and then my two seconds want a little something out of my money — so we settle on 45 cents worth of sandwiches and coffee, and I've got a nickel left. Next day I look at my shiner and that nickel and I say to myself, "What the hell, Whitey, those seconds got everything you did except a black eye. Get wise and be a second."[1]

Many of Bimstein's champions were also Arcel's, since the two train-ers decided in 1925 to form a partnership, what insiders came to call the Siamese Training Twins. As Arcel told it, their partnership grew out of a casual conversation at Stillman's in 1925. "He just said to me, 'You know, Ray, there's a lot of work around here. If we were together we could handle a lot of fighters.' I sure didn't have any money objections. Before the Depression, fifty dollars was a lot for a trainer to earn from a fight, and most of the time you ended up with no more than a couple of bucks."

The pair could have been called the Odd Couple as easily as the Siamese Training Twins. If Arcel impressed as an austere teacher who at most accepted the occasional drop of Harvey's Bristol Cream, Bimstein came across as a garrulous character with a vein of Yogi Berra–like obser-vations and an avid taste for what Prohibition had outlawed. In contrast to the rail-thin Arcel, who never let a fork approach his mouth without profound scrutiny, Bimstein's pot belly attested to his ongoing romance with food as much as alcohol. (One journalist described him as looking like "a clown without makeup."[2]) They didn't even particularly like the same fighters, Bimstein always saluting Gene Tunney as the best he had ever seen in the ring and Arcel listing the heavyweight as among those from the boxing world he wouldn't have minded never having met. So how did the partnership work in practice? "Maybe Whitey would get the guys ready in the dressing room and I'd be in the corner. Or vice versa. On a good night we'd go home with 20 dollars apiece, maybe 25. Whitey was an excellent trainer. There were days when we wouldn't say two words to one another because from ten to six we'd be working with different fighters. If we started with a kid, we stayed with him. There were days when he might lose patience or I might lose patience, and we'd switch."

As a rule of thumb, trainers like Arcel and Bimstein pocketed ten percent from the honey pot. But sometimes managers would stiff them, or bargain them down. "One of the worst I had to deal with was Ancil Hoffman, the manager for Max Baer and his brother Buddy. He was always insisting we make a deal up front before we got around to counting the gate. The guy never lost out that way. He was really cheap. I'd ask for something like five thousand for a fight where I knew he was pock-eting hundreds of thousands, and he'd say no more than $1500. I trained both Baers and both of them wanted me in their corner, but I turned them down as often as I accepted because I just wasn't up for more finagling from Hoffman."

Although most of their work on a given evening was in four-round preliminaries at different clubs, it wasn't unusual for the partners to be in opposing corners during a bout. ("It was kind of strange, but you always had different managers so nobody could ever accuse us of conflict of interest.") One of those who fell within their partnership orbit was the lightweight (or junior welterweight, depending on the occasion) born as Judah Bergman, rechristened for the ring as Jackie Berg, and sold by promoters as the Whitechapel Whirlwind. As indicated by his nickname, Berg was an Englishman — and in Arcel's eyes, at first, that was the least of his problems. "The first time I saw him was in 1928. He'd just come over with his brother Willie and found a manager named Sol Gold. Gold calls me at Stillman's and tells me I have to get over to the Harding Hotel on 54th Street nearby to meet the kid. Kid was putting it mildly. He was this fragile thing with big saucer eyes, hair parted down the middle and pasted down on the sides with grease. I had to say to Gold, 'My God, you're going to get arrested going around with him! He looks like a little girl.'"

What Arcel found out soon enough was that Berg's past, brief as it might have been at 18 at that juncture, had nothing in common with an innocent girl's. The fourth of seven children of Russian Jewish immigrants raised in the poor and frequently violent London East End district of Stepney, he developed an early affection for his fists through a daily need to defend himself. At the age of 14 he received his first money for boxing; by the age of 16 he had been through six 15-round fights. Arcel didn't doubt the record; he just found it hard to reconcile with the teenager he had been introduced to. "There were people in England I knew and whose opinion I trusted, and they said he was the best English fighter they'd ever seen, at least at that stage in his development. But he still looked like a kid playing hooky from school, and when Gold went on talking about how he was going to match him against the likes of Tony Canzoneri, I thought that was crazy. The kid looked so delicate, so young, so breakable."

When the three of them went to lunch and Berg touched nothing, Arcel had a different kind of worry. "He just stared out of the window with a far-away look in his eyes. 'How far is Times Square from here?' he wanted to know. 'Where are all the movie houses, the night clubs, the fluff?' Uh, oh, I thought, one of those wild guys."

What Arcel didn't know at that first meeting was that Berg had once wondered the same thing about London's West End, and had gotten into the habit in his early teens of cruising the night spots for a little adventure. In the meantime it could not have been altogether reassuring to hear that Berg's hero was none other than the trainer's own early influence, the larger than life Kid Lewis. But Berg's Lewis wasn't Arcel's. The Lewis the kid was most taken with was the one whose time outside the ring was spent doing advertisements, appearing on the stage, and generally making it clear that he regarded himself as an entertainer more than merely a fighter.[3] But all these early red flags notwithstanding, Berg ended up so endearing himself to Arcel that the trainer had no compunction saying he "loved him like a son." (Another claim that it was in order to convey this feeling that he originated addressing him with the affectionate Yiddish term *Yiddle* was not true. Berg had been called *Yiddle*, or the kids' champion, since his East End days when he had attracted neighborhood boys whenever he was in public.[4]) What that also left him with was enough personality baggage to make Charlie Phil Rosenberg seem like low maintenance by comparison. "When he was on his good behavior, there was nobody gentler or sweeter. I took him into my home for awhile as a member of the family, and he was always the first one to put out the garbage, open doors for the women, all that. But then there was the wild Jackie where I ended up having to be a cop. He considered himself God's gift to women, and if I didn't keep my eye on him, he'd end up with the wrong woman."

One of those wrong women got him involved with the gangster Legs Diamond. As Arcel recounted:

> We were at the Harding Hotel because that was close to the gym. I'd heard stories that Diamond was the actual owner of the place, but I never knew for sure. Anyway, one day Jackie sees this woman in the lobby and starts flirting with her. What he didn't know was that she was Diamond's girl friend. A few minutes later, there's a knock at our door upstairs and two guys come in with guns. They're there to kill Jackie for making time with Diamond's girl friend, and if I'm there too that's too bad for me. Jackie can't get a word out, and I'm not making speeches, either. But I finally convince them he meant nothing serious in the lobby and promise we'll check out as soon as we can get packed. I liked thinking it was that deal that got us off the hook, but it helped a lot that these henchmen had taken it on their own to go after Jackie, that Diamond really knew nothing about it. And if he did have a piece of the hotel, shooting up the guests wouldn't have been good for business. But we got the hell out of there that day.

After Arcel had put Berg through a few weeks of work at Stillman's, Gold took the fighter to Chicago for his professional debut in America. Arcel, who also had to be in Chicago for a Frankie Genaro bout, got his first good look at the Englishman in action. "There were very, very few fighters who were able to fight so frequently, ten-twelve days apart, and show the stamina and endurance he had. He never looked to be a powerfully built man — he was just a slim, good-looking kid. But we found out one day he had a six-inch chest expansion! When he took a deep breath and expanded his chest, we stood there in absolute amazement. We couldn't believe it. It was like pumping up a balloon!"

After winning seven out of eight in Chicago, Berg returned to London to build up his stamina (and native fan following) in two 15-round victories. Only then, a few months before the Depression hit, was Gold ready to turn the Englishman loose in New York. Arcel wasn't as sanguine as Gold. "No matter what he had done elsewhere, Madison Square Garden was Madison Square Garden. You could really lose control of yourself once you climbed into that ring and had 20,000 people screaming and hollering at you."

New York also meant prowling for women, as Berg himself admitted years later. "Sometimes I'd sit in movie houses hour after hour. But then there were the dance halls. There was one place in particular on Broadway, called the Orphean Dance Hall. You paid as you walked in upstairs, top floor. You went over to a girl and you gave her a dollar and she gave you ten tickets for the dollar. Ten cents a dance, like the old song. You picked out a girl and you went to dance with her and while you were dancing, well, she sort of masturbated you. Really! By the time two choruses had gone by you'd blown your pants. So I used to go up there every day, sometimes twice a day."[5]

If those out-of-ring New York diversions exasperated his handlers, Berg was much easier to like within the ropes. His first — and second — opponent was Tiger Flowers, an African American from New Rochelle who had already cleaned the canvas with the best in the division. Nat Fleischer of *Ring* magazine described the battle almost 20,000 people saw at Madison Square Garden on the evening of May 10, 1929: "It is doubtful if any alien ever crashed the Big Time in more spectacular fashion. Berg proved to be a veritable human windmill in action. From the opening gong, he was perpetual motion personified. The fans were amazed at his speed and aggressiveness. Though bewildered at times by his opponent's furious attack, Flowers fought back desperately with everything he had and the battle developed into one of the wildest slugfests ever seen in the Garden."[6]

The fight ended in a decision for Berg and prompted so much talk that promoter Tom McArdle immediately scheduled a rematch for the Garden two weeks later. When Berg took that bout from Flowers, too, there was a new name to reckon with in the New York boxing world. Moreover, the fighter wasn't good only for wins and losses newspaper copy; some of his idiosyncrasies kept feature writers going for days afterward. In fact, if his charge's chasing after women posed one problem for Arcel, it wasn't any more taxing than the need to anticipate Berg's plethora of superstitions:

> There was one night in particular that I thought I had him totally relaxed before a fight the next day. I take him to the movies, we have no misadventures on the way home, then I go upstairs and take a look in at the bed where he's going to be sleeping. Right in the middle of the bed is my black cat all curled up asleep. I was ready to choke the damn thing. When Jackie saw him, he almost hyperventilated. Then I remembered something somebody had once told me about how the bad luck black cats were supposed to have little patches or streaks of white, while the perfectly black ones like mine were supposed to be omens of good luck. I don't know if he bought it. I know I didn't while I was saying it. But he calmed down and went to sleep. Which was more than I did all night thinking about that damned cat.

As it turned out, Berg not only bought it, but when he won his bout the following night, he insisted during his stay with Arcel that the cat be allowed to sleep with him every night.

At least to Arcel's mind, it was also Berg's superstitious nature that led him to enter the ring for his fights in the trappings of the most observant of Jews:

> He'd come into the ring with a *talaith* [sacred shawl] hung around his shoulders and *tvillan* [strips of leather worn as a reminder of God's presence] strapped around his arms and forehead. Then he'd go through this long dramatic ritual of unwinding the straps from around his body, kissing them and placing them in this embroidered gold bag he carried. "Please take care of this for me, Ray," he'd say, handing me the bag. At first you wouldn't hear a pin drop in the crowd, most of whom were Jews. Then just as fast they'd go crazy to see one of their own. When people found out he wasn't a particularly observant Jew, they assumed that entrance was all gimmick. It sure worked like one. But more than anything he was superstitious beyond reason. When I put the question to him one day, he seemed embarrassed. "It's comforting to have God on your side no matter what you're doing," was what he told me.

But Arcel's assertion to the contrary, everything suggested that Berg *was* deeply observant, that however much superstition and/or gimmickry were ingredients of his entrances, they were also afterthoughts. Even starting out as a teenager in London, he was known for the Star of David sewn onto his trunks. Reflecting his upbringing in a strictly religious family, throughout his life he was a regular presence at Jewish events, and at a plaque ceremony in Stepney after his death the keynote speaker was the Chief Rabbi of London.[7] For its part, however, the New York State Athletic Commission didn't care how religiously sincere the entrances were, it wanted them stopped. Arcel took credit for staving off that order by reminding Commission officials that they had never stepped in against Catholic fighters who made it a practice to kneel down in their corner and bless themselves before going out for the first round. Was the Commission about to show favoritism to Catholics and alienate all the Jews who flocked to Madison Square Garden and elsewhere to see Berg? No, the Commission was not.

Berg's most famous fights were probably those on January 16, 1930, against Tony Canzoneri at Madison Square Garden and on June 28, 1930, against Kid Chocolate (Elgio Sardinias) at the Polo Grounds. Although it had been a couple of years since the idea of a match against Canzoneri had been Arcel's notion of a dangerous fantasy, and Berg had become a ring star in the interim, the trainer still wasn't all that sanguine when the two boxers finally met for a contest to see who would get to take on Sammy Mandell for the lightweight title. "Jackie suffered making weight for the fight, and he appeared drawn and pasty-faced. Canzoneri, bouncing up and down across the ring, was heavy-chested, tanned, powerful, and dripping with confidence. Few people bet against Tony. He was a solid 16-to-5 favorite. We told Berg to swarm all over Canzoneri, the way he had with Flowers. 'Stay on top of him, Jackie,' I kept yelling to him. 'Don't let him get set.'"

With the result? "In the first round he fought completely the opposite of what we'd been telling him. Instead of swarming Tony, he stood straight up, jabbing, trying to outbox him. Canzoneri had a field day weaving low and pounding both hands into Jackie's body. Gold was beside himself. 'What the hell is he pulling?' he said to me. 'He's gonna get himself killed!'"

Despite the pleading reminders of his manager and trainer between rounds, Berg attempted the same approach in the second round, suc-

ceeding only in getting a split nose and bloodied mouth for his stub-
bornness. "But that was it," Arcel liked recalling. "He was taught his
lesson and for the next eight rounds he put on the greatest exhibition of
raw guts with skill I ever saw. Tony never again got a chance to set himself.
Berg kept him reeling back on his heels with snake-like jabs and machine
gun volleys to the head and body. Not once did he stop. Not for breath,
not for a fraction of a second. The crowd never used their seats. When it
was over, they had to half-carry Canzoneri back to his corner. Berg got
one of the longest and loudest ovations I ever heard in the Garden. I was
so excited I picked up the skinny little runt and kissed him."

After the Canzoneri fight, it didn't take long for Hollywood to come
calling with offers, and for Berg to be associated in print with Mae West
and other actresses. But Gold put his foot down against any serious
moviemaking for his fighter. Instead, Berg was whisked off to London
to take on Mushy Callahan for the title in the recently created (1922)
junior welterweight division. As crowns went, it was hardly the most
prestigious, with many boxing authority boards refusing to accord it
recognition and the title defender Callahan three years between defenses
because of lack of valid opponents. But Berg's new transatlantic fame
gave the bout all the energy it needed. With Arcel in his corner, the
Whitechapel Whirlwind battered Callahan around for ten rounds before
the latter's handlers threw in the towel. Shortly afterward, Berg successfully defended his new-won title against Joe Glick back at Madison
Square Garden in a bout that was most famous for his refusal to be
declared the winner because of two ugly fouls by his opponent. Waving
off that path to victory, he only increased his popularity with the crowd
and sportswriters by going the full 15 rounds to outpoint Glick.[8] Soon
enough, though, even that controversial bout was eclipsed by the duel
with the Cuban Kid Chocolate.

Although Bimstein drew the assignment as corner man for the fight
at the Polo Grounds, Arcel proved equally valuable as a detective.

Berg and Gold left New York for their training, but then Sol called me up,
saying he was worried. He said he'd heard Chocolate's camp was working to
get a certain referee to the fight, but he couldn't find out who it was. Since the
ref wasn't going to be named until the afternoon of the fight, that wouldn't
leave us time to change anything that had to be changed. He implored me to
get the name of the ref. Just by luck, that very same day, I ran into a guy on
42nd Street who I knew had a pipeline into Chocolate's camp. When he said
Chocolate would kill Berg, I had my opening. I told him that not only would

Berg win, but that I knew the name of the referee. I pulled out $200 and said to him, "I'll give you 2-to-1 the referee's going to be Lou Magnolia." The guy couldn't laugh loud enough. "Smart guy!" he said. "The ref's going to be Mister So-and-So. See you at the fight. I'll be there to collect."

Mister So-and-So, as Arcel confined himself to identifying the arbiter even 40 years later, had been associated with dubious Chocolate decisions, so Gold wasted little time getting on the phone to talk to an acquaintance of an acquaintance in the Athletic Commission's higher councils. But as late as when the two fighters entered the ring for their bout in front of a hyper Polo Grounds crowd of 36,000, Mister So-and-So was prancing around ready to fulfill his role as the third man. "The announcer was already going into his routine," Arcel recalled. "My heart bumped downward, and Gold was cursing to himself. But just when everything seemed lost, a member of the Boxing Commission climbed into the ring, waved So-and-So out, and waved in Patsy Haley as the referee. Sol's connection had come in by a nose!"

Even without a referee who might have been leaning in his direction, Chocolate was no treat. The most modest version of his record was that he had gone 66–0 in his professional fights; boosters claimed it was much closer to 100–0. But whatever the number, everybody agreed that Chocolate had never ended up on the wrong end of a decision. Through the first three rounds against Berg, there was little indication that he wouldn't keep his spotless record intact, especially after a third-round right that Berg later admitted "turned my head completely around."[9] But the longer the battle went on, the more the Cuban ceded ground under Berg's body blows, so that by the last round both fighters were staggering themselves as well as each other with every punch they threw.

Arcel: "When the final bell had torn them apart, I was drenched in sweat. Sol had cut his hand on one of the ring wires, he had been so tense about what he was seeing. We didn't say a word as we watched the announcer collect the decision slips from the two judges and the referee Haley. Then he walked toward our corner and held up Jackie's hand. The two judges had split their vote, but Haley — the last-minute substitute for ref — voted for Jackie."

As important to Berg's career as the Canzoneri and Chocolate fights were, Arcel always insisted that the moment that shone most brightly in his relationship with the Englishman came during the bout following the one with Chocolate, an October 1930 match at the Garden against

Billy Petrolle. Undoubtedly fueling that particular reminiscence was the fact that this was the fight that was preceded by the black-cat-in-the-bed episode.

Arcel: "They're going at it hook, line, and sinker with about a minute left in the round when Petrolle nailed him with the hardest punch of the fight, a left hook squarely under the heart. I saw it coming and turned away. I didn't want to see him drop. Whitey Bimstein noticed my frustration. 'He's okay,' Whitey said. Sure enough, Berg was still standing.... But I couldn't get it out of my head. That punch surely must have had some effect. As soon as the round ended I leaped into the ring, dropping the swabs out of my mouth in the excitement. 'How do you feel, Yiddle?' I yelled at him. Without batting an eye, he said, 'Lovely, thanks. And you?' If I live to be a million, I'll never forget those words."

10

The Family Man — Not

For all the anecdotes he helped sportswriters fill their columns with, next to none of them touched on Ray Arcel's home life. When his second wife Stephanie says he "wasn't really much of a family man," she is putting it mildly. Interview asides over the years — and they *were* always asides — generated little more than vague descriptions of his grandmother's settlement in Terre Haute, his mother's fatal diabetes, and his father's zeal for morning rolls. Beyond that, some of the recollections he volunteered for print have raised more questions than provided answers, beginning with those about his own formal education. To hear other members of the family, his often-stated praise of his step-mother Rebecca was at best an exaggeration. His niece Lila Libero, for example, heard nothing but the opposite from her father Solomon, Ray's younger brother, who spent most of his life as a foreman–truck driver for a New York winery. As she put it, "My father always said he and Ray had a tough time with [Rebecca]. He never went into too much detail, but I think it already says something that both of them were out of the house when they were in their mid-teens. I've also always had the feeling that their father wasn't the presence he might have been in those days. Maybe that's just my imagination, but Rebecca seemed to rule the roost."[1]

Arcel himself suggested the same thing about his father in the course of a series of tapes made in 1983 for the American Jewish Committee's project of recording the memories of American Jewish sports figures. "What I don't want to see I turn away from," he acknowledged to interviewer Elli Wohlgelernter. "My father was that way. He was always very evasive about things. There was a sadness about him. I never figured out about what, exactly. The old days, I suppose."[2]

Rule it or not, Rebecca didn't enter the roost by herself— she also brought along a son Sydney from a former marriage. Lila Libero: "The little we ever knew was that she was a widow. You might have thought that would have made for some problems between the boys and Sydney, but, apparently, just the opposite was the case. They both liked Sydney a great deal, and we had several Jewish holidays where all of them were together. They were very much at ease with one another."[3]

However at ease Arcel might have been, he never bothered to mention his step-brother to second wife Stephanie during their 38 years of marriage. He also lost sight of his half-sister Mollie. According to Libero, that might have been due to more than forgetfulness. "Whenever my father would mention Mollie in later years, it was always in annoyance over some fight they'd just had. A lot of it seemed to be about money, but I don't know about what exactly. It always seemed to be my father and Ray against her. They really didn't ever get along."[4]

Whether in regret for what it had come to mean for him personally or in self-assurance for what it meant for the ring, Arcel never disguised his feeling that family and boxing simply didn't mix. Most strikingly, he once told sportswriter Dave Anderson:

> Any fighter that has his father or any of his relatives around him can never make it. I once had a kid ... that I was trying to teach. He was a lovely young man. I put him in there to box in the gym and I told him, "Keep your right hand up and jab with your left. If this guy tries to jab you, catch his jab in your right hand." He went out there and instead of trying to do what I asked him to do, he was trying for a knockout. In the dressing room later, I told him, "I'm your friend. I like you very much, but I don't want you to box anymore. If you want to do it for fun, okay, but I don't want you to come here and get your brains knocked out." He started to cry, then he went home and told his family.
>
> Next thing I hear, his father and his brother are coming to the gym to beat me up. That didn't bother me. If anybody took a punch at me, I knew how to make him miss and counter. But now they arrive and they're screaming at me. "You're taking advantage of him! You're taking his money!" "What money? He hasn't earned any money!" Then I told them, "You're his father and you're his brother. But I'm his friend and he should never box again. He can't make it. He's going to get hurt." They walked out, calling me a Jew bastard, all that stuff. The kid went to somebody else's gym and had one fight. He got knocked out. His father and his brother wanted him to be a fighter for them, not for himself. The worst enemy a fighter has is his family.[5]

Similarly, in his 1983 interview with Elli Wohlgelernter, he stressed how "boxing is a poor boy's sport. Most of the time, you get the boxer's father taking all the money and you don't know what happens to it. Bad investments, stuff like that."[6]

If there was ever a nexus in Arcel's disclosures about family, the hardships of the Depression, and his discretion about personal affairs, it was in his reminiscence about a fighter who entrusted his savings to his mother during the economic crisis. "I'm not going to mention names because he still has descendants alive and the story is really none of my business," he said in his conversation with Wohlgelernter for the American Jewish Committee:

> But there was a fighter who earned quite a bit in the ring during the Depression and gave every penny of it to his mother. He didn't trust the banks and figured the money would be safe with her. Then a few years pass and he wants to get married, so he goes to his mother and asks for some of the money back. She says no, he gave it to her, so it's hers. He ends up having to take her to court to get back his own money. Just before the judge is about to rule in the mother's favor because there had never been any talk of a loan or something like that, he says to the mother's lawyer, "You can't let this man walk out of this courtroom without a penny in his pocket. I know what the law says, but there's also a moral question, and I think you and your client would be well advised to address it." So the mother gives the son $10,000. One day, after he's told me this story, I ask the guy how he felt about it all, and he still had this dumbfounded look after it's all over. "You're supposed to be able to trust your mother, aren't you, Ray?"[7]

What usually got lost in the telling of such tales was that Bimstein wasn't the only partner Arcel took on in the mid–1920s. After what he once admitted had been "a long period of being alone," Arcel married Hazel Douglas, a divorcee with a tow-headed five-year-old son named after his father, August Masterson (or simply "Gus"). It was a situation not unlike what David Arcel had inherited with his second marriage — except for the fact that Hazel wasn't Jewish. ("My father and step-mother were taken a little aback by that, I suppose, but there was never any big problem, and he ended up loving her.") According to Arcel, Hazel, shown by family photos to have been a thin, elegant brunette with sharp facial features, was "one of the angels on earth," though he never went into detail about how and where he first met her. In 1928 the couple adopted a daughter, Adele. For the most part, the family (which also extended to Hazel's mother) remained within the New York City area in the Queens township of St. Albans. But that largely meant Hazel and the two children remained there since the breadwinner was constantly on the road — a fact he reflected on ruefully with Anderson in a rare admission many years later: "One thing I would have to say about myself, the fighter was the most important part of my life. Which was wrong. But

Stepmother Rebecca with first wife Hazel in Queens.

Arcel with Hazel and her mother.

I didn't realize it at the time. It was wrong because I had a family, my first wife Hazel and our two children. I would go to training camp for months." And then, rationalizing the rationalization and tying it up with one of his pet axioms, he went on: "They weren't just ordinary fights. They were important fights. Mostly championship fights. Tough times make monkeys eat red peppers."[8]

Neither of Adele's daughters, Susan Molloy and Jill Bloch, was around when their grandmother was, though Jill recalls stories from her mother about Hazel's own mother having been a prim and proper Episcopalian and member of the Temperance Society. As for their experiences with their grandfather, both women use words like "courtly" and "gentlemanly." Even when he was in his nineties, according to Molloy, he did his utmost to open doors before women reached them. "It was really charming and old school," Molloy laughs. "But at the same time you never felt like he let his hair down. From what I've read about him, he was the same in public as he was in private. He wasn't somebody who was going to get down on the floor and play Cops and Robbers with kids. What you saw was what you got."[9]

And that included his ideas about what should and shouldn't be put into the body. "You shouldn't drink water or anything else during meals, that was one thing," Bloch recalled. "And he was really wary of vitamins. He was always warning about not taking too many of them."[10]

A day's outing with Arcel, according to both women, might be to a museum like the Met or the Frick or to a play like *The Front Page*. "He was really interested in a lot of cultural things," says Bloch. "When we knew him, he was already pretty much away from boxing, but he still wasn't the image of what you think of when you think of a boxing trainer. He liked to *observe* things. He was interested but always a little distant. And when you think about it, that was his whole life in the boxing world, wasn't it? He watched and he observed. After doing it so long, it wasn't something he could just turn off when he wasn't in a gym or at ringside."[11]

11

Paybacks and
Comebacks

With the 1929 Wall Street Crash and the onset of the Great Depression, the firm of Arcel and Bimstein made itself more available than ever for work, getting involved in bouts it might not have in other economic circumstances. ("There were no days off. You had to try to pick up a five-dollar bill some place. You learned how to starve quietly.") In one particular case, this led Arcel to bumping into one of the most notorious gangs in the United States, while in another he wasn't nearly as emphatic as he later admitted he should have been in discouraging a champion from coming out of retirement.

Around the time stockbrokers were jumping out of windows in lower Manhattan, fight fans in Detroit were organizing a boisterous fan club for bantamweight Carlo Mazzola, whose knockouts of opponents were reviving boxing in the city. According to Arcel, he was contacted by a Michigan promoter to propose an opponent for Mazzola that "isn't any kind of champion, but is still a fair enough fighter to give the bout more than just local attention." Arcel's candidate was Terry Roth, the first Golden Gloves champion and yet another immigrant who had ended up on the Lower East Side. Roth's manager, Danny Brown, agreed to the fight with Mazzola but only on condition that Arcel take over his training. If Brown didn't sound all that confident about what he was getting his fighter (who ended up with an overall record of 18–9–6) into, he at least wanted his bad judgment shared with the person who had put the idea into his head.

As it turned out, though, the real trouble didn't start for Arcel until the day before the fight in late November. Watching Roth work out in a Detroit gym, the trainer was approached by a character who inquired as to whether he thought the New York import could beat Mazzola. Arcel's reply, as he told more than one columnist over the years, was, "Well, we didn't come all the way out here to lose. Of course he's going to win."

After the questioner had walked away from that optimistic prediction, Arcel was reprimanded by a gym rat who had overheard the conversation: "You shouldn't have told him that. That guy is with the Purple Gang. He's gonna tell all the rest of them and they'll be betting on your fighter. Your guy loses, you and him both are in a lot of trouble."

Arcel didn't have to be told what the Purple Gang was. From the early 1920s a loose confederation of Jewish gangsters had been operating under that umbrella name in the Detroit area, specializing in the hijacking of bootleg whiskey being brought across the border from Canada; as often as not, they had taken their booty by shooting the traffickers transporting it. Because other mobs had been the favored targets of the Purples, local authorities took a long time deciding that the easy recourse to gunplay and other forms of terrorism posed an urgent civic threat. By the time Detroit police and Federal agents began zeroing in on them, the Purples had taken a qualitative leap into such other areas of expertise as shakedowns, strikebreaking, and contract murder. Al Capone, for one, was said to be so intimidated by the Gang's ruthlessness that he reached a pact with it for peaceful coexistence, thereby insuring no problems with his own speakeasy supplies in Illinois.[1]

Arcel acknowledged being "shaken" by what the gym rat had told him but also insisted that he had never wavered from concentrating on the best way to have Roth carry the night at Detroit's Olympia Stadium. Their strategy was to let the usually frenetic Mazzola wear himself out in the opening rounds while replying with nothing more than body blows. Roth did exactly what he was told, and in the sixth round he scored a TKO.

Negotiating their return to the stadium dressing room was a little harder. Arcel: "There was no room for us to get in. The whole Purple Mob was there, including the guy who'd come up to me in the gym. He gave me a card and said, 'I want you to come down to this restaurant, we're having a party.' Then he left and took all his guys with him. Danny Brown thought it was a nice invitation, that it was payback for the tip I'd given the guy in the gym. I told him it was no payback, it was a command, and unless we went, we'd probably not get out of town."

When Arcel, Brown, and Roth arrived at the restaurant, they found three empty chairs waiting for them around a huge table of revelers:

> Then this master of ceremonies got up and said, "Ladies and Gentlemen, we have a real treat for you here this evening — the young man who knocked out our local boy Carlo Mazzola. I take great pleasure in introducing the next featherweight champion of the world — Terry Roth!" Well, Terry jumps up and goes to the middle of the floor and takes this big bow. And I'm thinking to myself there's only two things wrong with that introduction — Terry is a bantamweight and he's never going to be the champion because he's on the down side of his career. When he comes back to the table, he leans over to me and whispers in his broken English: "Vot a bizness dis iz, Ray! In New York I'm going, but here in Detroit I'm coming!"

Although Arcel usually concluded the Purple Gang anecdote by pointing out that Roth was indeed soon out of the game, he left out the small detail that Brown and the fighter were not allowed to cut their ties to Detroit so easily, that the mobsters anticipated a lot more pay days and weren't about to cut them short. In the end, Roth fought five more times in Olympia Stadium but with such mediocre results that the Purples were finally relieved to let him go back to New York for his last couple of bouts before retirement.[2]

If Terry Roth prompted scary moments for Arcel, at least they were free of the melancholy that enveloped him in Los Angeles near the end of 1931 when he received a call from his ring hero Benny Leonard in New York. Training a Naples-born featherweight with the name of Kid Francis (Francesco Buonaguno) at the time, Arcel was dismayed to hear Leonard say he needed a trainer for a comeback. What made this announcement doubly stupefying to Arcel was not only that Leonard had been out of the game for years but had also been repeatedly cited as one of the few boxers to invest his purses wisely so that he would never lack for money. But that, as the former champion pointed out immediately when they met back in New York, had been before the Wall Street collapse.

Even decades later Arcel was given to shaking his head at what had happened to Leonard. His idol simply shouldn't have ended up like, say, his first three champions — Abe Goldstein, who had to drive a cab after Wall Street crumbled; Charlie Phil Rosenberg, who turned into a small-time bookmaker; and Frankie Genaro, who was forced to tend bar in Staten Island to make ends meet. On July 24, 1923, Leonard had successfully defended his crown in Yankee Stadium against Lew Tendler before 58,000 fans who had anted into a then-record gate of $450,000.

The ensuing months were all bathos, and in August 1924, at the age of 28, and following a desultory bout in Cleveland with Pat Moran during which both fighters were booed continually, Leonard retired as undefeated lightweight champion. There were no money worries on the horizon. He owned an auto parts store in New York and several apartment houses in New Jersey, and was still able to earn conspicuous sums through a vaudeville act in which he mixed stories of his career with exhibition matches. He was so popular that *Time* magazine named him, along with the likes of Babe Ruth and Hollywood stars, as illustrative of the personality cult sweeping the United States. As the magazine put it, "It is not only the physique which he so delights in displaying.... It is the curious quality of personal magnetism shooting across the footlights into the hearts of every fluttering little gum-chewer in the audience."[3]

But then the stock market crashed, taking Leonard's savings along with it. Thrown into the collapse were the failures of two night clubs, first the Ringside and then the Wigwam. With the additional problem of an ailing mother, he saw no way to stay afloat without returning to the ring. Arcel sought to dissuade him, pointing out that his long inactivity, plus the seven years added to his age, promised no good. But when Leonard insisted that he had no choice, Arcel relented, and for once agreed not only to be a trainer but to book whatever fights he could get.

> There were really two problems. The first was with Whitey, and I could see that wasn't going to work. Bimstein just had a different disposition from me, and it wasn't one that went well with Benny. So I did all the training myself. Then there was the manager problem. By the time Benny came back, his old manager Billy Gibson was in a sanitarium, out of the game. He then took up with Doc Kearns. Nobody had a bigger reputation as a manager than Kearns after his years with Jack Dempsey and Mickey Walker, but Doc was always thinking big, and in this case that wasn't the right way to go. He wanted to bring Benny back in Chicago against Dave Shade, who had already beaten some of the top contenders of the day and who would end up with more than 100 victories [*ed.: 130*]. The Illinois Boxing Commission took one look at that matchup and said no. At that point Kearns lost interest in managing the comeback, and I agreed to do double duty.

Arcel's first task was to bring Leonard's weight down from an initial 175 pounds. They managed it, after a fashion. "I knew he had nothing, he was washed up, but he was dead broke. I knew he wasn't going to make the money he was hoping to make, either. Maybe at the beginning, maybe as a novelty for the same people who had gone to see him in vaudeville, to see what he had been. But after that? I couldn't see it lasting long."

Within those limitations, Arcel set out a program calling for Leonard to fight twice a month for somewhere between $400 and $500 a bout, or 25 percent of the gate, whichever was more. He also devised a training regime that would give his charge the necessary workouts but simultaneously expose him to young gym fighters who would learn something from their sparring. "What I wanted was for Benny to be as much of a teacher as he was a boxer in training for a match. He'd always been a big influence on others, and I didn't see any reason for that to stop."

Other managers agreed, seeing little to lose by matching their up-and-coming fighters against someone with Leonard's reputation. "They knew Benny couldn't hurt their boys," as Arcel put it. "He wasn't going to look to go after some knockout record, and they would have exposure."

The one flaw in the program was what took place in the ring before a paid crowd. The first of the comeback fights took place on October 6, 1931, against Pal Silvers at Queensboro Stadium in Long Island City. The 15,000 people who contributed more than $25,000 to the gate ended up unleashing an angry cascade of booing and catcalling for a debacle that was compared to the tank jobs associated most often with Primo Carnera. As Nat Fleischer described it in *Ring* magazine:

> Leonard walked into the ring to the acclaim of a returned hero, but he left with the hisses of those thousands. The less said about the fight the better. Silvers, after outclassing Leonard in the opening round, in which four straight lefts in a row had Benny's face smeared with blood, apparently suddenly figured that it wouldn't do to make Leonard look bad. Instead of following up his advantage in the second round, he forgot how to fight and left himself open to severe criticism. When he received three light blows on the jaw and went down after first locating a soft spot, he acted like one who was dead to the world. But when Arthur Donovan, the referee, had counted ten, up leaped Pal and dashing about the ring, sought to continue the 'battle.' What a fiasco that was!"[4]

Arcel never commented on suspicions of a fix or on who might have been in on it, stressing instead how embarrassed both he and Leonard were by the Silvers bout. In the meantime, they pursued their original program, working toward "the one big one" with 19 more preliminaries in small clubs in places like Albany that sought to capitalize on the boxer's reputation. Although the official record credited Leonard with victories in every one of the matches except for one draw, none of them qualified as being among the Greatest Fights of the Century. Nowhere in sight was the Leonard who, according to *New York Mirror* columnist Dan Parker, "moved with the grace of a ballet dancer and wore an air of arrogance that belonged to royalty."[5]

There was more than one Arcel version of what happened when "the one big one" finally came into view. In a rare instance of espousing different viewpoints on the same event, he told some reporters that Leonard's brother Willie, who had begun to take more of an active managing hand in the scheduling of opponents, was the primary promoter of a bout against prominent welterweight contender Jimmy McLarnin, a 24-year-old Irishman whose record at the time was 50 wins and 8 losses. McLarnin also brought along some simmering ethnic tensions insofar as his handlers had never shied away from noting that he had made a career out of dumping Jewish boxers. For Willie and others, the idea of Leonard avenging all the defeated Jews could have only added to the box-office appeal of the fight. Arcel didn't see it that way — at least sometimes. "It was typical of Benny to search for the toughest and hardest road. I was dead set against such a match. Not only had McLarnin smooth boxing skill, but he was strong. Fit as he was, I couldn't see Benny giving away so much in age without being hurt. But Benny was obstinate ... and his brother was for the McLarnin clash."[6]

In his unpublished memoir, however, Arcel offered another explanation for the McLarnin bout, pointing the finger directly at the New York State Boxing Commission and its growing impatience with Leonard's often-cheesy comeback bouts. "One day we received a call from the Commission. They weren't pleased with Benny's comeback at all. Where they were concerned about was that he was making a fool of himself in these small clubs and that did nothing for the sport as a whole given who Benny was. They said it straight out, 'We've watched you going along as you have and we want you to stop. Why not take one fight where you can earn a lot of money, and then retire?'" According to this narrative, it was only after the Commission call that Arcel and Leonard began hunting around for that one final opponent, and that they came up with an offer from Madison Square Garden for a match against McLarnin. The offer was exactly what boxer and trainer had been hoping for since launching the comeback — a clean 25 percent of the net receipts on a projected $60,000 gate.

The bout was set for October 7, 1932. What Arcel remembered most vividly about the training camp they set up at Pompton Lakes in New Jersey for preparing for the fight was a conversation with Leonard one evening. "He got very reflective one night and talked about how when he was champion for eight years, the big business tycoons were falling over each other to invite him to functions where he was a drawing card for big fund raisers. 'But when I retired and the Wall Street crash came, Ray,' he told me, 'not one of those millionaires ever asked me how I was doing, how I was handling my money. Don't ever let anybody use you the way they did me.'"

The bout with McLarnin turned out the way most sportswriters had pegged it going in — with the referee declaring the Irishman a winner by TKO in the sixth round. But Leonard had his consolation, both in and out of the ring. Fleischer told his *Ring* readers:

> It was not the one-sided battle that most critics had predicted. At times Benny was so cool and agile that it seemed he might not only last the route but slip across a sleep-producing punch. There was plenty of reason for that in Leonard's showing the first two minutes of the opening round when Benny drove a right to the heart that caused McLarnin's knees to sag. Jimmy, infuriated, tried to retaliate, but Leonard spun him halfway around with a left that was most damaging. Benny demonstrated in that round that he was not simply in there for the money. He was in there to prove "they can come back." And this he went out to do. The crowd was with him, but Nature was against him. Twice in the first three minutes Leonard almost upset McLarnin, and those who have seen Jimmy in action know that only a good puncher can do that. But it was Leonard's one desperate stab for victory.[7]

However purple Fleischer's description of Leonard's motives, it was a far cry from the same writer's description of the Pal Silvers fight that had launched the comeback. And TKOed or not, Leonard himself painted the McLarnin bout as the fulfillment of the objective he had set out to reach with Arcel more than a year before. Talking to *New York Sun* sports editor Wilbur Wood on the eve of the fight, but referring to his guarantee from the gate, he declared: "You ask me if my comeback has been worth the effort? Since I started boxing little more than a year ago, I have put $65,000 into a savings bank account. Show me another business into which I could have gone and have made that much money in a year."[8]

Leonard never fought again after McLarnin, but he did remain in the ring for some years as a referee. That was also where he died, on April

18, 1947, while serving as the sole arbiter for six bouts held at St. Nicholas Arena on Columbus Avenue and West 66th Street. Just as the last fight on the card was about to begin, Bill Corum, who was broadcasting the fights to millions for the Gillette Razor Company, noted that Leonard was suffering from the heat in the Arena, to the point of taking off the Athletic Commission's regulation tie. Then, in between gasps and long silences, Corum reported that Leonard had collapsed and failed to respond to an immediately arriving doctor. One of those hearing Corum's pronouncement of death was Leonard's wife Jacqueline, who always listened to the fights her husband refereed.[9]

12

Citizens of
the Depression

Benny Leonard wasn't the only one forced to change plans because of the Great Depression. With fight crowds drastically thinned out by the need to watch how every penny was spent, not even the steady requests of managers to entrust their fighters to the Siamese Training Twins could keep the Arcel-Bimstein partnership together. In Arcel's telling, it was Bimstein who asked for the divorce, and strictly for economic reasons. "We had to split up in 1934. Nobody was making anything. Whitey came to me one day and said, 'Ray, I think we better go out on our own again. You're not making anything and I'm not making anything. If I make ten bucks, I gotta give you five. Same with you. That's just no good."

But others have told a different story, citing the economic squeeze as only one reason for the breakup. Amateur and professional trainer Vic Zimet, for one, attributed it mostly to the back-biting atmosphere at Stillman's — specifically, to the jealousy of other trainers that they weren't getting the boxers that would have kept *their* heads above water and to a collusion with Lou Stillman to level off the competition. "The others complained to Stillman about all the boxers being brought to the Gold Dust Twins," Zimet said. "So Stillman concocted some story, and he got Arcel and Bimstein into an argument with each other. I wouldn't say they ended up as bitter enemies, but they didn't talk to each other for years. I think it was pretty inevitable. It was a wonder they had lasted together for so long. Whitey was a nice guy, a fun guy. Ray was much more serious and much more trustworthy. I don't mean Whitey was a thief, just that he liked to play, he was really a playboy. But if you had to send a fighter out of town, you'd send him with Ray, not Whitey."[1]

One of the last of the fighters who fell within the partnership orbit was bantamweight Sixto Escobar, Puerto Rico's first world boxing champion. But though often listed as one of Arcel's titlists, Escobar was primarily trained by Bimstein. Around the time of the breakup Arcel was devoting most of his attention to Bob Olin, then a 28-year-old light heavyweight who had risen higher in division ranks than his accomplishments had merited. The Brooklyn native first attracted attention in 1928, when he won the Golden Gloves Open Championship. When he turned professional, he was a sure thing against the middle-level talents in his class, but very much a dubious proposition when it came to opponents with good records. In the span of three months in 1934, for example, he came out on the losing end of two bouts with former middleweight champion Lou Brouillard. But mainly because he was perceived as a smooth transition to a Hollywood career, Olin drew the nod in November 1934 as a challenger to light heavyweight champion Maxie Rosenbloom.

Rosenbloom, known as "Slapsie" for his habit of slapping opponents with an open glove, had held the title since 1930. At first this had opened more night life doors for him than he would have eagerly marched through on his own, and he had developed a reputation of going directly from his latest groupie's bed to some improvised ring for a midnight workout session. But after a few years that routine had begun to pall, and he had declared his intention of trying to make it in the motion picture business. Providing the last nudge was a ruling by the New York State Athletic Commission that his slapping habits were ridiculing opponents and, by extension, the promoters who had selected them as challengers, so it had to be stopped immediately. Instead of doubling the mockery for the ruling, as might have been expected, Rosenbloom acted suspiciously chastised while his manager sifted through candidates for a title fight. The weeding out process rested on two cardinal assumptions: that the champion was headed for California as soon as the bout was over and that the light heavy title would be remaining in New York for what other sports were given to calling "the best interests of the game." It was through this process that Olin, popular because of his roots in Brooklyn's Borough Park, rather than a couple of potentially more threatening opponents with little local following, was chosen as the challenger. Maxie might not have had his pride, but he wanted everybody to know he could have had it if he wanted to have it.

The bout, held in Madison Square Garden on November 6, 1934, has been recorded by chroniclers of ethnic events as the last championship bout between two Jews. It might have been just as well there wasn't another one. Rosenbloom would have been accused of defending his title half-heartedly if it hadn't been closer to quarter-heartedly. Within a couple of rounds the Garden crowd became one large hooting section. When Olin was awarded a split decision for the 15 rounds, it was largely because he had initiated the few exchanges inside the ropes. Even at that, some sportswriters thought the incumbent's superior nimbleness entitled him to hold on to the crown.[2]

For the next several months Olin barnstormed the country for matches that sometimes pitted him against fighters of comparable weight and sometimes didn't. All local promoters cared about was the draw of a champion against some local hero. In general, the bouts produced little revenue for even the celebrity champion because of the Depression, and Arcel always insisted that their chief value was in keeping Olin in condition. Finally, the Athletic Commission had had enough of the traveling carnival and ordered Olin to defend his title. The opponent was John Henry Lewis, an African American protégé of Joe Louis who had already defeated Olin in a non-title match during a barnstorming stopoff in San Francisco. The date chosen for the meeting was Halloween, October 31, 1935; the place was the St. Louis Arena in Missouri, where Jim Crow still governed and where black and white boxers had never mixed it up in public before.

By that point, Arcel had developed a sense of *déjà vu* where Olin was concerned vis-à-vis Benny Valgar. Like Valgar, Olin twisted himself into a physical mess on the eve of major bouts. "He would wake up in the middle of the night and have a very bad anxiety attack. He just went to pieces physically and emotionally. Not even doctors could explain it. What I usually had to do, and what seemed to work for awhile, was to give him a teaspoon of aromatic spirits of ammonia in a glass of water. He'd take a few sips, and that usually let him go back to sleep."

The trainer admitted this wasn't his only concern about the title bout when he arrived in St. Louis a month early. The whole rationale of the St. Louis promoters was that the fight would bring out black fans in unprecedented numbers in anticipation of seeing Lewis knock Olin to the canvas. What they had blithely overlooked was that potential black audiences were scraping the bottom economically even more than urban whites, raising the prospect of a sparsely filled house of white rednecks who wouldn't have cared how badly Lewis was beaten just as long as he was. None of this did anything for Olin's normal anxiety attacks, and only a couple of days before the fight he had one so badly that Arcel decided to take him to a doctor. As he told it: "I introduced him to the doctor as Ray Arcel. I couldn't tell him his name was Olin because word would get out that Bob was sick and that would get back right away to the promoters. The doctor put 'Ray Arcel' through all kinds of tests, then finally sat him up on the examining table and said to him, 'Mister Arcel, if I had your physical condition and build, I'd be a prize fighter. There's nothing wrong with you.'"

When Halloween came, few fans came with it. The crowd at the St. Louis Arena was so small that Lewis, with the double disadvantage of not being the reigning champion and being black, didn't see a penny from the gate. His cheering section consisted of Louis with his usual coterie and his manager Gus Greenlee, the racketeer noted for his influence in baseball's Negro leagues. The fight itself was a slugfest. Olin followed Arcel's advice to avoid Lewis's grab-and-move style and to force him into a brawl. The fighters kept at it before a screaming crowd until Lewis floored Olin in the 13th round. Even Arcel said later he thought the knockdown had ended the fight. But thanks to the intercession of the bell it didn't. "When I got him back to the corner, I started yelling at him, 'Don't let this guy take away your title!' Olin became what I could only call vicious. He walked out into the center of the ring and starting punching as if there was nothing in front of him. Lewis had to retreat, and Olin stayed right on top of him. This went on for the entire 14th and 15th rounds. You can imagine what the house was like. Even Louis and his friends were on their feet for the last two rounds."

In the end, though, Olin's late surge wasn't enough to prevent Lewis from getting the nod from the judges and the referee. The depressed Olin's consolation prize was a visit from Louis in his dressing room congratulating him for the battle. Over the next few months the deposed light heavyweight took his act as far as England and Australia, but without Arcel. A title rematch with Lewis had to wait until June 1937, but it was over more quickly, with Olin going down for keeps in the eighth round. While hardly praising Olin as one of the best ever in his charge, Arcel always acknowledged him as "a real fighter." Lewis ended up retaining the title until 1939, when he had to retire because of an advancing peripheral vision problem that had made some of his victories improbable if not incredible. Ironically, his last ring opponent, in an attempt to reach up to seize the heavyweight title as well, was Louis. The heavyweight champion had campaigned for the match as a way of helping the economically pressed Lewis pay off some of his debts — a situation that would be repeated in his own case some years later. What newspapers played up as the first heavyweight title fight between blacks didn't last long, with Louis battering his friend mercilessly into submission in the very first round. It was the only time in his officially recorded 117 fights that Lewis suffered a TKO. Coming full circle, his trainer for the bout was Arcel.

The trip to St. Louis for the first Olin-Lewis bout turned out to be an eye-opener for Arcel in a way he hadn't foreseen. Shortly before leaving New York, his father asked him to stop off in Terre Haute to pick up David Arcel's citizenship papers on file there. The elder Arcel was anxious to obtain the documents because of a recently passed pension law requiring proof of citizenship for collecting a government check. Arcel contacted a friend of a friend and was assured of help when he stopped off in Indiana. But after burrowing through documents dating back to 1880 at Terre Haute's City Hall, there was no trace of David Arcel's citizenship papers; of his deceased brothers, Ramil and Solomon, yes, but not his own. What further digging turned up was that David had filed first papers only, never the second ones that would have codified his citizenship. When Arcel protested that his father had even served for a short time as a city councilman, the local contact merely shrugged that "in those days they didn't keep accurate records."

Back in New York after the St. Louis match, Arcel broke the news to his father that, as far as the Federal Government was concerned, he had never been a recognized citizen. David took the news with what his son described as "enormous disappointment" but then quickly changed the subject to ask whether Ray had looked up the Levines, fellow immigrants to Indiana back in 1883. When Ray replied that they had built their original handkerchief sales trade into a large department store in Terre Haute but had otherwise only asked in general about him, David cackled in somewhat bitter self-satisfaction and replied, "Maybe they were afraid you were going to ask for the money they owed me." In true Arcel style, Ray never asked what money his father was referring to.

13

Out on Limbs

Panic attacks were not the only problem Arcel had to deal with during the 1930s with his fighters. Three of his most noted charges had physical impairments that should have disqualified them from all ring activity but instead set off intricate maneuvers to cover up the injuries and allow them to climb through the ropes as scheduled. The trio included two fighters whose struggles ultimately attracted Hollywood screen treatment and a third whose ministrations from Arcel probably stood as the single most striking example of the trainer's absorption with those for whom he felt responsible.

The first case was that of Barney Ross, who would at one time or another hold the titles in the lightweight, junior welterweight, and welterweight divisions. Ross's storied career already had several chapters written when he arrived in New York in 1933 for his first meeting with Arcel. The third of six children of parents who had fled a pogrom in what today would be Belarus, Beryl David Rasofsky, as he was born, barely got to know New York before his father Isidore moved the family to Chicago. There the elder Rosofsky served as an Orthodox rabbi while making ends meet in the poorest section of a Jewish ghetto by operating a small vegetable store. Beryl's ambitions to follow his father's strict Orthodox ways ended abruptly when Isidore was shot to death during a botched robbery of the grocery. When his mother suffered a nervous breakdown over the killing, and the social services officials of the day packed the youngest children off to an orphanage and basically left the three older boys to fend for themselves, the streets beckoned far more seductively than the local temple. Within a short time Beryl was running with a roughhouse gang that also included Jack Ruby, the future Mob-connected assassin of Lee Harvey Oswald in Dallas. Whatever he was doing, and little of it was good, he did it conspicuously enough to attract the attention of Al Capone, who used him as an errand boy for everything from fetching cigars to carrying messages to other thugs. Through it all, though, the future Barney Ross maintained the goal of accumulating enough money to buy a house for himself and his scattered siblings. Convinced boxing offered a surer path to that end than small-time thuggery, he entered the Golden Gloves and emerged as the welterweight champion. In 1929 he turned professional, but, at least initially, to so many yawns that Capone was rumored to have bought out the arenas where he fought so that Ross would have the beginnings of a nest egg. True or not, that these rumors even got started persuaded many that the gangster regarded the boxer as more than just one more fetcher of cigars.[1]

By the time Ross met Arcel in 1933, there was no need for Capone or anyone else to buy out arenas. Only a few weeks earlier he had defeated Tony Canzoneri for the double lightweight and junior welterweight titles along the road to a career record of 81 matches without ever being knocked out. Moreover, his ring dynamics had inspired publicists to point to him as the anti–Hitler answer to the anti–Semitism then being propagated in Nazi Germany.* Arcel came into the picture when Ross's managers, Sam Pian and Art Winch, asked him to take over the training for a return bout against Canzoneri slated for the Polo Grounds in September. When Ross defended his titles successfully in a 15-round decision, he insisted that Arcel remain in his corner. This Arcel did through three fights against Jimmy McLarnin, Benny Leonard's last ring opponent, for the welterweight championship. Still Number One after the third of the matches, Ross qualified for a September 1937 extravaganza against Ceferino Garcia at the Polo Grounds organized by super-promoter Mike Jacobs and ballyhooed as the "Tournament of Champions" because of the four title bouts on the card. As related by Arcel, it was almost his undoing:

> Two days before the fight, after his last round of sparring, Barney went to slap his sparring partner on the head the way boxers do and he hurt his right thumb. Barney's personal physician, who always came in from Chicago for his fights, took him right away to the hospital for X-rays that showed a hairline fracture. We all said immediately the fight was off, there was no way we should risk the title and an even worse injury to his thumb. But not Barney, he didn't want

*A similar theme prevailed in the heavyweight division where the gentile Max Baer was persuaded to wear a Star of David on his trunks in his winning bout against Germany's Max Schmeling on June 8, 1933.

to hear about any cancellation, and Pian and Winch gave in. Barney must have seen I wasn't very happy about that decision because he took me aside from the others and said, "You're always telling me to jab and hook and to make the other guy miss and counter. Well, now I'm going to show you everything you've been hollering about all this time." And that's what he did! We gave him a shot of Novocain and he went through the whole bout using just one hand. It was one of the most masterly exhibitions of boxing and feinting I ever saw. Garcia never caught on that he could only fake with his right hand, never actually punch with it. But that was Barney. The more pressure he was under the better he always was, and he was never under more pressure than that night.

Ross's luck ran out eight months later, in May 1938, when he lost to Henry Armstrong, the only professional boxer ever to hold three titles (featherweight, lightweight, welterweight) simultaneously. In a brutal and largely one-sided affair, Ross stubbornly refused cries even from some of his ringside supporters to quit as he staggered from one round to another. Arcel: "Ross was really hurt in the twelfth round, and we were going to stop the fight. There was no sense in him getting hurt anymore. But he told us, 'You stop this fight and I'll never talk to you for the rest of my life.' He meant it, too. And the referee was standing nearby and he heard it, and even he warned Barney. 'You're on your own from here on in, Ross,' he told him."

But he wasn't on his own following the fight. For three days after the bout that marked the end of Ross's ring career, Arcel remained with him in a hotel room, applying hot towels and salves to bring down the swellings from the Armstrong beating. "You don't leave a guy like that," the trainer said. "You especially don't leave a tremendous person like Barney Ross."

Although the Armstrong beating put an end to his boxing, Ross had even tougher days ahead. When World War II broke out he joined the Marines and insisted on combat duty instead of the celebrity recruitment role the Corps had planned for him. Before being shipped overseas, however, he was brought up for court martial for whacking a sergeant who had made an anti–Semitic remark to him. It was only thanks to a Jewish member of the military court and arguments that imprisoning a Jew for reacting against anti–Semitism was hardly ideal advertising for the Marines in combating the Axis that the panel agreed to go through with shipping Ross overseas — to Guadalcanal. Shortly after arriving in the South Pacific, he found himself with three other Marines isolated one night under heavy Japanese fire. All four men were wounded, but Ross, the only one able to return fire, fought an estimated score of Japanese until dawn, killing most of them. By then, two of his companions had died from their wounds, but he carried the third man — almost a hundred pounds heavier — to safety. For his bravery he was awarded both the Silver Star and a Presidential Citation, conferred by Franklin Delano Roosevelt personally in a Rose Garden ceremony.

Even that didn't end his travails. Because of his wounds he was given heavy doses of morphine during his hospitalization, leading to a craving for it that, with his release from medical care, evolved into an addiction to heroin. Arcel recalled running into him on the street several times and being struck by how shaky he looked. "I never really suspected drugs, I thought he'd just had a long night drinking or something. I'd tell him he needed to go home and get some rest, but he'd just shrug it off, tell me he was fine. I'd seen other drug addicts, but somehow he didn't seem like one. Maybe I just didn't want to believe it." Ross's protracted battle to overcome the addiction became the central drama of the motion picture *Monkey on My Back* (1957), with Cameron Mitchell portraying the boxer. In fact, as during his fight with Armstrong, he left little incomplete. After overcoming his heroin problem, he was able to enjoy the reunion of his siblings that he had sought for so long. He also appeared as a character witness for Ruby in the Oswald shooting trial. For Arcel, though, it was Ross who had the character. "I rank him right up there with Benny Leonard as a human being," he declared more than once. "When you look at his whole life, the enemies he had in the ring were the least of it. But he beat them all."

When middleweight Teddy Yarosz came to Arcel in 1935, he had only one opponent in mind — Babe Risko, a club fighter to whom he had lost a non-title fight on New Year's Day and who he was scheduled to meet again for the title at Pittsburgh's Forbes Field in September. The only problem with manager Ray Foutts's request for Arcel's help was that Yarosz had not only lost his January battle with Risko, he had lost it gruesomely by fracturing his kneecap and tearing a cartilage in the first round and then going down a few more times on his bad leg until the manager had thrown in the towel. Although Arcel had been impressed by Yarosz's skill in the ring, that had been before the bout that had torn up his leg, and he acknowledged being dubious about the clearly gimping figure who showed up the first day for gym drills. To make matters worse,

In a Philadelphia gym in the early thirties with Barney Ross.

Yarosz showed no enthusiasm at all for Arcel's plan to move to a training camp out of the public eye. Only under his new trainer's pressure did he mention a rural area known as Alum Rock Park, about 10 miles from his Pennsylvania home in Monaca. "I was no more enthusiastic about that idea than Teddy was about a training camp in general," Arcel admitted. "It was still the Depression, and it was hard enough to find a properly outfitted gym in the mountains or the woods without talking about some remote cabin that had never been used for that purpose. I only went to see the place when Foutts insisted that was the only place Teddy would go."

What Arcel found was the barest of accommodations: three rooms and three beds, not even a toilet. At this point it was Yarosz who had all the answers for a skeptical Arcel. "I told him we needed clean bedding for the beds. He said his sisters would come over with it from Monaca. I told him we needed a bath. He said no problem, there was a cold spring nearby and he'd always felt refreshed after using it. And what about food, I asked. No problem, he said, his brothers would bring canned food."

That was where Arcel finally got him. "No way, I told him. We don't eat canned food. On the way to the cabin I'd seen some farms, so I headed for the nearest one. The woman there was very obliging. They had a nice porch where we could eat. I told her there were only two of us she had to cook for. Her one condition was that it had to be dinner at 5:30 sharp because she had to feed all the people she had working in her fields. As far as the food went, I brought steaks, chops, and chicken from a butcher. She supplied the vegetables. We never had any trouble on that score."

The game leg was another matter. Arcel had seen enough of Yarosz's reduced mobility to know he couldn't follow his traditional routine of running fighters for gradually longer distances every morning. "We started off by simply walking, a little further every day. That was all right as far as it went, but when I moved on to jogging, you could tell he didn't have a very firm step. I told Foutts I wasn't going any further until I could sit down with the doctor who had operated on him."

As it turned out, the doctor was all reassurance. Arcel acknowledged still having his doubts but stepped up the training regimen. "I still didn't want him running much so stuck to the walking, but if the doctor who operated on his knee said he would be all right, what was I supposed to do? Actually, the worst part of that time at Alum Rock Park was those cold springs. But if Teddy did it, I had to do it."

Ever skeptical, Arcel insisted after a couple of weeks of training that the surgeon again examine Yarosz to see if his leg had held up. Once again the doctor said the boxer was equal to the challenge of a match, and once again Arcel, by his testimony, left his office not completely convinced. By the night of the fight, Yarosz was under 160 pounds and giving every appearance of living up to his reputation as a nimble boxer who relied on speed for confounding opponents. The appearance lasted through two rounds, but in the third the troublesome leg buckled. "It's gone, Ray," Yarosz admitted when he returned to his corner. Arcel's improvised solution was to tie a plastic bandage around the leg for support and to advise his boxer to stay away from Risko. On an up note, the sight of the bandage and Yasosz's obvious pain as he tried to bounce up and down on one leg won the Forbes Field crowd over to him, and they cheered him through to the end of the 15th round. Back in the real world, there was little surprise when Risko was awarded the decision.[2]

After the fight, Arcel pleaded with Foutts to get a different medical opinion on the state of Yarosz's leg than that provided by the original physician. Finally relenting, Foutts took Yarosz to Philadelphia to see John Royal Moore, an orthopedic surgeon connected to Temple University and noted for unorthodox ways of dealing with fractures. For weeks Arcel heard nothing, his calls to the manager eliciting little more information than that Yarosz was under Moore's care. Then in December, according to Arcel: "I was in Stillman's and I see the elevator door open. This guy comes out. He's got a steel brace on his leg and is carrying a cane. He's as disabled looking as anyone I've ever seen. Then I recognize him. It's Yarosz, and he tells me this Moore has operated on him. I think that's great, but what's he doing at Stillman's? 'I came here to see you,' he says. 'I've got to fight. There's nobody at home earning money, and there're six of us with my mother. We have to eat, and I'm our best shot.'"

Arcel's first move was to call Moore in Philadelphia and set up an appointment for the very next day. With Yarosz making the two hour–plus drive, he was ushered into Moore's office to hear that his uneasiness about all the earlier assurances had been well-placed, that the first surgeon had erroneously operated on the fighter for a torn cartilage when, in fact, the problem had been torn tendons. At that point, according to Arcel, he reached back into the lore of Grupp's Gymnasium for the story of Freddie Welsh, the lightweight champion who had lost the title to Benny Leonard in 1917. As the trainer recalled the story, Welsh, serving as a boxing instructor in the Army during World War I, had used a combination of heat, weights, and massage to help an officer who faced discharge because of his inability to bend a knee. Thanks to that therapy the officer eventually regained flexibility in his joint and was able to remain in uniform. In Yarosz's case, wouldn't it be possible to seat him on a table and put a wooden clog on his foot and attach a bag of salt to the clog? ("I wanted to use a bag of salt because I wanted to add a safe amount of buckshot every day to gradually work up the knee's resist-ance.") When Arcel asked Moore whether that might work, the surgeon said "in due time" but when exactly depended on Yarosz's body. "'But I'll tell you why I think you've got something,'" the doctor was said to have gone on in Arcel's telling. "'When I operated, I didn't sew the ten-dons, I knotted them, like a piece of string. Even if you knot them and then pull, there's always a little give, and if weights force his knee to bend, then he'll still have enough room to make it possible.'"

On his way back to New York with professional approval for the planned therapy, Arcel reflected that "Doctor Moore almost made my father's dream of me becoming a doctor come true." An immediate prac-tical problem confronting him, though, was Lou Stillman. "I needed a lamp to bake Teddy's knee, but I knew Stillman wasn't going to let me use the gym's electricity for that. He didn't even need the excuse of the Depression to say no. But then I remembered all elevators have little red lights on them, so I got a long extension cord to plug into the socket from the elevator light to the small room I had at the gym. Once Stillman heard that I would be stealing power from the building and not from him, he had no objections."

Yarosz submitted to the treatment every morning from eight to eleven. "There was no pain involved. He sat on the table with his leg extended. The leg was as stiff as a board. I kept turning him so he could rest it a little. Every day I added a quarter of a pound of buckshot. When I saw we were making some progress, I took him down to see Doctor Moore again, and he was thrilled, kept encouraging us not to stop. I was up to 16 pounds of buckshot when it happened. The knee started to bend! Teddy got so excited he started pleading with me to let him go outside and punch the bag a little. He insisted so much I said okay, but only on the condition he keeps his steel brace on because we weren't going to undo all our work for a couple of bag punches."

If there was a note of black comedy in the exhausting routine, it came when Yarosz began punching the bag, and one of the street toughs attracted to the gym approached Arcel to praise the fighter's style. When Arcel replied that Yarosz was a world champion, the tough said, fine, he was going to be his manager. Arcel: I tell him Teddy already has a manager. If he's going to horn in, he's going to have to tell the manager. The guy says okay, give me the number of his manager. I give him the number for Jack Dempsey's restaurant, and he goes off to the phone booth. Only at the last second does he think to ask me for the manager's name. "I tell him to ask for Frankie Carbo, a notorious underworld character at the time. The guy turns absolutely white and comes running back out of the booth. 'Hey, forget it, forget it,' he's yelling at me. 'I never said anything.' The guy ran out of the gym so fast I thought he was going to fall over his own feet. Never saw him again."

There was such steady progress in Yarosz's condition that by April 1936 Foutts was asking whether his fighter could get back into the ring. With Moore's approval, the middleweight took on Bob Turner at Hickey Field in Millvale, Pennysylvania. Not only did he win that 10-round decision, but it was the first of seven consecutive victories that were held in gradually larger venues, such as Forbes Field, Griffith Stadium (in Washington), and Madison Square Garden. All told, he had about 40 more fights before retiring in 1942 with a record of 106–18–3, and not once did his leg again prove troublesome. "It was really hard to explain everything that went into it," Arcel said. "Of course we were all ecstatic — me, Moore, Foutts, Teddy himself. But it was still hard to get across to others the courage and determination he put into his comeback. In one sense, the wins were just the cherry on the cake. And I got to feel a little like the doctor my father had wanted."

When Yarosz first came to Arcel in 1935, the trainer already had plenty to keep him busy. Although the partnership with Bimstein had broken up the year before, the pair still had converging interests on several fighters. One of these was heavyweight and light heavyweight James Walter Braddock, identified on boxing cards as James J. Braddock (a publicity ploy for likening him to the legendary James J. Corbett and James J. Jeffries). He also became known as "The Cinderella Man" thanks to writer Damon Runyon, who gave him the sobriquet for his fairy-tale career. Braddock didn't particularly enjoy the fairy tale. He brought more than eight years of professional bouts when he crossed paths with Arcel and Bimstein, and the more wasn't all good. For starters, he had been written off on two different occasions for howling defeats just when he had appeared to be on the verge of being recognized as a serious heavyweight contender. He also had a manager, Joe Gould, who had a somewhat cavalier attitude toward his fighter's injuries. Informed on one occasion that Braddock had broken his hand during a bout and would require a second break for resetting it properly, Gould decided the cheapest way of realigning the bones was to send the fighter back into the ring and hope that he broke his hand a second time on the head of his next opponent. Only when that didn't happen did he agree to have doctors perform the readjustment. Most of all, though, there was Braddock himself, a devout Catholic who waxed and waned on his ring ambitions and who couldn't keep his family above the poverty line by working as a longshoreman with practically only one hand because of the ring break. The necessity of accepting government welfare ($19 a week to feed his wife, himself, and three children) incensed him more than most of his ring adversaries and marked the extent of his interest in boxing (and its purses) after earlier disillusionments.

When Gould brought Arcel into the Braddock camp, it was in the run-up to a title bout against heavyweight champion Max Baer. The least of Arcel's problems was that he had always liked Braddock and that he regarded Baer as a friend whom he had already tutored more than once. Like most other experts, he gave Braddock little chance against the incumbent and knew he had been maneuvered into the role of challenger only through a series of untimely defeats of other heavyweights regarded as more formidable opponents and the refusal of the most credible of them all, the German Max Schmeling, to travel to the United States for the match. Never one to let a sports page headline opportunity go by, Baer was quoted as saying: "Braddock? You're kidding me. With all due respect for my elder, he's over the hill. He was over the hill five years ago."[3] Braddock's own take on his situation? "Funny racket, this. Bum one day, headliner the next."[4]

The headliner was almost old news before the headline. Still aching from the broken hand that had developed arthritis, Braddock took on a series of sparring partners in his Catskills training camp whom Gould might have selected from a chain gang. One of them hit the challenger in the ribs so hard Braddock tore a muscle. Fortunately for Gould, if not for Braddock, the press was so captivated by Baer's machinegun one-liners that every reporter assigned to the fight was over in the champion's camp for more quotes. This enabled Gould to whisk Braddock off to a doctor without being noticed and also to fit him out with a pneumatic corset under his sweatshirt for protecting the fighter's midsection. And, as Arcel was to note, if Braddock had to suffer such an injury, he couldn't have chosen a better opponent for it since Baer was notorious for ignoring torso punches in favor of going for the head.

The night of the fight, Baer was considered such an overwhelming favorite that odds makers were demanding at least 10 to 1 on him. What didn't emerge until much later on, though, was that the champion had gone through his own training with an uncharacteristic moodiness that his handlers never succeeded in lifting and that, given his evening social habits, might have had something to do with one of the women habitually drawn to him. Baer never said what was bothering him, but he brought enough of his distractedness into the ring to lose his title to Braddock in a unanimous 15-round decision. Braddock's ribs were never endangered — nor was the new champion's fanatical sense of rectitude. One of the first things he did with the money gained from the fight was to pay back the state for the welfare checks that had kept his family alive. It was a gesture re-applauded with gusto by anti-entitlement politicians when Russell Crowe portrayed the fighter in the 2004 film *Cinderella Man*.

14

The Cool and
the Crude

Given his penchant for laconic, if not altogether evasive, answers, it was easier to read Arcel's likes more than dislikes while he was an active trainer. Even distaste for Billy Grupp's anti–Semitism was regularly deflected to the opinions of Benny Leonard and the other Jewish boxers who protested against it by moving over to Stillman's gym. At least until he got around to talking about promoters late in his career and in retirement, he was loathe to pronounce himself against anyone and had moments of candor admitting as much. But there were exceptions.

In style and personality, Arcel and Whitey Bimstein had little in common during their partnership; they also had little in common when it came to their opinions on two ridiculously different heavyweights — Gene Tunney and Tony Galento. For Bimstein, Tunney, the victor over Jack Dempsey in the infamous "long count" championship bout of 1927, was the "finest fighter I've ever seen. He was cool, calm, and collected. Nothing ever bothered him. He was always underrated. In my book he could have licked them all, from John L. Sullivan to Rocky Marciano."[1] While he never held back from praising Tunney's biggest ring moments, particularly his revenge victory over Harry Greb after Benny Leonard had given him punching advice in the gym, Arcel begged to differ with Bimstein. Asked by *New York Daily News* columnist Michael Katz in 1985 to name the 10 greatest fighters he had ever seen, the then-retired Arcel insisted on naming 12: Willie Pep, Henry Armstrong, Pete Herman, Benny Leonard, Mickey Walker, Harry Greb, Tiger Flowers, Jack Dempsey, Joe Louis, Ray Robinson, Barney Ross, and Roberto Duran — a group that included two heavyweights who had floored Tunney. And he didn't stop there, either, telling Katz he would like to add seven others to his personal Hall of Fame list: Rocky Marciano, Muhammad Ali, Tony Canzoneri, Ike Williams, Lew Jenkins, Johnny Kilbane, and Marcel Cerdan. In short, Tunney couldn't even make the Top 19, while the relatively unknown Herman and Jenkins, as well as the Kilbane who had supposedly been "too scared" to fight Benny Valgar, could.[2]

Arcel's reservations about Tunney were hardly unique. The fighter had always struck a remote figure, interpreted by gym rats and many sportswriters as a snobbishness toward his own profession (and them). For sure, his marriage to the socialite niece of steel magnate Andrew Carnegie, his tendency to pontificate on one and all subjects, and his reluctance ever to say "while" when he could say "whilst" didn't build up his credit in the spittoon world. Nor did Tunney lose points to Arcel in particular because of his generally defensive approach in the ring; how could he have, when the trainer himself had guided more than one fighter to a title with such tactics? But even when he wasn't making lists of his favorite fighters, there was inevitably a hesitant tact in Arcel's tone when the topic turned to the heavyweight. Perhaps he came closest to explaining his attitude in the tapes he did with Elli Wohlgelernter for the American Jewish Committee in 1983, making it clear he saw Tunney as a somewhat bloodless character with a short memory:

> For a lot of years, whenever Tunney was going into training or was just having a down time, he'd depend on this sometimes–sparring partner to cheer him up. The guy was named Billy Wallace, and he did some exhibitions with Tunney. Wallace always managed to get a laugh out of Tunney and put him back in the mood for training or whatever he was doing. Then a few years pass, and Wallace hits the skids. He finally goes to Tunney to ask for his help. Tunney's got money, he's got plenty of it. He married very well. But the only help he gives this guy is to tell him he should go join the service because the Army would give him a bed and feed him. I don't know how you say something so heartless like that to somebody you were depending on for so long. It's the kind of mentality I've never understood.[3]

From his veiled remarks over the years, it was apparent that Arcel was also irritated by how the public initially warmed to the ex–Marine Tunney in his confrontations with good friend Dempsey, accused of having been a slacker during World War I for not having joined the armed services. Although Dempsey erased much of this reputation (also a source of gossipy publicity during his fights against French war hero Georges Carpentier) with his training accomplishments during World War II, Arcel was always quick to point to testimony that confirmed Dempsey's story that he had been kept out of the Army only because of bureaucratic snafus, leaving the suggestion that the Tunney camp had exploited what was basically a smear.

At the opposite end of personalities who would have never been invited to an Arcel party was heavyweight Tony Galento, as proudly crude as Tunney sought to impress as refined. If Tunney was accused of thinking of himself as above boxing, Galento conveyed the idea that the sport was about as sacred as going to the toilet. But that didn't change Bimstein's view that Galento should have put a quick end to Joe Louis's reign at their Yankee Stadium title bout in June 1939. "I still think Tony Galento would have licked him if he obeyed orders," Bimstein said a year after the fight. "We had Tony bobbing and weaving in the first two rounds, and he had Louis dizzy. He even knocked Louis down. Then he thought he was John L. Sullivan and came up straight to slug, and you just can't do that with Louis. If Tony had fought the way he was told, he might have kept Louis down for keeps — and I don't think Tony was the greatest fighter in the world, either."[4]

About the only part of that Arcel agreed with was the last part about Galento not being the greatest fighter in the world. "I never had much time for that guy," Arcel declared in a 1948 column floridly ghosted under his by-line for the *New York Journal-American*. "He was as strong as an ox, and his powers of endurance and his ability to soak up punishment and absorb pain bordered on the freakish.... But outside the ring he was nothing but a comic, noisy man whose circus tent antics and crazy eccentricities certainly brought no credit to the game. Trying to get Galento fit was a farce. The New Jersey Fat Boy dragged his training down to a comic strip level."[5]

Arcel's attitude was forged from more than one personal experience. And it mattered not at all to Galento, whose moniker of "Two Ton" came not from the substantial gut he carried into the ring but from an excuse he once gave a manager that he was late for a fight because he had been busy delivering two tons of ice on a part-time job. If it hadn't been ice, it would have been bay leaves, since nobody spat on the rigors of training more outlandishly than the heavyweight whose every accomplishment between the ropes in the 1930s became instant fodder for the talk in the saloon he ran, and ran raucously, on Day Street in Orange, New Jersey. "Nobody liked him except maybe the guys who hung out in his saloon," said Arcel. "To call him crude was putting it mildly. He resorted to all kinds of foul tactics to win a fight."

In the weeks leading up to his confrontation with Louis, the tactics included making late night calls to the champion to whisper threats and shriek racial epithets. More publicly, his camp had little compunction about accusing Louis of hiding an iron bar in his glove in a fight against Max Schmeling. The Day Street bar also featured a giant poster of Louis that Galento periodically approached for unleashing a punch or two to get a rise out of his patrons.[6] Even Bimstein acknowledged that the Orange saloon was headquarters for gluttony and a few other capital sins. "The first time I was called upon to take charge of him," Ronald K. Fried cited the trainer as saying in his *Corner Men*, "I watched him work out, then we went back to his tavern for dinner. And what do you think he ate? A big platter of meatballs and spaghetti! Just before he fought Max Baer. And two days before the fight they called me and told me he had a fight with his brother and that his brother shoved a broken glass in Tony's face and split his lip. We fixed that up and the day of the fight, at three o'clock in the afternoon, he ate more meatballs and spaghetti and drank a dozen bottles of beer. Baer walked right out, smacked him with a right in the mouth and dug a left hook into his stomach. After that was repeated a few times Tony was through."[7]

Arcel wouldn't have had it any other way. Certainly he had heard the same Galento stories that Bimstein and the bar patrons in Orange had. Like the night in Oakland in 1931 when Galento had fought three bouts, dropping two opponents in the first round and the other in the third, pausing between fights only to fill himself up with beer. Or the night a year later in Newark when he had floored Arthur DeKuh in four rounds and then immediately had taken up a challenge to eat 50 hot dogs for 10 dollars (he collected). At various times he wrestled an octopus and boxed a kangaroo in the ring. When he wasn't being a clown, he was being a bore, if not worse. Several times his fights were ruled no contests because of suspicions they had been pre-orchestrated with bookmakers; when arena crowds weren't laughing at him they were booing him out of the ring. On two occasions fans resorted to throwing trash into the ring to put an end to sorry spectacles. His September 1939 match against Arcel charge Lou Nova has been chronicled by boxing historians as perhaps the foulest bout ever held, and for some years it earned its venue the name of Filthydelphia among sportswriters.[8]

None of this did much for a lasting relationship with a manager, and Galento had nine of them between 1929 and 1943. In 1933, the optimist who thought he could restore order was Dempsey, and, six years before the Nova bout, he asked Arcel to sign on as the trainer. "I told Jack it was a waste of time and money, but he was convinced that Galento could be shaped into a world beater, and so, since we were friends, I agreed. But right from the start it didn't work. Galento was just bone lazy. Half the time he didn't even bother to turn up at the gymnasium, and when he did he only loafed around." Scolded for his gargantuan eating habits, Galento told Arcel, "Aw nuts, Ray. I'm a big guy. When I'm hungry, I just gotta eat."

It didn't take Arcel long to back out of his agreement with Dempsey. If he had any satisfaction at all from the experience, it was in being in Stillman's a few days later when Dempsey had his own moment of decision:

> Dempsey strolled quietly into the gymnasium and walked up to the balcony while Galento was going through the motions of "working out." He was fatter than ever, hopelessly out of condition, and quite obviously doing nothing about it.... He didn't see Dempsey and continued waddling around the ring, clowning and wisecracking as he fooled with his sparring partners. After watching a couple of rounds, Dempsey came down to ringside. He was wearing a beautifully cut light gray suit, tan and white shoes, and white silk shirt. When Tony caught sight of him, he gave him a big hello. "You look like a million bucks dis afternoon," he says to him. "Never mind how I look, you big bum," Dempsey answers. "Let's see you do some work."

When Galento didn't take the hint, Dempsey turned to Arcel for boxing gloves:

> He took off his coat and stripped right down to his white silk monogrammed underpants and vaulted into the ring: "Now, Tony," he told him. "It's you and me. I'll show you how we used to do it." He began humming a little tune — an old Dempsey mannerism — and then, as Galento backed away, he flashed into action. Jack was turned forty but his body was as lean and hard and tanned as ever, and for three memorable minutes we saw the old Dempsey, the murderous, tear-away Manassa Mauler.... What he did to Galento in those three minutes was nobody's business. He ripped punches into the pudgy torso from all angles, split his lips with a terrific left, and sent the blood squirting from his nose with a right.

Even when Galento threw his arms up for Dempsey to stop, Arcel said, the former heavyweight champion kept going. "He chased after him, throwing punches until I called time. Still breathing easily, Dempsey ducked under the ropes and began to dress while Galento stood shaking his head in a semi-daze and trying to wipe the blood from his face with the backs of his gloves. When he was dressed, he threw Galento a contemptuous look. 'That's how we used to fight, Galento,' he said. 'Now I'm through with you. You can find yourself another manager.' Then he turned to me and said, 'You were right, Ray. It's a waste of time trying to make a champ out of that chump.'"

Not that Arcel had any illusions about the long-range impact of the beating. As his bylined column ended: "I don't suppose Galento lost any sleep over the incident. In or out of the ring he wasn't the worrying kind. And my guess is that within an hour he was probably established in a nearby tavern, lining up the empty glasses and belligerently flourishing a cigar as he related how he'd given the brush-off to those bums Dempsey and Arcel."[9]

The trainer had one more moment of satisfaction where Galento was concerned — at Roosevelt Stadium in Jersey City in July 1940. The heavyweight's opponent that night was Max Baer, another charge who drove Arcel crazy and for a grocery list of reasons. Baer was making a comeback after a full-force assault on Hollywood to become a leading man. But as exasperated as Arcel had been in the past with the night-fly Baer, he distinguished him clearly from Galento. "Max was always out for a good time. I don't know how many times I had to go looking through hotel corridors for him when he was supposed to be training with me. I don't think it's any secret that's one of the reasons he lost the championship to Braddock. One time he put these giant arms of his around me and said, 'Hey, Ray, I'm a lover, not a fighter.' Why didn't he bother me like Galento? Call it his heart. He was just a basically nice guy. Except for the time he fought Galento."

On that evening in Jersey City, according to Arcel, fans in the tenth row could hear the continuous insults being swapped between the heavyweights as fast as their punches. "Max really *hated* Galento, and it was *guinea bastard* this and *guinea bastard* that until he finally brought him down. Why he hated him in particular I don't know, but he was hardly alone in that."

If there was any managerial equivalent of Galento for Arcel in midcentury, it was Hymie Caplin, handler of such champions or contenders as Sid Terris, Allie Stolz, Lew Jenkins, and Al Singer. Another product of the Lower East Side, Caplin had no compunctions about breaking the gym code by calling out opposition managers or trainers when he felt like it. In the specific case of Arcel, he groused to reporters more than once that the trainer was overrated. "What makes him smarter than me? His secret is that he never wants anyone around who's smarter than he is."[10]

Even if he hadn't been called directly into cause, Arcel had more than one reason for not sharing a meal with Caplin. Even his most successful fighters, for instance, had a tendency to slide quickly into oblivion shortly after their peak performances — according to Arcel because of the capital sin of not having been managed or trained properly. Then there was Caplin's indictment in 1940 for financing a major gambling ring that linked him directly to Organized Crime figures. But maybe worst of all, not only did Terris defeat Arcel favorite Benny Valgar under his manager's bombastic tutelage, but Caplin had also trumpeted the lightweight for considerable time as the boxer most likely to take the division crown away from the favorite of favorites, Benny Leonard. Terris never got to meet Leonard in the ring, and Arcel never voiced doubts about how such a match would have ended, but there weren't too many other nightmare scenarios for him equal to a Terris win in such a bout. As for why Caplin targeted him more than once for being overrated, he was content to say that the manager was "just jealous."[11]

15

Bums of the Month

Despite his knockdown of Joe Louis in Yankee Stadium (preceded by his often quoted prediction that "I'll moida da bum"), Tony Galento was a full-fledged member of the "Bum of the Month Club" — the shorthand used by sportswriters for describing the opponents hastily lined up against the heavyweight champion in the late 1930s and early 1940s. It was a group that Arcel had a particular connection to since he repeatedly found himself in the corner of the fighter Louis demolished. Moreover, the Bum of the Month Club was chartered in good part thanks to another Arcel boxer, Jim Braddock, and the heavyweight's reluctance to defend the title he had taken from Max Baer in June 1935.

For most of two years after the Baer match, Braddock barnstormed the country for exhibitions with Jack McCarthy and for picking up as much product endorsement money as he could. Midway through 1936, Madison Square Garden called Braddock and his manager Joe Gould on a contractual obligation to defend the title against Germany's Max Schmeling. But then Braddock and Gould signed with promoter Mike Jacobs, who had convinced them that losing a title bout to the Nazi icon Schmeling would have been disastrous for the image of the United States. What Jacobs didn't have to spell out was that he exercised control over Louis and had every intention of having him take the first shot at Braddock's crown. The last one to hear about all these manipulations was Schmeling, who had already arrived in New York for what he had been told would be a September face-off at Madison Square Garden with Braddock.

Thanks to the Jacobs intervention and a recurrence of his hand arthritis, more months elapsed before Braddock found himself actually in the ring — on June 22, 1937, in Comiskey Park, Chicago, against Louis. Arcel, for one, had predicted nothing but catastrophe, not least because of the champion's two-year layoff since the Baer fight. As he told Dave Anderson, "I honestly didn't think Jim had a chance. Jim had been laying off, he was broke. Louis was already a great fighter. I didn't tell Jim much, just don't get hurt. Jim knew how good Louis was."[1]

The odds-makers agreed, making the champion a 3-to-1 underdog when the fight began. Braddock's moral victory was flooring Louis in the first round, but not so devastatingly that the challenger didn't immediately get to his feet again before the referee had counted up to two. The blow was the best Braddock had in him, and Braddock was gone by the eighth round. The win was Louis's eighth in a row, and once he had his championship belt, he reeled off another 26 wins, straight up to Ezzard Charles in 1950. Some of those he met had familiar names — Schmeling, Max Baer's brother Buddy, Nova, Billy Conn, Jersey Joe Walcott — but most of them were destined to be known chiefly for hitting the canvas against Louis during his heavyweight reign. Some of them, like Johnny Paycheck (John Pacek), appeared to know that even before their fight. Regarding the March 1940 bout held at Madison Square garden for the benefit of invasion-torn Finland, Arcel told an interviewer, "Before we started for the ring, I said to him, 'Johnny, you're a pretty good boxer. A boxer can always do things a slugger can't. Go out and box your fight. Remember, you're boxing a human being. He's only got two arms.' It was like talking to a wall. When we were in the center of the ring getting instructions, he shook like a leaf. His knees actually shook, he wasn't a live body."[2]

Nat Fleischer took it up from there in *Ring* magazine: "He was more scared than any pugilist I had ever seen in my long association with the sport. Paycheck, the bald chap from the Corn Belt [*ed.: He was from Iowa*], was a jitterbug from the time he sat in his corner to don his mitts. He proved that he needed help more so than the Finnish Fund.... Three times he was stretched on the canvas in the first round before the *coup de grace* was delivered. It was pitiful. For shame, Paycheck should have turned over his entire check, less his expenses, to the Finnish Fund."[3]

Even fighters with more dubious credentials for membership in the Bum of the Month Club displayed similar nerves. One was Lou Nova prior to his September 1941 meeting with Louis. For some years Nova had been making his own copy in and out of the ring. There had been celebrated battles with Max Baer (including the first televised fight, on

June 1, 1939), his foul-a-thon with Galento in Philadelphia, and the wide publicity given his study of yoga and practice of standing on his head for a few minutes before every fight. On top of that, he had begun listening to a quack named Walston Crocker Brownhis who had persuaded him that he was a "Man of Destiny" whose "cosmic punch" straight from the seventh vertebra would level any opponent, Louis included. "From that time on," Arcel said, "I couldn't get through to him. His mind was too crowded for what I was trying to tell him. I was fit to be tied. He would start posing in this John L. Sullivan style and do all his shadow-boxing that way. Then to make matters even worse, the newspapers picked up all the 'cosmic punch' stuff, and he had to give one interview after another to explain it to them. It made for a lot of press, but it was absolutely impossible to get him on a schedule. He bucked me every step of the way. I had great respect for Lou as a man. I could see him as a potential heavyweight champion. I felt I knew what he needed. But he never really gave himself a chance."

Not even belief in his cosmic punch could settle down Nova the night of the fight. Arcel: "He was always nervous in his dressing room, but this time he was acting as though it was execution day and he was the guy who'd be strapped into the chair. The day of the fight it was obvious he just didn't have the spirit he'd had when he fought Baer and Galento." And, in fact, Nova was declared a TKO loser in the sixth round.

If Arcel's fighters were regular losers to Louis, the trainer never gave the impression that he thought he was as well. On the contrary, one of his most repeated stories was about the night he walked to the center of the ring with his fighter to hear the referee's instructions. (Depending on his listener, he said the exchange occurred when he was seconding Al McCoy, Paulino Uzcudun, or Nathan Mann.) Seeing Arcel, Louis declared, "You here again?" Arcel said he couldn't help bursting out in laughter.

He didn't mind lampooning his situation either. He certainly couldn't ignore it when the press began to refer to his regular retrieval of fallen fighters as turning him into a "Meat Wagon." Following Louis's battering of the enormous Buddy Baer in January 1942, he lent his name to a story that ran in the *New York World-Telegram* under the head "Baer Haulage Arcel's Best: Ray at Peak While Retrieving Buddy." Arcel said, in part:

I am happy to say I retained my title as champion hulk carrier last night in the garden. I handle big propositions best, and Buddy Baer, at 250, gave me a chance to prove that I haven't slipped a bit. Of course, I was in great shape. I never underestimate Joe Louis. I was ready to pick up whatever came my way. I can divulge now that I underwent secret practice before the fight. I worked with [heavyweight contender] Abe Simon at Stillman's Gym and set an unofficial record of two seconds flat in bringing him across his locker room. Unfortunately, there was nobody holding a clock on me last night. I think I was sharper than I've been in some time.[4]

Arcel never disguised his admiration for either Louis or for the long-time champion's trainer, Jack Blackburn. On the other hand, he had little good to say about Mike Jacobs, the promoter who liked to boast he had "Louis in [his] pocket" for making any matches he felt like making. More than once Arcel emphasized to interviewers that he was no regular on "Jacobs Beach," the Midtown area around the Brill

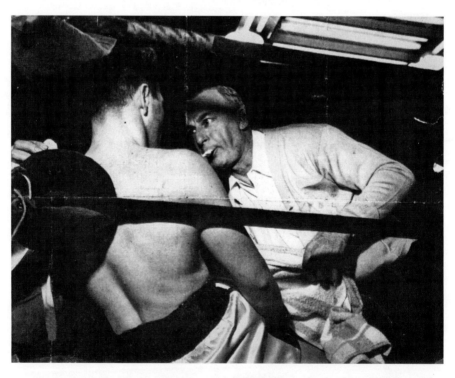

Ray Arcel, with cotton swabs in his teeth, works over Tony Pellone between rounds. He has handled more champs — and more victims of Joe Louis — than anyone.

Building where Jacobs had his office and where managers and trainers idled away hours. If there hadn't been warm feelings between the men previously, they turned absolutely icy in the run-up to the February 1938 Louis fight against Nathan Mann. As he told Dave Anderson in *In the Corner*: "The night Louis fought Mann, they had Everlast make up form-fitting gloves for Joe, but they just had a pair of ordinary gloves for Nathan. I had trained him ever since he was a kid, but when I squawked about the specially-made gloves Joe had, Mike Jacobs interfered. I knew Mike. I knew all about him. It was none of my business what he did, but when he said, 'You don't like this, do you?' I said, 'No, I don't, because I build up and you destroy.' Mike didn't talk to me after that, but I wasn't surprised. Mike was never concerned with fighters, only with money."[5]

Years later, however, Arcel had a more nuanced, sentimental opinion of Jacobs, undoubtedly influenced by the interim ascent of James Norris, a pure foe, as professional boxing's primary business figure on the East Coast. As recorded by Budd Schulberg in *Ringside: A Treasury of Boxing Reportage*, Arcel was quoted as saying: "He was a lone operator. He played all his cards close to the chest. I don't think he ever let anybody get very close to him.... Some of the biggest people in this city call him Mike, and yet he hasn't got a single close friend."

And again: "Sure, maybe it was a monopoly and all that, but Mike knew how to fill a house. And the more money he made for himself, the more he made for our fighters.... He drove the toughest bargain he could, but once he said you had a deal, it was like money in the bank. You didn't need a contract. If Mike said 25 percent, he didn't pay off on twenty-four and a half. He stabilized this business."[6]

Arcel's admiration for Blackburn, on the other hand, knew no nuances. It was also notable because he often brought up the trainer's name without prompting and more often than not without including him in a laundry list of fellow professionals worthy of praise. Speaking with Frank Graham in 1946 some years after Blackburn's death, he said about the first significant black trainer:

> I don't have to say it because everybody has known about it for a long time. But Blackburn was the greatest trainer and teacher of boxers in our time, maybe anybody's time. As a fighter, he fought most of the good ones from Joe Gans to Sam Langford and Gunboat Smith. That was covering quite a range in weight since most of the time he was a real lightweight and I don't think he

ever weighed more than 160 pounds going into a ring, and he must have been as smart a fighter as ever lived. Nobody that I've ever known had the sound boxing knowledge he did, and no one I've ever known had the knack for teaching young boxers that he did.[7]

Arcel never stinted on his praise of Louis, either. Even more meaningful than the opinions he shared with journalists over the years on the subject of the champion was his gesture at the end of the September 27, 1950, bout at Yankee Stadium with Ezzard Charles. Louis, who had been in retirement for a couple of years, had been forced to return to the ring to pay off back taxes, the understanding being that whatever he earned would go directly to the IRS. Under Arcel's tutelage, the leaner, much younger Charles dominated Louis to an unsurprising decision. At the final bell, Arcel joined the two fighters in the middle of the ring, putting his arms around both. Louis immediately returned the gesture. "As glad as I was that Ezzard beat Joe," Arcel told the *New York Post* in 1989, "I was sad for Joe. I was very fond of Joe. He was an outstanding man, a real man."[8]

16

Home Away from Home

For most of the 1930s Arcel lived with his wife Hazel, step-son Gus, and adopted daughter Adele in a rented house in the southeastern Queens area of St. Albans, not too far from the Long Island border. For much of the time, Hazel's mother also lived with them, as did a series of dogs for the children. "We didn't own it," he laughed to an interviewer. "We just had to pay the bills for it every month like a rental."[1] Aside from what Arcel was making from boxing, the monthly income came from part-time waitressing jobs Hazel held down near the house while her mother watched Gus and Adele. Even at that, there were days when money was so tight that he had to get up before dawn and walk to Stillman's, a trek of some 12 or 13 miles through Queens and across the East River. "The Long Island Rail Road from Jamaica to Manhattan cost about $30 a month, and we didn't always have it."[2]

Much like his grandmother when she had first arrived in Terre Haute, he found himself more Jewish than his surroundings. "I always considered myself a Jew," he told Elli Wohlgelernter, "at least to the extent that I always observed the holidays and went to *shul*. But strange for a New York City neighborhood, St. Albans didn't have a temple when we first moved there, so we had to go to Hillside Avenue in Jamaica for services. Hazel wasn't Jewish, but she said she liked coming, too. To her, the sermons and the singing were the same as going to church. It was only later on they organized a Reform temple in St. Albans."[3] What he also insinuated on other occasions, however, was that his mother-in-law, a member of the Methodist-Episcopalian church in the area, didn't share her daughter's ecumenical enthusiasm, and that this sometimes made for a frosty atmosphere in the house. Conversely, it made for double holidays in the winter for the children. "Hazel always celebrated Christmas," Arcel's niece Lila Libero recalled. "Right up to the time she got sick near

103

Dogs were a constant presence in the St. Albans house.

the end of World War II, she observed all the holidays, Jewish *and* Christian, and I never heard of any objections from my uncle."[4]

Arcel's regular travels out of town for training stints and fights, sometimes lasting several weeks on the other side of the country, left him relatively little time to become a prominent resident of his neighborhood, in any case. But that was not to say he didn't have a home base. Indeed, one of the more consistent themes of the hundreds of interviews he granted over the years was how "familial" gymnasiums, and particularly Stillman's on Eighth Avenue, were for those depending on them. When he spoke of how fighters had little to do on normal days but work out and talk boxing from early morning to late at night, he was also talking about himself. Moreover, he was given to claiming that, in contradiction to the image of a gym as a hangout for seedy types with little on their minds but winning a few bucks from the right ring matchup, Stillman's promoted positive instincts not easily found elsewhere, including racial color blindness:

> I'd show up in the morning with a nickel in my pocket for a coffee and a roll during the day, and that was often all I needed. But then I'd tell some guy to get in the ring and he'd confess that he wasn't up to it because he hadn't eaten in a long time. That was especially true of the black fighters, and I'd always tip off the managers and the other trainers that so-and-so could use a couple of bucks as a sparring partner. Sometimes I'd take the fighter over to the lunch counter that Stillman's brother-in-law ran in the gym and get him a coffee and a roll. It wasn't much, but you had to do what you had to do. And since I was around there all the time, the brother-in-law put it on the books for me. Everybody there knew the score. And you could usually count on the managers and trainers finding sparring jobs for the black boxers.[5]

That said, he also conceded that it wasn't until champions Henry Armstrong and Joe Louis dominated the scene in the 1930s that black trainers were anywhere in evidence.

Another, emphatically paradoxical influence Arcel attributed to gyms was what he viewed as a relatively modest level of violence in professional boxing because fighters and trainers got to know one another in them and rarely had viciousness on their minds when they faced each other before a paying crowd. "Most of these guys came from rough backgrounds. You had stickup men, members of gangs, things like that. Anything at all to put food on the table. But then they became boxers, got to know the guys they would be facing in the ring. The opponent wasn't some faceless victim of a street mugging, he was the guy you were talking with about some fight the night before. They began to understand — at least the good ones did —

that they had to do more than try to mug an opponent. They had to analyze him, figure out his strong points and weak points. They had to do something they really hadn't done all that much of before — they had to *think*."

He never underestimated his own role in this. "Like Dai Dollings had always told me, a good trainer didn't just give orders to a fighter, he taught. A gym was a school where you learned your lessons, and I think I was a pretty good teacher dealing with most of the fighters."

Arcel's belief in this educational process sometimes led him to maladroit denials. "You get this image of the punch drunk fighter," he averred on one occasion. "But that's always been exaggerated, and really refers to the fighters around the beginning of the twentieth century when they were going thirty and forty rounds to make a living. That kind of thing really died out after the introduction of the Walker Law. A trainer or a manager who let his fighter slide down to that point just wasn't responsible." When pressed that this suggested irresponsible managers and trainers abounded since there had been plenty of fighters since the Walker Law to show symptoms of what was generally termed punch drunk (including his hero Joe Louis), Arcel fell back stubbornly on his "brains over brawn" mantra. "Then those fighters and their handlers just didn't do it right. The name of the game has always been out-smarting the other guy, not beating him to a pulp. If you can't out-smart him, don't use your brain, you're going to be a loser."[6]

Especially in the company of ductile interviewers, he had little trouble agreeing that the boxing trade was a "science" or an "art"; he never contradicted either premise. But if there was one term that he used far more than any other to describe a boxer, it was "performer"; just as often, a fight was a "show." At one time or another, everyone from Benny Leonard to Roberto Duran came in for appreciation for how he "performed," much as a stage actor or singer might have been judged. (And he wasn't the only one to make the comparison, given the enormous number of fighters who nurtured Hollywood ambitions, appeared on the vaudeville stage, or, in later years, turned up on television variety hours.) By extension, of course, that made the gym a rehearsal hall, and Arcel never shied away from using the language of directors or choreographers in recounting a boxer's preparations for a bout. "A trainer can only work with the talent that's there. He can't give some kid a talent for boxing. What he can give him, has been hired to give him, are the moves and steps that will help him give a good performance in the show when it counts."

Not all the gym habitués were fighters, trainers, or managers, and the veteran second didn't have to be nudged too hard to tell tales about some of the hangers-on. But it was also in relating the misadventures of the Congolese Beezy Thomas in particular that he inadvertently raised doubts about how far the claimed color blindness of Stillman's went*:

> One day a shriveled little guy walked in. He was barely five feet tall and weighed under a hundred pounds. He could hardly speak English, but we made out that he was looking for a handout. It just so happened that Stillman needed someone to help the locker man, so he gave this guy a chance to earn a few bucks so he could at least eat. We didn't know the guy's name, but after a lot of questions we thought we made it out as Beezy Thomas. The only other thing we knew about him was when we asked him what country he came from, he said something that sounded like the "French jungle." Anyway, he was very likeable, and we all kind of adopted him.
>
> What the locker man did was to sweep up and general maintenance things, and also take care of the boxers' clothes. One day, when the locker man was too sick to come to work, Beezy had to take care of all the wet clothes. When the fighters came in the next day, they couldn't find anything because he had put some clothes in the right lockers and others who-knew-where. The fighters spent the whole day trying to track down their stuff. Needless to say, that was the end of Beezy as a locker man's assistant.

But the normally crusty Stillman came up with another solution for the would-be black handyman:

> Stillman didn't want to send him away, so he got him a little shoeshine box. That might have sounded thoughtful of him, but it was actually pretty thoughtless because there was this big former heavyweight named Battling Norfolk who already had a shoe stand in the gym. Norfolk was a good 6'3" and 225 pounds, and he didn't like it at all when Beezy started being a competitor. The two of them spent all day arguing with one another, and the teasing from everybody else went on and on. I think that was as much Stillman's purpose as helping out Beezy. But the funny thing was that Beezy started to put together enough to pay the rent on a cheap room on the west side of town. The bad part was that he had enough money left over to start drinking. We didn't pay much attention to that at first. The guy was really mainly there for making everyone laugh, especially after he started putting on the gloves and asked some of the fighters to teach him a few moves in the ring.

Arcel himself wrote the next chapter in the plantation tale. "There was a church out in Hollis in Queens that was in bad shape financially and

---

*This Beezy Thomas was not to be confused with a similarly named flyweight in the 1930s who fought to the excruciatingly inept record of 5–41–6. Most likely, the Congolese was slapped with the boxer's name for lack of any established alternative.

thought it could raise some money by staging a boxing evening. I got them a few young boxers, then proposed they add a comedy routine between Beezy and Battling Norfolk. Everybody went for it, and Norfolk came up with his own idea of fighting Beezy on his knees to make up for the huge difference in their heights. What he hadn't counted on was that Beezy would throw a wild punch and knock him out! We had to use smelling salts to revive Norfolk. But at least he salvaged some pride because just about everybody attending this racket thought the whole thing had been planned."

As much as Beezy proved to be the star attraction that evening, however, it was only shortly afterward that his drinking got so out of hand one night that he created a ruckus in the gym, bringing the police:

> What came out of it was that we found out Beezy was an illegal immigrant who had jumped ship. Immigration got into the act and ordered him deported. The day before he was set to go, he came by the gym with two guards to say goodbye to his friends. He was in tears when everyone gathered around him and began wishing him well. "They're going to deporch me," he kept saying. I saw Norfolk hanging back, and I went over to him and gave him a nudge to say goodbye to the little guy. Norfolk went over and said, "Beezy, what're they doin' to you?" And Beezy said, "They're going to deporch me." And then Norfolk asks him, "Where are they sendin' you?" And Beezy, still crying, says, "Back to the jungle." And like it was the most natural thing in the world to say, Norfolk says, "Back to the jungle? What're you gonna do when you get there? The old monkeys forgot you and the new ones never heard of you." Even the immigration guards burst out laughing, but that didn't stop them from marching Beezy away. We laughed a lot about it all, but anybody who was there was really heartbroken.

At least stories of Benjamin Finkle, known to one and all at Stillman's and most other gyms in the East as "Evil Eye," didn't rely on racist japery for their humor. A street tough from New York, Finkle's brief professional career as a fighter (5–1–2) was mainly notable for the fact that one of his opponents has been listed as No First Name Boozerman. But as a manager he found his way toward boxing fame in the early 1930s by telling sportswriters that his perennially bloodshot right eye had evil powers that he could direct at will against opposition boxers. When some of the opponents confessed to being bothered by the sight of Evil Eye staring out at them from behind the ring post, he began getting so much attention for this "talent" that managers began requesting his services, paying him as much as three hundred dollars a bout. Before he called it quits, he had lent his hexing to such stalwarts as Jack Dempsey, Billy Conn, Sugar Ray Robinson, and Floyd Patterson.

Arcel's most vivid experience with Finkle came in November 1938 when Evil Eye was made part of the coterie accompanying featherweight champion Joey Archibald down to Washington for a fight against Tennessee Lee. Nobody will ever know whether the match at Turner's Arena would have sold out on its own merits, since for days leading up to the fight both Washington and New York papers had made Archibald and Lee sound like secondary considerations. As Arcel liked recounting:

> Lee's camp knew all about Finkle, so they had a character in their corner who called himself the Finger. He was a skinny little guy, and he said he had his own magic powers by positioning his finger in such a way as to neutralize whatever Finkle was doing. To hear all the talk, you'd think the real bout was between those two guys crouched behind the ring posts. There was even debate about whether the Finger should have his magic hand manicured. But no, somebody said, that might give the fingernail a glare under the ring lights and disrupt the Eye unfairly. Guys who supported the Finger didn't like the idea anyway. "You'll just spoil the bum by giving him a manicure," they said. "Let him go as he always has."

As it turned out, Finkle's eye proved stronger than the Finger's finger, with Archibald taking a unanimous decision. After claiming that Lee had been robbed, the Finger faded into obscurity. Not Finkle, however, who was still being heard from well into the 1970s, along the way serving as an inspiration for Al Capp's "Evil Eye Fleegle" in the *L'il Abner* comic strip, and appearing on numerous radio and television shows to flaunt his expertise. Just like any other performer from the boxing world.

17

Other Wars

When he wasn't functioning as the "Meat Wagon" for Joe Louis's opponents in the late 1930s and early 1940s, Arcel was training a few more champions. The most tragic of them was bantamweight Tony Marino.

A native of western Pennsylvania and the younger brother of another professional, Tommy Ryan (Charles Marino), Marino worked his way up through the division ranks mostly in California. Then, under Arcel's tutelage, he met Baltazar Sangchili at the Dyckman Oval in New York on June 29, 1936, for a bout that had a title meaning for every jurisdiction except New York State. When he knocked out Sangchili in the 14th round, pressure built for a unified title fight against Sixto Escobar, recognized as the bantamweight champion in New York. Only two months later, that fight too was held at the Dyckman Oval, with Marino again prevailing. But at a cost.

In both title fights Marino received almost as much as he gave, and he hit the canvas hard so often that both Arcel and the boxer's older brother Ryan advised him to retire. When Marino refused, Arcel withdrew as his trainer. Then, on January 30, 1937, Marino took on Carlos Quintana at Brooklyn's Ridgewood Grove. Before the fight was ended in the eighth round, Quintana had dropped his opponent four times. Sitting on his stool at the end of the bout, Marino suddenly collapsed, went into a coma, and died two days later. Over the years Arcel largely limited himself to shaking his head at mention of the bantamweight and saying, "There was no way he should have ever been in that ring against Quintana."

Middleweight Freddie Steele (Frederick Earle Burgett) was as much a "performer" as anyone Arcel ever trained. Reared in the Northwest and tagged by early promoters as the "Tacoma Assassin," he claimed the division title after long years in which he had already proven his athletic skills in everything from baseball to swimming, and before he embarked on a Hollywood career that, among other things, saw him doubling for Errol Flynn in *Gentleman Jim* (1942), playing a highly visible soldier in the Preston Sturges comedy *Hail the Conquering Hero* (1944), and sharing the screen with Robert Mitchum in *The Story of G.I. Joe* (1945). His struggle to the top started at the age of 13 when a local gym operator allowed him to hang out on the premises and gradually caved in to his nagging to be allowed to enter the ring. He reached the age of 20 (through some 40 bouts) before losing, then later on in his career went undefeated 56 straight times. His key bouts were against Babe Risko in July 1936 and Gorilla Jones on New Year's Day in 1937. But Steele was also beset by injuries during his career, especially because of an automobile accident that compounded an existing broken jaw and a broken breastbone received during a fight. It was because of this latter injury that he had to withdraw from competition for a while, moving the New York State Commission to strip him of his title. A subsequent attempt at a comeback against Al Hostak in July 1938 ended quickly in the first round, sending Steele off to Hollywood.[1]

Indicative of the fluidity that existed between trainers and fighters was the fact that Arcel also seconded Ceferino Garcia, two rungs on Freddie Steele's climb to the top and the opponent Barney Ross fought with his fractured thumb in defense of his welterweight title in 1937. A native of the Philippines, and the first boxer from his country to claim an internationally recognized title, Garcia was a middleweight by the time Arcel was calling the shots in his knockout of Fred Apostoli at Madison Square Garden on October 2, 1939. Ten weeks later Garcia defended his title successfully against Glen Lee in the first international bout staged in Manila. Garcia's box office cachet was the so-called bolo punch, which his handlers claimed he had invented but which has also been traced to earlier Filipino fighters. Garcia lost his belt to Ken Overlin at Madison Square Garden in May 1940. After a few more fights he followed the well-traveled trail to Hollywood, and specifically to Mae West, where he worked for some years as her driver and bodyguard.[2]

From his own ebullient reminiscences, there is little doubt that Arcel's favorite champion of the period was Billy Soose, a middleweight whose career was halved into more than amateur and professional phases. While still an amateur at Penn State, the Pennsylvania-born Soose won three Golden Gloves championships through sheer power, then repeated the performances in college tournaments. When the NCAA received too many complaints that his fights uniformly ended with knockouts of his opponents, it drafted a rule banning Golden Gloves champions from college matches. Shortly after turning professional, however, he split the tendon in one of the knuckles on his right hand, forcing him to abandon his power game anyway. From that point on he was considered a boxer more than a puncher.

Soose's handler was Paul Finder Moss, a writer of minor Hollywood musicals and the manager of actor-singer Dick Powell, who was said to have invested in the boxer as part of an image correction attempt to come across as something more than just a song-and-dance man. Powell and his wife at the time, actress Joan Blondell, were said to have been so taken by Soose's handsome looks that they offered to open doors in Hollywood for him, but the fighter politely declined.[3]

There are conflicting stories about how Soose and Arcel came together. The tale with the longest legs said that Soose and Moss were impressed by the trainer's personal nursing of Lou Nova in June 1939 after the heavyweight had defeated Max Baer and wanted him in their corner for an upcoming bout against Charley Burley. The problem with that story is that the Burley bout at Pittsburgh's Motor Square Garden occurred months before the Nova-Baer match. Whatever the calendar details, Arcel remembered being stunned by Moss's approach at Stillman's with a request that he train Soose for the Burley fight. If he didn't go as far as fellow trainer Eddie Futch, who called Burley "the finest all-around fighter I ever saw,"[4] Arcel didn't have to be reminded that the son of a mixed racial couple had become something of an embarrassing white-black elephant for promoters, who liked to pitch their ticket sales along simple racial and/or ethnic lines. Together with his raw talents in the ring, the result was a welterweight-middleweight who was forced to take on heavyweights for survival because every top contender, from Marcel Cerdan and Jake LaMotta to Sugar Ray Robinson, found reasons not to get into the ring with him (and help him maintain an inexplicable record of never having a title fight). "When Moss came up and said he had this fight against Burley scheduled for Pittsburgh, I thought he had to be a nut."

Ignoring his first instinct, Arcel gave Soose an advanced degree in footwork, and especially in the left jabs and hooks that he hoped would make up for the injured right hand. It worked — and didn't. Soose's more mature tactics enabled him to last the entire 10 rounds and in the process gain the cheers of the crowd for his doggedness. Those cheering, though, didn't include the judges and referee, who gave the fight to Burley. Back in the dressing room, according to Arcel, Soose broke down in tears. "I said to him, 'What the hell are you crying about? You just beat the best fighter in the world even if they didn't give you the decision. You know what you take from here? The knowledge that you've established yourself as a top-notch boxer.'"

The pep talk cemented the relationship between the trainer and the fighter, and for the duration of their time together Arcel worked on strengthening Soose's injured right hand so that it at least didn't become a liability in the ring. The payoff finally came in May 1941 when Soose took the middleweight title from Ken Overlin at Madison Square Garden. Mainly because he began filling out his six-foot frame, Soose never officially defended the title, though not for lack of trying on one occasion. In September 1941 he was scheduled to take on the declining Ceferino Garcia at Gilmore Field in Los Angeles for the crown. But the California State Commission, allied to the National Boxing Association in recognizing Tony Zale as the division's number one, refused to accord the bout championship status. The fight itself proved even more chaotic than its organizational footing. Up to the very end of the seventh round, Soose clearly dominated, but then he staggered back under a blow that some thought came from Garcia's fist and others from his head. The wound over the eye couldn't be closed, and Soose told his corner that he had no intention of risking his eyesight for a bout that was only a card-filler anyway. Garcia's cheering section erupted in celebration at a TKO victory — at least until referee Herb Roth declared an illegal butting that made for a technical draw. At this verdict a full-scale riot broke out among Garcia's supporters, and Soose and his people barely made it back to their dressing room safely.

Shortly after the Garcia fiasco, Soose relinquished his title to move up to the light-heavy division. That ambition got no further than a couple of bouts, and shortly after losing to Jimmy Bivins in January 1942 he enlisted in the Navy for the duration of World War II. Soose never had to have his arm twisted to attend a testimonial for Arcel. As he put it on one occasion, "He taught me many things other than boxing.... He taught me a lot of other values. Above all, he taught me that love and faith and trust were the most important things in the world."[5]

Soose was only one of scores of professional boxers who ended up in uniform during World War II. Aside from Louis's meetings with two more Bums of the Month in 1942 (Buddy Baer in January and Abe Simon in March), there were no further title fights in the heavyweight, light-heavyweight, middleweight, and welterweight divisions until February 1946. For Arcel, in his forties and with three dependents, the war years meant more scrambling for odd jobs.

In Black and White

Unlike the case with team sports, professional boxing in mainstream America did not have to wait until after World War II for black athletes to emerge as dominant figures. Ever since Joe Gans (Joseph Grant) had captured the lightweight championship in 1902 and Jack Johnson the heavyweight crown in 1910, African Americans were a highly visible part of the sport. But that was not the same thing as saying they were an integral part of it — a distinction Arcel encountered more than once in training black fighters. Whatever equalities might have been granted for the duration of a bout inside the ring were refuted by what was outside, starting with the all-white trainers and managers standing behind the ring posts, not to mention the promoters in the country's most sought after venues. For a majority of promoters, black fighters were acceptable box office precisely to the extent that they aroused racist blood lust in crowds craving to see them decked by some white opponent. Nobody embodied that attitude more than Tex Rickard, the organizer of the 1910 Reno championship fight between Johnson and James J. Jeffries. But Rickard was far from alone in appearing open-minded while actually fueling racial strife. And if in his business sympathies a Mike Jacobs could seem exempted from this kind of hypocrisy, it was principally because he had a far bigger interest than the gate from a single bout in having a Joe Louis defy racist instincts by continuing to reign as a ring king for as many years as possible.

As far back as the 19th century, long before Jeffries came out of retirement for his meeting with Johnson, prominent white fighters concluded they had nothing to gain and everything to lose by stepping into the ring against a skilled African American. One of the most conspicuous examples was how both James J. Corbett and John L. Sullivan dodged appointments with Peter Jackson. When Johnson came along at the dawn of the 20th century, he didn't come alone; indeed, boxing's white estab-lishment began to reel before the prospect of not only Johnson, but of Joe Jeannette and a couple of other black heavyweights vying with John-son for dominating the sport for the foreseeable future. It was as much to ward off that more comprehensive evil as to silence Johnson himself that Jeffries announced he was answering the call of "that portion of the white race that has been looking to me to defend its athletic superiority."[1] When that call to arms didn't work out so well, with Jeffries losing by a TKO before he suffered the ultimate indignity of being knocked out altogether, state after state sought to cover up the Reno result by banning films of the Johnson victory — a vindictive campaign that had the endorsement of the likes of former president (and amateur boxer) Theodore Roosevelt and that ultimately ballooned into a Federal law prohibiting the transporting of boxing films across state lines. This leg-islation, which remained formally in effect until 1940, dealt a heavy com-mercial blow not only to motion picture exhibitors who had counted on filmed bouts for a substantial part of their income, but to boxing itself and its use of newsreels as an important advertising tool. It was hardly surprising that the anti-boxing lobby (which also included new recruit Roosevelt) was invigorated by the backlash against the Johnson victory, leading to various state laws outlawing or severely restricting boxing competitions and leaving the industry pretty much in a shambles until the mid-twenties.[2]

It was also in the wake of the Johnson win over Jeffries that novelist Jack London lamented that the country needed a "great white hope" to combat blacks in the ring. As starkly paranoid as it was, it was a wail that through sheer repetition gained currency over time, in casual lan-guage if not in advanced civics. In the 1920s, Jack Dempsey was steered toward heavyweight championship bouts with Gene Tunney with the decisive help of a racist New York State Athletic Commission vote that had originally ordered him to fight the more deserving Harry Wills, an African American. In the 1930s it was the then-retired Dempsey who offered to finance a tournament that would produce a "great white hope" for preventing Joe Louis from dominating the heavyweight division. That notion died in farce when some of those drafted for the tournament turned out to be African Americans themselves. (Dempsey apologists denied he was a racist, contending that he personally admired Louis and was merely a shrewd businessman trying to make money from a ripe opportunity, but there was no mistaking the intent of the rhetoric that by then could be gleaned from the sports pages of the *New York Times* as easily as be heard at the bar of a corner saloon.)[3]

As though any other motivation had been needed for the firestorm that broke out after the Johnson-Jeffries bout, there was also the flauntingly aggressive character of the victor and a personal life that was marked by enough domestic violence to have one of his three wives commit suicide. But it wasn't domestic abuse that most rattled the authorities determined to get back at Johnson, it was his eagerness to grab headlines for marrying three white women in a row in between escapades with white hookers that he was never reluctant to brag about. When one of the hookers cooperated with authorities in charging that Johnson had taken her across a state border for sexual acts in violation of the Mann Act, he was sentenced to more than a year in prison — despite the fact that the alleged crime had taken place before the Mann Act had been put on the books. Johnson skipped the country rather than go to prison, spending years traveling the globe.

Twenty years later, with the arrival of Joe Louis on the scene, it was the Jack Johnson *character* that was the starting point for Jacobs and the heavyweight's handlers to win over the paying public — i.e., the need to be just the opposite. As Jeffrey T. Sammons noted in his *Beyond the Ring: The Role of Boxing in American Society*, manager John Roxborough told Louis:

1. He was never to have his picture taken alongside a white woman.
2. He was never to go into a nightclub alone.
3. There would be no soft fights.
4. There would be no fixed fights.
5. He was never to gloat over a fallen opponent.
6. He was to keep a "dead pan" in front of the cameras.
7. He was to live and fight clean.[4]

Once Louis accepted those premises — for public consumption anyway — he became as exploitable as a national symbol as a heavyweight fighter. His June 1935 fight against Italy's Primo Carnera was the black race getting back at Benito Mussolini's Fascist invasion of Abyssinia. His matches in June 1936 and 1938 against Germany's Max Schmeling were America rising up against Adolf Hitler. Most of all, he became a "credit to his race" precisely to the degree that he was dangerous within the ropes but otherwise no threat to existing white authority. Not that all sectors of the country were sure of even this. While the North generally applauded his reign as a lucrative social and financial investment, the Southern states weren't too keen to have the blacks within their borders adopt a hero who succeeded inside the ring with his fists and, however meticulous the ground rules, hobnobbed with rich and powerful whites outside it. Following Schmeling's victory in the first match between the heavyweights in June 1936, the *New Orleans Times-Picayune* hailed the outcome as a confirmation of white supremacy, Nazis or no Nazis. According to columnist William McG. Keefe, "The reign of terror in heavyweight boxing was ended by Schmeling. The big bad wolf had been chased from the door. It took the Black Uhlan to prove that the black terror is just another fragile human being." It was the kind of open door Berlin didn't hesitate to barge through, its propaganda machinery aligning the interests of Nazi Germany with the South's "white honesty" against "black brutality."[5]

The systematic compartmentalization of blacks was aided no little by sportswriters, very few of whom would have been mistaken for civil rights advocates. One notable exception was Nat Fleischer of *Ring* magazine. On a fighter-trainer level, aside from the Beezy Thomas kinds of stories, the rampant racism played out mostly in restaurants and at hotel desks. Arcel related several incidents that were striking for both their places (not rural areas but major cities) and times (not in the pre–Joe Louis era but well after World War II). They did not come as a shock to him; on the contrary, as he told Dave Anderson, "One of the trials and tribulations of the trainer who was in full charge, the one thing that always depressed me and made me feel miserable, was the fact that in those years, long before the civil rights movement, you couldn't always get decent living quarters when you traveled with a black fighter."[6] In the late 1930s, for example, he accompanied Puerto Rican featherweight Cristobal Jaramillo to Washington, D.C. When the pair walked up to the front desk at the Sheraton, they were confronted by a clerk who announced that "we don't allow niggers at this hotel." "I asked him," Arcel recalled, "who's a nigger? When he pointed to Jaramillo, I told him he was crazy, that Jaramillo was whiter than him or me. For reasons I never did figure out, he just shook his head and gave us keys to the room. Maybe it was because the room had been reserved by the promoter of the fight we were there for, and the hotel didn't want big trouble with a good customer. I never did find out."

But matters didn't end so simply a few years later when the trainer returned to Washington with Jimmy Bivins, a heavyweight and light heavyweight who, despite beating eight of the eleven world champions he met during his career, could never get a title fight. As Arcel told Anderson, Ronald K. Fried, and recorded in his own memoir, he was appalled to discover that Bivins had been given a "steam bath" of a room in a hotel for blacks. So he went to the manager of the Sheraton, where he himself had again been booked, opening his negotiations with the winking claim that he had brought along his "valet." The manager laughed off the lie.

"I said, 'Look, I'm gonna ask you as a special favor. I got a room up there with two beds. Let him sleep up there.' He says, 'Now listen to what I'm telling' you. I'm gonna let you do it. But when you order his meals, you order for yourself. Don't let anybody see him. Put him in the bathroom. When they come up to take the dishes out, put him in the bathroom. No hanging out in the lobby. When he goes down that elevator — out, completely out of the hotel. He made a delivery. Know what I mean? And as for you, you can take all your meals in the coffee shop.'"

Arcel never failed to recount the Jaramillo and Bivins stories without underlining how they had taken place in the capital of the United States. But they were anything but singular tales. In 1951 he brought heavyweight champion Ezzard Charles to Chicago for a title bout against Joey Maxim (Giuseppe Antonio Bernardinelli) with assurances from promoter James Norris that he would have no problem registering the boxer and his coterie at the Western Hotel, since Norris himself owned the place. It turned out to be not so easy. "Right away the manager tells us the usual — 'We don't let niggers in this hotel.' I ask him if he owns the place, he says no, he's just the manager. I tell him to hold on and call Norris in New York, then hand the guy the phone. He turns all kinds of colors as he's listening to what Norris is telling him. We never had a problem after that, and Charles won the fight."

The beginning, the middle, and the end were very different when Arcel went to Ogden, Utah, for an August 1952 bout against Rex Layne not too long after Charles had been dethroned as champion. Arcel:

The trouble with Charles was that he carried ten guys with him. That was his gang, and he wouldn't go anywhere without them. It was tough enough getting a room for him, but I was in effect the advance man who also had to get accommodations for them, too. I arrived in Ogden two days before Charles and his friends because he was afraid of flying and was coming on a train. I go to the mayor, who had assured us there would be no trouble getting rooms. The fight was important for the city, and he wanted to do everything he could to encourage it. So he sends me to this hotel, where the owner is sitting with a gun on his hip. I tell him I'm Ray Arcel from New York, that the mayor told me he had set aside rooms for us. He looks at me and says, "This Charles, he's a nigger, ain't he? I don't allow any niggers in my hotel." I tell him that's not what the mayor told me. He couldn't have given a damn. "The mayor doesn't own this hotel, I do," he says. The one good thing to come out of it was that he told me I might find something in a motel that had recently opened and was looking for business.

Sort of. Arcel paid for six double rooms in advance, then awaited the arrival of Charles and his party two days later. "The man and wife who ran the motel, I will *never, never* forget, they stood there and they *froze....* You think white is white? They were whiter than white. So I go over to calm them down before we're all thrown out. We agree there'll be no music and no girls in the room. I also have to assure them we'll be out of the place every morning by nine or nine-thirty in case their other guests start making trouble. They agree to it all."

Which still left two problems. "The first one was where to eat. I go back to the original guy who directed me to the motel, and he agrees to set up two private rooms for breakfast and dinner. I pay for the food and I pay for the waiters he's got to hire. Again, the first rule was that we come and go without being seen as much as possible."

This left the training problem, which turned out to be the thorniest one of all. "The guy who was supposed to be the promoter, he turns out to be a big *schlump*. Here we are in Utah, across the continent from New York, and the only things he can provide for us is a skating rink with a collapsible ring that we have to put up and take down every day. Same thing with a punching bag—we had to put that up when we arrived in the morning and take it away when we left." But then Arcel happened to run into an acquaintance on the street wearing an Air Force uniform. When he told him about the problems he was having with Charles's training, the airman immediately volunteered use of his base's gym. Said Arcel:

Not only. He acted excited about the idea of bringing up the former world champion. Would I do that for the guys, he asked. Would I do that! So I went up to the base, and the master sergeant in charge of the gym was a black guy. When I told him I was bringing Ezzard Charles, he couldn't have been more enthusiastic. Then I went to see his commanding officer, a colonel who almost kissed me for coming up with an idea for raising the morale of the men on the base. They did everything they could to make our training comfortable, and I think we paid it back. After every workout, we'd have Ezzard mixing it up with some of the airmen in the ring. I told him, I said, "If you land a single punch on any of them, I'll throw a bottle at you." He didn't, thank God.

For the fight itself, the Charles camp made sure there were enough tickets for all the officers on the base and for as many airmen who could be squeezed into Ogden Stadium. The final touch was the arrival of Jack Dempsey as the referee. "I don't know who was more popular. You had the legend Dempsey, you had Charles who had won over all these airmen, and you had Layne, who was a local boy from nearby Lewiston. I guess you could say anybody who was anybody in Ogden was there, including the original hotel guy who didn't want to put us up and the motel couple who really didn't want to. They all bought their own ringside seats. It would've been a great night except that Dempsey awarded the 10-round decision to Layne."

Arcel didn't have to go on the road to Washington, Chicago, or Ogden, though, to experience the racist attitudes prevailing in mid-century America. In what he intended as a positive, breakthrough anecdote, he told his AJC interviewer, Wohlgelernter, in 1983 that, as far as he knew, he had been the first person to introduce a black customer to Toots Shor's, the noted midtown Manhattan watering hole that served as a magnet for sports stars, sportswriters, and show business personalities, and where he had spent a lot of his own time in the post–World War II years. "You always had guys like Joe DiMaggio and Jackie Gleason in there, so one day I thought I would bring Charles in with me. I didn't think there would be a problem with Toots. He just wasn't that kind of guy." *But.* "Well, yeah, I cleared it with him ahead of time. I mean, Charles was heavyweight champion. Would any black guy in off the street be served without a problem? I don't know. But Toots knew me, and a heavyweight champion was a heavyweight champion."[7]

Regarding anti–Semitism, Arcel repeatedly asserted that, with one exception, he barely experienced it. "Oh, sure, you'd hear people muttering "Jew bastard" this and "Jew bastard" that, but you could hear that about any ethnic group and I never took it all that seriously. Besides, in the early years especially, the best boxers were all Jewish, so who was going to be stupid enough to taunt somebody like that?"[8]

The one exception was prior to the September 1939 bout between Tony Galento and Lou Nova when he was slated to train the latter at a private golf club outside Atlantic City. "We all arrive to register, and the guy running the place pulls aside Nova's manager, Ray Carlin, and asks if there are any Jews in our group. Carlin tells him I am. The guy says my name out loud, then says, 'Oh, I suppose we can get by with that name.' We didn't. We got right out of there and went to the Warwick Hotel in Philadelphia."

Beneath such single episodes, however, was a deeper discriminatory attitude based on prevailing racial and ethnic stereotypes, which Arcel was as vulnerable to as anybody else. In the July 27, 1940, issue of *Collier's* magazine, for example, he broke down boxers for the paraphrasing of writer Dan Parker as follows:

1. Negro fighters have a tremendous advantage over white boys in the matter of stamina. With fewer generations of the softening influence of civilization behind them than their white brethren and inured to hardships by the less favorable living conditions under which they are brought up, colored boys not only have more endurance but can take more punishment. The thicker skull of the Negro also helps make him a better shock absorber.

2. Of the white boys, the Italians have the sturdiest physiques. This is accounted for not only by the fact that Italians eat rough, wholesome food and are a race of hard workers but also because Italian children aren't pampered and learn to fight early in life.

3. The Irish and Poles excel in courage, determination, and initiative. Of late the Irish have softened up because the progress they have made in America has improved their mode of living immeasurably.

4. Jewish boys are the smartest fighters and fastest thinkers. Benny Leonard and Barney Ross stand out as the intellectuals of the ring.

19

Short Memories, Long Memories

In order not to penalize fighters who were drafted or who volunteered for military service, the major boxing titles were frozen for most of World War II. One estimate was that some 4,000 conscripts identified themselves as professional fighters on induction forms, though only a modest percentage of those who survived the conflict without consequential injury returned to the ring afterward. In many cases new careers beckoned, such as with Jack Brazzo, a heavyweight who won his first 15 fights before the war (12 by knockout), entered the service, and re-emerged as the actor Jack Palance.[1] At home, attention-getting bouts were few and far between, but one that did get in under the wire, scant weeks after the Japanese attack on Pearl Harbor, was Buddy Baer's second run at Joe Louis's title in January 1942. That fight, with Arcel in Baer's corner, was also the start of the horrendous problems Louis would have with the Internal Revenue Service after the war.

The rematch came about mainly because of the farcical unfolding of the first meeting between the heavyweights at outdoors Griffith Stadium in Washington in May 1941. For starters, it rained heavily throughout the day of the initial bout, prompting referee Arthur Donovan to watch the raindrops from a bar from which he emerged in questionable condition when the weather unexpectedly cleared and the fight went on as scheduled. Then the gargantuan Baer (6'6") had a moment of glory much like Tony Galento when he put Louis through the ropes with a punch, though Arcel was the first to say later that the chief culprit was the slack ring ropes more suitable for wrestlers than boxers. Then, at the end of the sixth round, with Louis unquestionably recovered from his brief plunge and firmly on his way to adding Baer to his Bum of the

Month casualties, the champion got in a punch that the challenger's manager, Ancil Hoffman, insisted had been leveled after the bell, amounting to a disqualifying foul. The shaky Donovan insisted that wasn't so and demanded that Hoffman get his fighter ready for the seventh round. Knowing only too well that Baer might never see an eighth, Hoffman refused, winning a verdict for Louis but also sparking enough controversy over the decision to all but guarantee the rematch that took place in Madison Square Garden eight months later, after the war had already begun.[2]

However skeptical he was about Baer's ability to dethrone Louis, Arcel had also picked up what he thought was the one flaw in the champion's ring movements — one that went back to his study of trainer Jack Blackburn. When Blackburn had been fighting as a lightweight, Arcel recalled, he had the vulnerable habit of jabbing, then bringing back his left hand low without stepping away from the straight line of the opponent's right-hand counter-punch. As he had in so many other ways, Louis had copied this movement from his trainer. "Did I think this would give Buddy an edge? Let's just say I didn't think it would hurt."

It was about the only thing that didn't. With the proceeds from the bout going to the Navy Relief Fund, the fighters had to wait through speeches from various dignitaries, including 1940 Republican Presidential candidate Wendell Wilkie, who referred to Baer as his brother Max. Because of Louis's known campaigning for Wilkie in the race against Franklin Delano Roosevelt, this slight made Baer appear all the more like an insignificant extra for the evening's entertainment. The heavyweight hardly needed that aggravation since he had already been complaining to Arcel in the dressing room that he didn't feel well. But even worse was the pre-fight scene in Louis's dressing room, where the ailing Blackburn had to be talked into accompanying his fighter to the ring. Louis's prediction that he would end matters in one round so his mentor could get home quickly proved accurate. It was the champion's last victory monitored by Blackburn, who died a few months later.[3]

But Louis's problems were only beginning. Although he had announced before the Baer match that he intended signing over his purse to the Relief Fund, and made a similar announcement a few months later for a bout against Abe Simon, the champion and his handlers were slow to catch the tax implications of having the proceeds assigned to Jacobs and then having the promoter write his own check to Louis. For the IRS after the war, this added up to a straight salary, and the agency was not responsible for how Louis wanted to dispose of his own income. But income it was and at a significantly higher taxable rate. Not even the fact that Louis had spent other money for 3,000 tickets for servicemen to attend the fights or had himself enlisted in the Army at the rank of private for the duration moved the Federal accountants with short memories. By the time penalties and other charges were added to an originally calculated bill of around $500,000, the man hailed as a "credit to his race" was in debt to the IRS to the tune of seven figures, forcing Louis out of an intended retirement and into some humiliating postwar bouts.[4]

Arcel's problems in the period also went beyond the ring. Already, on the eve of the war, he had lost both his father (in his early seventies) and step-mother Rebecca (mid-sixties). Inevitable problems between a father and teenage boy in the house led to what he referred to as "conflicts" with his step-son Gus, and these weren't helped by his long absences. At the same time, he never shied away from referring to his fighters as "sons," and with a pride seldom heard in connection with Gus. Given his own admissions about his family life vis-à-vis his profession, it is hardly a leap to suggest that the relations between the two males in St. Albans were at best distant, this in turn precipitating further tensions. One remedy proposed by Hazel's mother was a more defined religious upbringing for Gus — i.e., have him become a member of her Methodist-Episcopal church. Arcel's attempt to sound matter-of-fact about this move rang with defensiveness. "I didn't get into a fight about it, but she was there with him probably more than I was. He was her grandson. 'He'll be a better man for it,' she told me. I didn't get into words with her. Would I have preferred he went to temple? Sure. But what could I say?" His one peek at the issue revealed nothing about Hazel's attitude, not completely surprising since the subject of Gus was one he sought to avoid even more than most family matters. At one juncture in his interview with the American Jewish Congress, he admitted that he once threw the boy out of the house, but quickly moved on to another topic without offering details.[5]

The worst awaited him, however, on August 3, 1946, when Hazel died after a two-year struggle with cancer. For some time she had been battling her illness at her family home in Yardley, Pennsylvania — a situation not unlike that of Arcel's mother returning to New York with her terminal diabetes. On the road for a textiles company at the time, Arcel had hardly been in any position to contest Hazel's move back to the heartland of the Methodist-Episcopalian influences that had put him at odds with his mother-in-law over Gus's upbringing, among other things. Where exactly he was when Hazel succumbed has been lost to first-hand testimony, but he never left others in doubt about how her death sent him reeling. "She was one of the angels on this earth," he declared, as he usually did when referencing her, in his AJC interview. And 37 years after the fact, when the interview was recorded, he was still able to say that he "never missed a single August 3rd, going out to her tomb in Trenton, where we buried her. How could I not go?"[6]

Although Arcel frequently pointed to the Depression years of the thirties as particularly trying, he was at least working regularly during the decade — maybe not always to great economic gain, but at least regularly. The same could not be said of the war years of the early forties. With big card fights in abeyance and crowds drastically thinned, he was forced to find other work for a couple of years, becoming a salesman for the Julius Stark Textile and Embroidery Company. As when working as a trainer, the job called for him to be on the road a great deal, specifically in the Ohio-Michigan area, meaning little time at home.[7] The end of the war didn't bring instant financial relief. In February–March 1946 he had to take on an assignment as head coach of the amateur New York Golden Gloves team.[8] Not all the professional fighters he gradually resumed training were four-star caliber, either.

One was Tony Janiro, an amateur featherweight champion from Ohio who, like Max Baer and other past charges, spent a lot of time trying to prove he was as much a lover as a fighter. "He prided himself as God's gift to the lonesome ladies who were in need of sexual attention and was always more than accommodating.... Try as we might, we couldn't control him. He filled more ringside seats with adoring women than any other boxer I knew."

To keep an eye on Janiro prior to a scheduled bout against Kid Gavilan in 1946, Arcel moved him into the Great Northern, a West 57th Street hotel owned by Jack Dempsey. "He caused more delays in elevator service than the Otis repair men could handle. Elevators had a strange way of always getting stuck between floors." Matters didn't improve when it was time to set up the training camp at Greenwood Lake in New Jersey. Arcel:

One day I saw him sitting at a desk writing something. When I asked him what he was doing, he said he was writing a letter to his mother. Since he never wrote letters, I told him that would probably kill the woman, that he was better off just phoning her. But no, he said, he wanted to write the letter, then take it down to the post office. When I offered to go with him, he said no, thanks, accusing me of being a watchdog. So off he went to the post office by himself. When more than enough time had gone by and he hadn't returned, I went off looking for him. The post office had a front and back door. At the back door there was a flight of stairs leading up to second-floor apartments. The guy in the post office said that was how Tony had left. Needless to say, I found him upstairs in one of the apartments entertaining a mother and daughter at the same time. When he saw me, he jumped out of bed stark naked and just smiled. I realized then and there that training for Gavilan would have been a waste of time. I told the manager I was out, and I was angry and heartsick. So much work wasted. It was more than I could take. Years later, he did fight Gavilan, but lost a 10-round decision. Janiro had everything going for him except self-discipline.

More often than not, Arcel's recollections of Janiro led him to Lenny Mancini as a contrasting case in point. The original "Boom Boom" and father of the later lightweight champion, Lenny Mancini shared Youngstown as a birthplace with Janiro but nothing else. Indeed, he was so scrupulous about following Arcel's instructions that he sometimes gave third parties the impression that he was as intimidated by the trainer as Kid Lewis had once been by Dai Dollings. Mancini was drafted soon after a fight against Sammy Angott that would have made him chief lightweight challenger except for the fact that he was deemed the loser in a controversial split decision. While in uniform he was wounded at the Battle of the Bulge, sent to a nearby hospital for weeks, then immediately shipped back to the front line. When he suffered a second wound, he was hospitalized in Paris, where he ran into a second Arcel boxer, Paul Klang. One evening the two of them were sufficiently on the mend to commandeer a jeep and some wine and go prowling for French women. They soon found a couple, but, as Klang later recounted to Arcel, "There we were having this great time and Boom Boom suddenly turns to me and says, 'Promise me you won't tell Ray about any of this.'"

As extreme in opposite directions as the Janiro and Mancini attitudes toward sex within Arcel's purview might have been, they both encircled a hard-and-fast training mentality in which even recourse to an Evil Eye Finkle was more explicable than dalliances with women. "Women are the worst enemies of fighters," the trainer declared to Elli Wohlgelernter, forgetting similar assertions where families and fathers came in for the same indictment. "I never let them in a gym. After women comes liquor. They usually come together." Asked if that meant he insisted on total sexual abstinence during training, Arcel said yes, though he also conceded that "marrying a good woman never hurt any fighter. Marriage has helped a lot of fighters." So he made an exception for married fighters? "For Lou Nova. I gave him until about eight days before his fight."[9]

Arcel himself was the first to credit a story involving him with veteran manager Eddie Walker and writer Damon Runyon. Stricken with throat cancer and unable to communicate except through a pad and pencil, Runyon spent the final days of his life dependent on Walker for company. One day Arcel visited them and spent a couple of hours talking about boxing. As he was leaving, Runyon grabbed his pad, scrawled the words "NICE GUY," and showed it to Walker. "Yeah, Damon," the always acerbic Walker replied. "He's the only guy I know who would say 'Yes, Ma'am' and 'No, Ma'am' in a whorehouse." According to Arcel, he left Runyon still laughing.

20

More Champions

Among Arcel's prominent fighters in the years after World War II were middleweight Tony Zale and heavyweights Joe Baksi and Ezzard Charles. All three ended up with championship belts, although the truculent Baksi's was custom-fit only for Europe.

One of those whose title was frozen during the war while he served in the Navy, Zale (Anthony Florian Zaleski) was put into Arcel's hands in anticipation of the first of what would turn out to be three savage duels with Rocky Graziano. Although the so-called "Man of Steel" (he came from Gary, Indiana) had remained in trim during his service years as a boxing instructor of sailors in Puerto Rico, and Arcel always attested to his fine condition, Zale also had a bad left elbow that reminded his managers Sam Pian and Art Winch of how the trainer had once shepherded Barney Ross through physical problems to a championship. Aside from dealing with the elbow, Arcel laid out a fitness program that was principally aimed at not burning up his fighter's energy. "He was 32 and had had a long layoff from professional fighting. I just thought we had to be especially careful not to burn him out before he got back into the ring."

The one tip Arcel didn't have to pass on was Graziano's reputation as a rip-and-tear street fighter who was not above grabbing at throats and resorting to other fouls to get his way. Zale didn't need that reminder because he had never put much stock in style points, either. In fact, before the three fights with Graziano entered boxing lore as some of the bloodiest ever fought, Zale could have been mentioned in the same category for the three set-tos with Al Hostak in 1940 and 1941 that had made him champion.

The first match with Graziano was held at Yankee Stadium on September 27, 1946, and didn't disappoint anybody who had come to see a bout with the subtlety of a gang war. The trouble for the Zale corner was that the wrong gang was winning. Arcel: "The fifth round was just a murderous round. Graziano was winning hands down. But when Tony got back to the corner, I said to him, 'Tony, don't let this guy take the title away from you. This is the last round. Hit this guy with your best punch. Just load one up and take a chance.'" Which was exactly what Zale did, connecting with a left hook and knocking out Graziano.

When a rematch was scheduled for Chicago Stadium the following July, Arcel was in Stockholm, where he was losing patience on a grand European tour with Baksi, who had insisted on fighting a Swedish champion instead of returning home to face Louis. "When Sam Pian called and said they needed me back for the second Graziano fight, I didn't hesitate."

The second bout was hardly a sequel to the first. For openers, the Chicago Stadium temperature rose as high as 115 degrees at one point. "You could hardly breathe," recalled Arcel. "On top of the summer

Arcel and Tony Zale waiting to go to the center of the ring for the first of the three bloody battles with Rocky Graziano.

weather you had thousands and thousands of people filling the place with cigarette and cigar smoke, and it was all just laying there in the humidity. I brought out a pail of ice, but it melted before it did much good." By the sixth round, Zale was reeling against the heat and the punishment from Graziano's fists. When he began to keel over the ropes, even the referee reached for him to prevent a serious fall, and the challenger was awarded the middleweight title. After the fight, Arcel advised Pian and Winch to persuade Zale to retire, but the managers were noncommittal, saying they would wait a few weeks before deciding on their next move.

Their next move was to put Zale into the ring over the next several months against relatively undistinguished opponents to build up his credit for a third meeting with Graziano. Once the former champion had scored either knockouts or technical knockouts in the bouts, there was nothing preventing the next rematch at Ruppert Stadium in Newark on June 10, 1948. Once again Arcel was called upon to work on the challenger's balky elbow and supervise his training. This time around there was much less suspense, with Zale knocking out Graziano in the third round to reclaim his title. At least in retrospect, Arcel didn't find the outcome all that surprising. As he told his AJC interviewer: "The two of them were really street fighters, no holds barred. They came right at you and you had to make sure you didn't give any quarter. But I think there was a big difference in the importance they gave their conditioning. Zale was very Catholic, always saying a prayer in tough situations, and really didn't fool around the way Graziano did. And the other thing about Graziano was that, for somebody who could punch like he did, he got knocked down or knocked out an awful lot of times."[1]

Once again, after the third Graziano fight, Arcel implored Pian and Winch to talk Zale into retiring. But with nothing except victories to show since hearing the last such plea, the managers agreed instead to a fight against the Frenchman Marcel Cerdan a mere three months after the Graziano bout. Arcel had no doubt that was an invitation to disaster. "I really didn't think he had a chance against Cerdan. I'd seen Cerdan in Europe when I'd been there, and this guy was both tough and polished. Plus, the fight was right after the Graziano thing. Zale wasn't a kid anymore, and that was without getting into all the differences in style he had to learn so fast. Naturally, I didn't say that to anybody. I could fool the world, but not myself."

More to the point, Zale didn't fool Cerdan. With a crowd of 25,000 that included the Frenchman's lover *chanteuse* Edith Piaf looking on at Roosevelt Stadium in Jersey City, the titlist had moments early in the battle, but from the fifth round on it was mainly a question of when he would fold under Cerdan's volleys. The answer was at the end of the eleventh round, when he collapsed from what was called "exhaustion," and Arcel and Winch had to drag him bodily back to his corner. Although Pian signaled the referee that they were throwing in the towel, New Jersey rules stipulated that the next round had to be belled, so that the fight was formally recorded as a knockout in the twelfth round. The good news for Arcel was that the decision finally persuaded Zale that it was time to quit. The bad news was that members of Zale's family insisted for some time afterward that there would be a rematch against Cerdan. If that satisfied Arcel's opinions about how boxers were usually ill-served by family members, it also left room for Zale's own claim 12 years later in a magazine interview that he had lost to Cerdan because he had been "over-trained."[2] As expected, the apparent dig at Arcel raised little response from its target. "Working with him was an education in itself" was about as far as Arcel went.

In later years Arcel would say that his relationship with Baksi came at the right time, while he was still grief-stricken over the loss of Hazel, and was spending most evenings at Toots Shor's until bedtime and in need of a work diversion. The record doesn't quite support that timeline, since he was already at work on the first Zale-Graziano match mere weeks after Hazel's death and didn't become involved seriously with Baksi until many months later. In any case, he was asked by manager Natie Wolfson to accompany the fighter to England in February 1947 for a scheduled bout against British heavyweight champion Bruce Woodcock. It didn't take him long to discover that London was still operating under severe power and food restrictions stemming from the destructive consequences of the war, and this brought out more crankiness than sympathy. "It was all very difficult. The hotel where we were staying, I had to memorize the hours when the electricity was on, otherwise the elevators weren't working and I had to go up and down seven flights of stairs. For things directly related to the fight we were at the mercy of the English boxing promoter Jack Solomons, and he took a long time to realize that we couldn't train in the gym he had for us because the place was like a barn without heat. You just couldn't train properly."

Facing a public relations fiasco, Solomons contacted a friend, Billy Sinclair, who lived more than an hour outside London but who owned a small gym where he and his friends worked out regularly. "He was a big boxing buff, and he had all the necessary equipment — ring, punching bags, everything. It was as well-equipped as a lot of places I'd seen in the States. And every day Billy would have his three sons go out to the nearby railroad tracks to pick up all the wood and coal they could. Between that and what he got on the black market, we kept the gym pretty comfortable."

For all that, Arcel didn't ever quite make his peace with the cold or with the British response to it during the postwar austerity years. "Of course we were glad to live at Billy's lovely home. We couldn't really commute back and forth from London every day. But there was no central heating, as there wasn't anywhere, and the cold could be fierce. Going to bed at night was like sleeping between two cakes of ice. I needed hot water bottles the whole time. Going into the bathroom was like walking into the ice box. We couldn't wait to get to the gym and use the bathroom there."

The temperatures didn't help Baksi's eagerness to do roadwork in the morning. "It was an ordeal trying to get him out of bed in the morning. In order to protect him from the cold and wind, I had to pack newspapers between his heavy woolen underwear and sweaters. And like that wasn't enough, we also had to be careful about where exactly we did our roadwork because it was an area where the Germans had dropped a lot of their buzz bombs during the war. I had to lead all the way, keeping my eyes on the ground to be sure there wasn't something on the road that shouldn't have been there. We were warned that a lot of those bombs could still be active."

None of this did much for Baksi's attitude, and Arcel found himself in a situation similar to that with Charlie Phil Rosenberg a couple of decades earlier:

> This one day was the worst of all. It was drizzling and it was cold. I woke Joe up and he looked at me with hate in his eyes. He finally got up and I could see trouble ahead. I found out he was determined this was going to be the last time I'd do any roadwork with anybody. He started out as if he was on a sprint. He ran me ragged for four miles. With about half a mile to go, he stopped running, and started jumping up and down. He shadow-boxed. Then he looked at me to see if I was dying. Believe me, I was. He was 24, I was twice that. But I knew if I let on, he would know he had me and wouldn't do any more

road work. So I told him, "Let's finish this half-mile with a sprint."... He looked at me for a long moment, then screamed out: "Even a work horse gets tired!" We ran back together. I didn't have any more trouble with him about road work on the trip.

But he did have time to do a lot more than had been scheduled. It turned out that the champion Woodcock also had problems getting used to the bitter weather, and his camp filed one request after another for a postponement of the fight originally scheduled for February 28. First it was moved to March 15, then to March 29, then finally April 15. This played havoc with Baksi's nicotine habit. "I wouldn't let him smoke. But Mrs. Sinclair smoked and kept her cigarettes on a little shelf in the kitchen. There was this opening between the kitchen and the room where we had our meals, and unbeknownst to me Joe was stealing a couple from the pack whenever my back was turned. I suppose I should've suspected something when he told me after a meal he wanted to take a walk by himself, but the light didn't go on until Mrs. Sinclair came to me one day and told me what had been going on."

Arcel's solution was to get Sinclair to take him to the local tobacco shop and to talk the proprietor into giving him some packs of stale cigarettes that had been destined for the garbage in any case. "I brought them back to the house and told Mrs. Sinclair to put them where she normally put her own cigarettes. After a couple of days, she came to me and said, "Mr. Arcel, you will never believe this, but Joe asked me where I bought my cigarettes because he thought they were the best he had ever smoked in his life."

When April 15 finally arrived, it turned out to be the least fatiguing day of Arcel's stay in Europe. Baksi made short work of Woodcock in Harringay Arena, decking the English champion three times in the first round and twice more in the second before finally being awarded a TKO verdict in the one-sided battle in the seventh frame. The British press wasted little time in jumping on the Baksi bandwagon, and the American heavyweight was lionized for his convincing display against Woodcock. The social whirl was on for manager and trainer as much as fighter, and it extended to a side trip to Dublin where Baksi was the special guest at a church benefit and played to the crowd by boxing one-minute rounds with some local boys.

For Arcel, though, the highlight of the trip came when the party returned to London and was invited to the House of Lords. Over and over again in subsequent interviews, he pointed to the invitation as the true mark of how far he had come from East Harlem. "Who am I? Just another bum, really. But how many people can say they've been introduced in the House of Lords? Makes no sense, but that's what happened. That's the kind of thing I owe to boxing. Would I have ever been at the House of Lords without it?"[3]

It was also during his visit to Parliament that he was approached by Adrian Gerald Foley, a peer of the Lords and a composer for minor British films. Then and there Lord Foley merely raised the hope that Arcel, Baksi, and Wolfson would find the time to visit his estate for tea. As it turned out, it was only the trainer who was available the very next day when a chauffeur came around to the hotel to make the vague invitation an imminent appointment. "When I arrived, he greeted me warmly and introduced me to his mother. She was sitting there smoking a long cigarette, and he said, 'Mother, I would like you to meet Mr. Arcel. Mr. Arcel is a famous trainer of American prizefighters.' As soon as she heard that, she rises from her chair. I thought it was to greet me, but instead she just gives me this long look and says 'How disgusting!' and leaves the room."

Arcel returned to the estate several times during his stay in England to placate the aristocrat's hunger for boxing stories. "The funny thing was that he wanted to talk boxing all the time but didn't want his mother hearing us. So we used to sit down at his piano, and the more excited he'd get about what I was telling him, the louder his playing got. I really think he wanted to be a boxer more than a musician."

But while Arcel was entertaining Lord Foley, Baksi was partying as hard as he could back in London. Then, to the trainer's surprise, Wolfson agreed to a bout in Stockholm against reigning Swedish champion Olle Tandberg. "I kept reminding them that they had nothing to gain by going there, that the win over Woodcock was a clear path to taking on Louis back in the States. But they didn't want to listen. So we go to Stockholm, and Tandberg gets the decision. That's when the Zale camp calls me and asks if I want to go to Chicago for the second Graziano fight. I couldn't get out of Sweden and away from Baksi fast enough."

Arcel's problems with Charles weren't only of the racist kind mentioned earlier. In August 1949 he was contacted by Jake Mintz and Tom Tannas, managers of the NBA champion, to work with Charles for a bout months down the road with the returning Joe Louis for the internationally recognized crown. Arcel stepped into a medical brouhaha before he ever got close to the Yankee Stadium ring, and with tones familiar from his experiences with both Barney Ross and Tony Zale.

Arcel's reputation as a trainer seeped over to comic strips when Ham Fisher depicted him out jogging with Joe Palooka.

To get a better look at his new charge, Arcel went up to Buffalo where the heavyweight was due to meet Freddie Bashore in a warm-up bout for Louis. But a week before that fight, Charles suddenly interrupted a gym sparring session to complain of a pain in his lower left rib. The Commission doctor from Buffalo diagnosed a heart condition that made a fight against Bashore, Louis, or anybody else moot. Pressed by the Charles camp to conduct another examination, this time including x-rays of the rib region, the doctor merely reiterated his initial finding and sent his report on to the Boxing Commission in New York City. Not trusting the physician's evaluation, Mintz and Tannas put up $10,000 of their own money for a heart specialist in Manhattan who came back with what Charles himself had said from the beginning — that he had a severely bruised rib and that there was nothing wrong with his heart. Years later Arcel recalled the episode as "an outrageous example of how doctors like the one in Buffalo will not admit their errors even when contradicted by more thorough examinations."

Since the Bashore fight had already been postponed, Mintz and Tannas had no choice but to have Charles get back to his warm-ups by going on a brief tour of the country, the most prominent stop-off of which was for an eighth round knockout of Pat Valentino at the Cow Palace in San Francisco. At this point the original promoter of the Bashore fight re-entered the picture and agreed to an August 1950 bout at Memorial Auditorium. Back within the jurisdiction of the misdiagnosing doctor, Mintz and Tannas submitted Charles to another full physical in New York City that confirmed he was in perfect health, had those findings served on the State Commission, and filed a formal request that a second doctor be assigned as a control on the Buffalo man. "We wanted no problems. At the weigh-in there were three Commission doctors present, and the night of the fight every single member of the Commission was at ringside. Charles battered Bashore until Freddie had to quit in the 14th round because of a dangerously inflamed ear. The fight was very important to Charles personally because the Buffalo guy had scared him with all the talk of a heart problem. Once he got through Bashore, he regained his confidence for taking on Louis."

And defeated him soundly, on September 27, 1950, to leave no doubt who was the world heavyweight champion. Over the next several months, Arcel remained in Charles's corner as he swatted away the likes of Nick Barone and Joey Maxim as challengers. His toughest title defense came against Jersey Joe Walcott in Detroit in March 1951. For Arcel, though, the worst part of that battle was what came after it, when Tannas promised the Walcott camp a rematch in Pittsburgh within four months, even though the pair had already squared off with the same result four times. The trainer admitted to being furious, especially when he heard the vast loopholes Tannas had left in the contract that failed to commit Walcott's manager Felix Bocchicchio to a rematch should the contender win. And, in fact, Walcott did unseat Charles with a seventh-round knockout, and Bocchicchio used the lack of a rematch clause to become one of the first boxing figures to hold up James Norris and Madison Square Garden with some success. When the two fighters met again about a year later, Walcott again prevailed. For Arcel, though, the moral of the story wasn't how Norris had been outflanked or even how Bocchicchio had deceived Tannas with verbal pledges of never pulling a fast one. As he told Milton Gross of the *New York Post* on February 1, 1952: "[This hustle] has taken a nice guy like Tannas and turned him sour.... All I know is the boxing business. There's nothing else I can do, nothing else I guess I'd want to do. But sometimes ... sometimes...."[4]

21

Separated from the Mob

Arcel did not suffer easily questions about the Mob's influence on professional boxing. His usual response fell somewhere between exasperation and dismissiveness, especially when the questions came from somebody not within his circle of sportswriter friends. When down to it, though, he could hardly deny the underworld's presence in the industry, especially when it came to the financial investments of Owney Madden (1920s and 1930s) and Frankie Carbo (1940s and 1950s) in boxers Arcel had trained. On the contrary, he went on the record in relating his own use of Mob reputations to get himself out of ticklish situations — such as when he encouraged the would-be gym hustler to call Carbo to say he was moving in as the manager of Teddy Yarosz, and, more significantly, when he appealed directly for Madden's help against Segal and Rosenberg. In the course of several interviews he also made it clear that he and Madden considered each other friends, and that he frequently dropped around to the gangster's midtown office at Broadway and Seventh Avenue "to talk about boxing. All the managers and trainers did. Owney could never talk enough about it. As for any other business he was involved in, that was his business, not mine. The closest we ever came to that was one time he asked me to taste some [bootlegged] beer. I told him it was lousy, and he just waved me off, saying I was no expert because I didn't drink anyway."

The "talk about boxing" was verse and verse from replies in other contexts when he was asked about his proclaimed friendship with Abe Attell, the early-century champion who was up to his neck in the scandal around the 1919 Black Sox World Series and who introduced Arcel to Arnold Rothstein, the reputed organizer of the baseball fix. What made this response especially disingenuous was that he acknowledged spending hours a day in such midtown eateries as Lindy's that professional gamblers like Rothstein used as offices away from offices.

Then there were the dogs. "I always had dogs, knew something about them. One day Madden says to me his dog is acting sick. I just needed one look at the animal to see it had distemper. I took care of it for Owney, brought it to the vet, made sure it ate right. That kind of thing."[1]

By Arcel's recounting, the line between what he had heard about ("you know, the talk around") and what he could accept professionally was marked by a single piece of paper. "When a manager asked me to train a fighter, the first thing I asked was to see his manager's license. If he had a license, that meant he'd been approved by the licensing commission. If the commission didn't have a problem with the people behind that manager and his fighter, why should I?" Given the shady connections of some members of the licensing commission over the years, this was a stance verging on tautology. But Arcel nevertheless maintained it into the 1950s through major scandals linking Carbo and his cronies to James Norris, the czar of the International Boxing Club and a big stockholder in Madison Square, twin positions making it impossible to organize an important fight in the East without his say-so. But on two different occasions in the decade his mental nimbleness didn't save him from physical confrontations.

The first incident revolved around Rocky Castellani, a middleweight from Pennsylvania. Early in his career Castellani attracted the attention of Thomas Eboli, a hood who belonged to the Vito Genovese crime family and who swaggered around under the street alias of Tommy Ryan. With Ryan calling the shots, Castellani, who had fought as a Marine at Iwo Jima in 1945, had a couple of false starts toward what his handlers were confident would eventually be the middleweight championship. Then on January 11, 1952, he came to a crossroads in a rematch with Ernie Durando whom he had out-boxed a few months earlier under Arcel's supervision. Despite his nickname, Castellani was anything but a Rocky, lacking a big punch. On the other hand, Durando had scored 24 of his 32 victories up to then by knockout. None of this, of course, was new to Arcel, who had coached numerous boxers past sluggers to titles in just about every division.

Trouble began in the sixth round when Durando dropped Castellani with a right to the jaw that kept him down until referee Ray Miller had reached a nine count. After the round, while Arcel worked on the fighter, Ryan lashed into him for leaving himself open for the right. Castellani didn't take the scolding much to heart because midway through the seventh round he again hit the canvas from a Durando right. Once again he managed to regain his feet as Miller was calling out nine, but this time the referee didn't like what he saw. "When I looked into Rocky's eyes," Miller said afterward, "they were completely glassy. He dropped his arms and fell wobbly toward the ropes, and as Durando came charging in with a fury that might have had a tragic outcome, I halted the battle and awarded the fight to Durando."[2]

The decision infuriated Ryan. Charging into the ring, the thug threw two punches at Miller, who dodged them easily enough for an ex-fighter who had once fought the likes of Barney Ross and Jimmy McLarnin and who managed to pin Ryan's hands to his sides until security officers came to his aid. "If I'd swung a blow," the arbiter said, explaining his failure to take out Ryan himself, "his friends at ringside would have stormed into action, my friends would have followed suit, and some terrible, maybe tragic, things could have occurred. I was proud in that instance of what I didn't do."[3]

But the brawl was just getting started, anyway. Surrounded by reporters at his ringside seat, New York State Athletic Commission Chairman Robert Christenberry announced within Ryan's hearing that the purse for the fight was being held up because "we will not tolerate hoodlum tactics." Christenberry left it at that for the evening, not following Ryan back to Castellani's dressing room. The one who made that mistake was Al Weill, a matchmaker for both Mike Jacobs and James Norris, and for that reason alone not one of Arcel's favorite people. When Weill showed his face in the dressing room, the still-seething Ryan and his brother immediately attacked him, punching him over a bench, breaking his glasses, and taking turns at pummeling him until Arcel dove into the pack to protect the matchmaker. "What was I to do?" he said to reporters after some peace had been restored. "I dislike Weill, but there are things you don't tolerate, even against your enemies. I couldn't just stand by and see them hurt him."[4]

In the wake of the tumult, Christenberry decided Castellani had not been responsible for any of it so released his share of the purse. He fined Ryan $3,000 and suspended his license for life, though it was Pulcinella's secret that the thug remained behind the curtain calling the tune for new manager Tex Sullivan. When even that charade didn't bring Castellani any closer to the title, they sold the fighter to Cleveland contractor Al Naiman. Under Naiman, Castellani got as far as a bruising battle with champion Bobo Olson sometime later, but no further. The assault victim, Weill, moved on to managing, becoming more well known for his handling of Rocky Marciano and tingeing the heavyweight champion with his ongoing underworld associations. Ryan also moved up the ladder, taking over as acting boss of one of the five Mafia families in New York for jailed *capo* Vito Genovese. But when Genovese died behind bars in 1969, Ryan began to lose much of his authority to Carlo Gambino. The payoff was his slaying in the Crown Heights section of Brooklyn in July 1972.[5]

As for Arcel, the Ryan-Miller-Weill episode was one more goad to a steadily building desire to do more than roadwork and bandaging. Without knowing it at the time, he had set the foundations for his first major career move in more than 30 years when, in addition to Zale, Baksi, and Charles, he had also worked in the corner after the war for Cuban welterweight Kid Gavilan (Gerardo Gonzalez). His task, as outlined by manager Angel Lopez, was to keep Gavilan focused on ring business more than on the pleasures to be had before and after it. Arcel delivered on the assignment through three headline fights pitting Gavilan against Beau Jack in Chicago, Lester Felton in Detroit, and Laurent Dauthille in Montreal. They turned out to be only the preface to a May 19, 1951, meeting at Madison Square Garden between the Cuban and Johnny Bratton. When Gavilan emerged from the bout with the title, no one was happier — or more grateful to Arcel — than Lopez.

When Lopez wasn't managing Gavilan, he was operating the Chateau Madrid supper club on West 52nd Street. In March 1952, Arcel received an invitation to have lunch with the owner at the restaurant. When he walked in, he found Lopez already sitting with three men, introduced as Hal James, Burke Crotty, and Pete Jaeger. They were all representatives of the Ellington Advertising Agency and were looking for somebody to head up a weekly one-hour TV boxing program for Philadelphia's Bayuk Cigar Company (Phillies brand) that could complement the bouts already being aired by Norris's IBC from Chicago on Wednesdays and from New York on Fridays. Impressed by how he had organized the rambunctious Gavilan, Lopez had recommended Arcel for the position. Neither Madison Avenue nor television broadcasters regarded such an undertaking as some minor appendage to the boxing industry. As Jeffrey T. Sammons observed in *Beyond the Ring*, "While television helped the monopolistic and criminally infiltrated IBC to expand, it also captured high ratings and exerted influence over the IBC and boxing in general. In 1952 televised fights reached an average 5 million homes, representing a whopping 31 percent of the available audience; by 1955, that figured climbed to 8.5 million, with the IBC pulling in $90,000 per week. In less scientific terms, boxing in the 1950s reportedly sold as many television sets as Milton Berle, and it rivaled *I Love Lucy* in the ratings."[6]

After a series of screenings of other candidates, the agency agreed to proceed on a conditional basis with Lopez's recommendation of Arcel, setting January 24, 1953, for launching what would be called *The Saturday Night Fights* on the ABC network. The rest was up to Arcel.

And there was plenty of "the rest." Arcel's most immediate task was to set up the main events that would assure ABC it had a viable program at least for an initial 13-week investment of air time. There were no commitments from anybody until that had been done. Complicating the question was the fact that boxing managers had little incentive to risk even the few dollars they had been pocketing from the Norris shows by offending the East Coast czar for a project yet to reach its larval stage. Arcel's solution was to call a meeting of the New York chapter of the International Boxing Guild, which included the sport's most prominent managers and of which he was vice-president. Armed with forms supplied by the Ellington Agency, he made the case that the managers could only profit from an additional opportunity to give their fighters national exposure. Not only shouldn't this have jeopardized their relationship with Norris, he contended, it would have ultimately been to his benefit as well since it would have created a larger pool of fighters with name recognition for bookings at Madison Square Garden and (why not, since there was no exclusivity involved?) on his own TV fights.

In Arcel's telling, it was this argument plus the general skepticism of Guild members that they would never again hear about the ABC project once their meeting was over that prompted them to shrug and fill out the forms provided by the agency. That explanation would be scoffed at by just about everybody a few years later before detailed accusations that the trainer had also made his own commitment of cash to the Guild for being able to walk out of the room with the signatures Ellington had been after. One way or the other, though, he did have the completed forms. The next obstacle to be negotiated was New York City — too important a market for ABC or the projected sponsor to agree to black out and the center of the Norris fiefdom. Here again, Arcel used the same argument with Norris that he had at the Managers Guild meeting, telling him through the press: "I'm your best friend. I'm developing talent for you."[7] For public consumption anyway, Norris said he was satisfied none of the ABC fights would originate from the city. That was enough for Arcel to form his own production company with two other industry veterans. One was Sol Gold, Jackie Berg's one-time manager. The second was Dewey Fragetta, regarded as the first international matchmaker and who at the height of his activity had on a single calendar day arranged for bouts being held in South Africa, Latin America, Europe, Asia, and three North American cities; all told, Fragetta was said to have organized 8,000 bouts in his career. Among the three of them, Arcel was confident, they had enough contacts with regional matchmakers to make their exclusion from New York a minor inconvenience, especially with the show's city of origin being blacked out so as not to jeopardize the local gate.

Then reality kicked in, and it didn't at all resemble Norris's pose as a good sport. The fighters scheduled for the main events on the first couple of telecasts from Boston not only developed mysterious ailments, but did so tardily enough to prevent their replacement by headliners or even semi-headliners. Arcel acknowledged that the results were a "disaster," but also refused to point a finger at Norris, at least one with a nail on it. He was very much in the minority. As *Ring* magazine put it sometime afterward, "As most of the fighters who were taken ill by the strangest of maladies wound up on IBC productions several weeks later, suspicious persons became even more so, but that austere body was given a clean bill of health, which should satisfy everyone, even if it doesn't."[8]

The knight in shining armor who saved the day was San Francisco promoter Sid Flaherty. "Sid was an old friend, and he managed Bobo Olsen, the middleweight champion. Even before the second show went on the air, I told him the trouble I was having lining up bouts that could attract an audience, and he agreed to send Olsen to Boston to box Joe Rindone, a local fighter, in an over-the-weight match. Olsen came, met the press, charmed everybody, and that was our salvation. The Boston Garden was sold out, giving us instant credibility. From that point on the promoters in every city we contacted wanted to be part of the TV show."

Well through the summer of 1953 *The Saturday Night Fights* drew good press and creditable ratings, despite operating on a budget little above shoestring for its telecasts to 29 cities. Among the fighters it brought initial serious exposure to were welterweight champions Carmen Basilio and Tony DeMarco. (Indicative of the publicity pizzazz the Arcel production team sought in its presentations was a main event from San Francisco pitting DeMarco against unrelated namesake Paddy DeMarco, and a quest, ultimately unsuccessful for budgetary reasons, to have the DeMarco Sisters, a popular singing group of the era, show up to sit ringside.) ABC was so satisfied that it extended its commitment from the original 13 weeks to a full year. Its glee wasn't shared by Norris, and more than once Arcel had to deal with managers who had received hints of envelopes if they turned down an opportunity to appear on the ABC telecast. There were also more direct approaches. In March, according to Arcel, he received a threatening phone call warning him to "get out of the TV racket if you know what's good for you!" Then, in September 1953, he was summoned to the Ellington Agency to hear that the TV boxing wars had escalated yet another notch thanks to the gossip columnist and weekly ABC broadcaster Walter Winchell. "When I arrived, Hal James told me that Walter Winchell had advised him that our Saturday program was controlled by the Mob. I was astounded, and asked him where Winchell had gotten his information. I was shocked to hear it was from Robert Kintner, ABC's own network president! I didn't waste any time getting an appointment to see Kintner. I was really hot. I asked him straight out why he had made such an accusation against me to Winchell, one without any basis in fact. He couldn't answer me. He just sat there looking at me with no expression at all. I was so enraged, I said, 'Do you ever look in a mirror? ... I don't even want to look at you.'"

The trainer had grim reason to remember that his meeting with Kintner took place Monday, September 14, 1953. By that Saturday, the 19th, he was back in Boston trying to balance his observance of Yom Kippur and the fights scheduled to be televised from Boston Garden that evening. While standing outside the Hotel Manger next to the Garden with manager Willie Ketchum, he was suddenly approached by someone wielding a lead pipe, whacked on the forearm and head, and dropped to the ground. Although the Boston Garden area was filled with pedestrians at the time, the closest police got to a description of the assailant was that he was in his early thirties, about six feet tall, and wearing a brown suit. Ketchum, the witness closest to the assault, insisted that it had happened too fast for him to see anything.[9]

Arcel was taken to Massachusetts Memorial Hospital, where he was initially listed as being in critical condition and where he remained for 19 days under police guard with a brain concussion and various lacerations. Like Ketchum, he said he couldn't provide police with a description of his assailant, despite alleged promises from one unidentified cop he had known previously that if "you tell us who it is, there'll be a funeral."[10] During his hospital stay he received a steady stream of visitors that included not only fighters and fellow trainers, reporters and columnists from Boston and New York, but also Red Sox star Ted Williams. If that attested to his standing in the sports world, it still didn't make him secure enough to say what was on everybody else's mind — and typewriter. Among those professing no doubt that the lead pipe had Norris's fingerprints on it were Red Smith of the *Herald Tribune*, Frank Graham of the *Journal American*, and Tim Cohane of the *Saturday Evening Post*. (Not joining the chorus was Jimmy Powers, sports editor and columnist for the three-million circulation *New York Daily News*, who moonlighted as an announcer for Norris's Friday fight telecasts.) For Dan Parker of the *New York Daily Mirror*, "all of the evidence points to the conclusion that the brutal assault was motivated by revenge for Arcel's refusal to be intimidated by one of the several factions which resented his Saturday night television show." Parker also made the points that independent Boston promoter Sam Silverman had also been the object of threats from suspected Norris associates, and that the lead pipe used on Arcel was precisely the kind of weapon favored by Carbo's kind of henchmen.[11]

But it was all to little avail, even after Boston sportswriters offered a reward for information on the assailant. The case was never closed, and Arcel went on claiming in interviews that "I didn't know who I had offended. Things happen, and you never know why. How can you explain it?" A typical exchange on the incident with the AJC's Wohlgelernter went like this:

> RC: When those things happen you don't know why. You can walk the street and somebody'll stick a knife in you, you don't know what happened.
> AJC: True, true. But there was a strong rumor that it was the Mob that did it.
> RC: They always say a Mob. I was never associated with any Mobs. I knew all of them and I'd walk on the other side of the street. When you were in boxing in the Fifties and Jim Norris was ruling the industry, why, he was

associated with many unscrupulous characters.... [But] nobody knows the why or wherefore. Maybe it was some disgruntled bum that wanted a fight and I wouldn't give it to him or something.[12]

At another juncture in the same 1983 interview, the trainer sought to justify his stance not only in the name of the "code" prevailing in sectors of the boxing industry but also as the fruit of paternal wisdom. "I learned a long time ago," he declared, "what could I gain [by making accusations]? I had enough experience in my early years when I had to fight to exist. My father was a great teacher, a very smart guy. He always told me, 'Watch your step and never try to get even. Because you never get even.' So what I learned early in life held me in good stead when I got hit in the head."[13]

There has been scant consensus around that opinion, either in the immediate wake of the attack or ever since. On the contrary, wiretaps from an investigation into a reputed Carbo threat against California promoter Jack Leonard a couple of years later turned up (Honest) Bill Daly, a manager never far from considerations of Carbo and Norris, and treasurer of the International Boxing Guild, confirming Dan Parker's observation on the weapon used in the Boston assault: "They use a water pipe ... lead pipe ... and they just get an ordinary piece of newspaper, see, newspaper don't show fingerprints.... And you sitting in a crowd ... and they try to give you two bats, and they'll kill you with two if they can. But they whack you twice and split you — fracture your skull. And knock you unconscious, and they just drop it.... And after they drop it — the law — they're protected by the law. They have to have witnesses."[14]

But however much that described the attack on him, Arcel held to his line. The nearest he came to wavering was when he was once asked about his appeal to Norris that the Saturday shows on ABC would have ultimately benefited Madison Square Garden cards as well, and he replied that "[Norris] was too greedy to understand. He wanted to be the sole ruler and emperor of the whole dynasty, so we had problems with them."[15] On the other hand, he received at least retrospective sympathy for his position a couple of decades later from Jimmy Breslin when the columnist said of the links of trainers with criminal elements: "Nobody mentioned them. It was like the hidden, secret sin. That's the business and your job is just the fighter. What are you gonna do? Are you gonna make statements and change America? It couldn't be done. I mean, what shot did you have causing trouble?"[16]

Released from the hospital, Arcel went back to partners Gold and Fragetta, who had continued to produce the weekly fight telecasts with success during his rehabilitation; for a few weeks the highly publicized assault had even brought larger audiences to the bouts. But for the duration of the show there was a decided accent on West Coast venues, especially San Francisco, San Jose, Sacramento, and Salt Lake City. If that wasn't a calculated move to stay away from Norris's centers of control, it was certainly open to be read that way.

22

Vows and Disavowals

For worse and better, Arcel's life in the 1950s wasn't defined solely by *The Saturday Night Fights*. He wasn't even the only Arcel in the period to be admitted to a hospital in critical condition.

On March 7, 1951, Ezzard Charles defended his heavyweight title in Detroit against Jersey Joe Walcott. A few hours after Arcel had guided Charles to the successful defense, he received a call from New York reporting that his 23-year-old daughter Adele had tried to commit suicide with an overdose of sleeping pills at the Great Northern, the West Side hotel owned by Jack Dempsey to which the Arcels had moved after Hazel's death. The shaken Arcel flew immediately to New York, and when he got to Roosevelt Hospital, where Adele had been taken, he found a wall of reporters waiting. At first he could honestly say he didn't know what had happened so had nothing to tell anybody. Later on, though, with the press siege extended to his own room at the Great Northern, his silence stemmed more from his nurtured aversion to talking about family matters with outsiders (or, in some cases, even insiders). When the doctors spoke about Adele's "acute depression," he had nothing to add except the conjecture that "she never got over her mother's death" five years before.[1] He was still elusive on the subject 40 years later in his memoir, in which there is no reference at all to the attempted suicide. But in 1983, 10 years earlier, he did speak about the episode, if reluctantly and in very familiar terms, under Elli Wohlgelernter's cajoling for the American Jewish Congress:

> RA: I didn't know if I was coming or going. It was just one of those things. I had to wait around at the airport to get a plane and get me in, and then when I got to the hospital, why, there were newspapermen there and they were shooting cameras and pictures, you know, what the hell. I went in there and talked to the doctor and I looked at the kid and.... You know, it struck me. I felt for her. I mean I couldn't explain it because I was torn between

trying to make a living and trying to take care of her and assuming she had some friends she could be with, and it wasn't that she needed anything because I gave her whatever she needed. I mean as far as her money was concerned, she had no rent to pay. All she had to do ... even if she didn't have any money, she could always go down to the restaurant in the hotel and sign the check. You know, it was Dempsey's hotel, so I could do anything I wanted.

AJC: Did you suddenly feel that you were a bad father?

RA: Well, you feel that way, that this is.... I felt like I was guilty, that it was my fault, that I was probably.... When I said to you that I was away from home so much, that my fighter was very important to me, and at that time I was tied in with Ezzard Charles, who was a great fighter and he had beaten Joe Louis for the heavyweight title, and I was upset after the fight [*ed: the Charles-Walcott bout in Detroit*] because they told me they were going to make a return match with Jersey Joe Walcott and I told his manager, I said I wouldn't walk on the same side of the street after this fight. I said, "This is the most dangerous fight that you can take." He says, "Well...." We called him Snooks, you know. He says, "Snooks beat him a couple of times," he says, "and you saw what happened tonight." I said, "Yes, I saw what happened tonight, and I still say to you don't make the match." But he went it and did it and....

And on he went along that sidetrack about Charles, making no further mention of Adele's overdose in that response or anywhere else in subsequent years.[2] On the other hand, the avalanche of reporters and photographers he described didn't prompt any sensationalistic coverage. On the contrary, a typical two-line item in *The Daily News*, barely visible atop a page of jewelry store ads, went little beyond the tiny headline "GIRL FELLED BY PILLS" and the identification of the victim as Arcel's daughter.[3] Adele overcame the crisis and later married and had two daughters.

It was also in the 1950s, during one of his trips to San Francisco for *The Saturday Night Fights*, that Arcel met Stephanie (Steve) Howard, the woman who became his second wife. A 34-year-old divorcee at the time with a resume that included acting in Hollywood B movies and running a ranch in Arizona with her ex-husband, the England-born but California-based redhead had a small business representing the lines of East Coast dress and sportswear manufacturers at a showroom in Los Angeles's Biltmore Hotel. By her own admission, she knew absolutely nothing about boxing when she received a call from one of the New York manufacturers saying that two acquaintances would be in San Francisco at the same time that she and a partner would be there for a show. "It was something they did all the time," she recalled, "but when I heard these people were involved in boxing, I didn't know what to think. So I told my partner we should meet them at the St. Francis Hotel, then bring them over to the Palace Hotel where there were always lots of people and where it would be easier to lose them after a little while. We'd be happy in San Francisco, and they'd be happy back in New York that we showed their friends around town."4

It didn't quite work out that way. "When Ray walked into the Palace, everybody in the place seemed to know him. There were reporters, people who recognized him from being in the corner of champions, just those who thought of him in terms of the TV show he was producing." The evening's next unexpected development came when Arcel asked Howard to accompany him to the popular night spot Bimbo's, where he was to meet another reporter for an interview about the ABC show. "I sat listening to it and not really understanding all that much," the next Mrs. Arcel said, "and after he was finished, we got out of Bimbo's and started walking around the North Beach area. Then he said he was hungry and we walked into a place, and I couldn't believe what he ordered. A cup of tea and prunes! I didn't know what to say. And I still didn't when the waiter looked at me and asked what I wanted. Naturally, I said a cup of tea and prunes!"

While Arcel was still in Northern California, he brought Howard along to her first fight, in Sacramento. "That first time I covered my eyes with my hands and just peeked through them the whole time. It took only about two more bouts to be standing up and yelling at the fighters what they should be doing and hearing it from the people sitting around me." For all that, though, she insisted that Arcel, neither then nor during their married life, "talked very much about boxing to me. We talked a lot about the people involved in it, but not really about the sport itself. With me he always seemed more interested in talking about the theater, music, world affairs, things like that. From the very start I always took him to be a very cultured person, not somebody who only knew who had knocked out who when and where."

Over the next couple of months Arcel called Howard regularly from New York and the other locations where he was producing *The Saturday Night Fights*. Finally, on the transparent pretext of getting a closer look at the new lines she would be representing in Los Angeles for the coming season, Howard flew to New York. ("Nobody believed me when I used that as an excuse.") In August 1954, she and Arcel were married at a City Hall ceremony conducted by a rabbi, without friends or relatives in attendance. ("We thought of it as our private thing.") For the next nine months they lived at the Beaux Arts Hotel on the East Side near the United Nations. Then they moved into a newly constructed apartment building at Lexington Avenue and East 37th Street where they spent almost 40 years of married life. But it wasn't as a TV producer that Arcel moved in.

Despite the steady audience attracted by *The Saturday Night Fights*, the Phillies cigar sponsor informed ABC and Arcel's production company in November 1954 that it was going to call it quits in January after two years on the air. The reason given for the decision was heightened production costs. The bottom line was that, for all its appeal to fight fans, the show barely laid a glove on the Norris productions elsewhere on the dial. Although some boxing writers credited Arcel with at least having encouraged local, independent fight clubs through his program, he himself never quite bought that argument, basically contending that *The Saturday Night Fights* was part of the problem, not anything like a solution. "TV is a monster," he told one interviewer. "It's chewed up and destroyed independent promoting, and independent promoting is the lifeblood of the game because that's where fighters are developed for the big time."[5] Whether the weekly show boosted or helped to suffocate the independent fight clubs, it didn't translate into significant enough profits for Phillies, making ABC equally unenthusiastic about going on when no other sponsor could be found.

For a short while Arcel and his partners, Gold and Fragetta, sought to maintain their company by promoting fights in some of the locales where they had organized their bouts for ABC; but without a TV outlet and a sponsor to underwrite the costs, they were soon forced to disband. The dissolution of the partnership brought Arcel back to the same crossroads where he had found himself prior to taking on the weekly fights — no particular desire to go back to a gym to tutor fighters. That he did go back temporarily to seconding Ezzard Charles was due to a lack of any immediate practical alternative for earning money. Then Harry Kessler came along.

Kessler was hardly the average boxing referee. For one thing, he was estimated as having arbitrated a good 6,000 fights from the 1920s onwards, including what would eventually add up to 13 championship bouts, into the era of Muhammad Ali. For another, he wasn't averse, especially in his early days, to throwing a kick at a drag-footed boxer if, in his irritated judgment, the fighter wasn't giving his all. But what singled out Kessler more than anything from his bow-tied brethren, earning him the sobriquet of "The Millionaire Referee," was his career outside the ring, where his knowledge of metallurgy had enabled him to set up a flourishing foundry company called the Meehanite Metal Corporation, among the largest engineering consulting firms in the world. One of the most prominent clients for the New Brunswick, New Jersey–based firm was Mack Trucks, for which Meehanite supplied all the castings. Kessler's reputation in the field was such that President Dwight Eisenhower's administration sent him to the Soviet Union at the height of the Cold War to look into the purity of Soviet steel. And with all that, he still had time — *made* the time — to go back to the ring on special occasions, such as when he refereed Ali's unanimous decision over Ernie Terrell at the Houston Astrodome in 1967.[6]

Listening to Arcel's indecision about his next career move one evening at Toots Shor's, Kessler floated the idea of having him come work for Meehanite Metal. When Arcel pointed out that he knew nothing about the foundry business, Kessler advised him to think about it for a few days. What Arcel didn't know at the time was that, thanks to their last meeting in the ring, the referee had not come up with the idea on his own; in fact, Kessler had rejected it when originally proposed by his brother Saul. Friction between the men dated back a couple of months to February, when Arcel had been seconding Charles at Madison Square Garden in a heavyweight match against Charley Norkus. As Kessler recorded the episode in his inevitably entitled as-told-to memoir *The Millionaire Referee*:

> The only trouble I had with this fight was with Charles's trainer, Ray Arcel.... That night, for some reason, this experienced ring man was ignoring the 10-second warning buzzer which means "seconds out of the ring." Ray Arcel just didn't bother to get out on time. I went over to his corner before the start of Round 2 and said, "Seconds out, please!" But the same thing transpired after the second, third, and fourth rounds. Finally, my patience thinning, I went over and yelled at him. "If you don't get out of the ring, I'm going to throw your fighter out." Threats often do work, and I had no more trouble with Mr. Arcel.

According to Kessler, it was with that episode in mind that he exploded shortly afterward when his brother suggested hiring Arcel. "'I'm not going to hire that man,' I said emphatically. 'Not after all the trouble he gave me in the ring.'"[7]

So what changed his mind? *The Millionaire Referee* claims it was because he belatedly learned about the assault in Boston, but that doesn't hold much water since the lead pipe attack had occurred in September 1953 — anybody reading a newspaper (let alone somebody connected to the fight game) would have known about it — and the conversation at Shor's didn't take place until the late winter or early spring of 1955. All indications are that it was Saul Kessler, who had come to know Arcel separately, who pressured his brother into suggesting the foundry job, and that Harry's evocation of the Boston beating was so much cant. That still left Arcel himself to say yes, though, and he admitted to having more than one doubt. Not only didn't he have any knowledge of the foundry business, but he got the distinct impression from Kessler that he would have been brought into Meehanite's purchasing department in White Plains as a replacement for the man holding down that position. "I just didn't want a job at the cost of somebody else losing his," he told one interviewer. On this score he didn't have to worry. Hired initially as an assistant purchasing agent, he followed Kessler's advice to "keep your eyes open and learn" for almost three years before taking over the department and seeing his predecessor promoted to another sector.

First as a purchasing agent operating from administrative offices in Westchester and then as boss of the casting subsidiary Sorbo Cast in New Brunswick, Arcel remained associated with Meehanite until 1980, when the company moved its main quarters to Tennessee. But that did not leave him out of boxing, though in more than one case he would have preferred to stay out of it. In 1957, for instance, he wasn't too happy when, more than two years after it had been cancelled by ABC, *The Saturday Night Fights* came back for a rerun bearing the wrong kind of residuals.

For almost a decade there had been every conceivable kind of probe into the activities of Norris and the IBC. On Federal and Congressional levels there had been looks into the IBC's reputed monopolistic practices in violation of anti-trust laws. These investigations encompassed not only the my-way-or-the-highway ultimatums given to managers if they wanted their fighters booked into Madison Square Garden and other prominent venues, but Norris's manipulations of the television networks that carried his fights and his practice of beaming closed-circuit fights to select theaters for a heavy admission price if he didn't think he stood to make enough profit from the broadcasters. In New York, District Attorney Frank Hogan convened grand juries to hear evidence on corruption charges that initially touched on stooge organizations like the

Managers Guild but that were mainly aimed at setting the groundwork for a broader inquiry into the IBC's links to Frankie Carbos, Blinky Palermos, and other gangland figures. Similar investigations were undertaken in California and Illinois. The heat became so intense at one point that the spotted New York State Athletic Commission thought it was prudent to open its own inquiry, although that, predictably, largely ended with the finding that the overall structure of professional boxing would have inspired the saints themselves.[8]

Given the volume of legal papers flying around for so long, it could not have come as a complete shock to Arcel, especially after his misadventures with *The Saturday Night Fights*, when he was subpoenaed by a grand jury in 1957. But what definitely did disconcert him was the sight of Minneapolis sportswriter George Barton waiting in an anteroom to give his own testimony before the jury. "I asked him, 'What are you doing here?' and his reply was, 'I came here to testify against you.'"

In his memoir, Arcel said Barton's response "hit me across the face. I could not have been more stunned. I was speechless." According to the trainer, the last time he had seen the newsman had been in 1954 in Milwaukee, where he had gone to produce one of his Saturday bouts. "The *Milwaukee Sentinel* was having a retirement dinner for one of its writers, Sam Levy. Many people were in town to honor him. Both Levy and I were friends of Ernie Fliegel, an ex-boxer who had lost an eye in the ring but had then gone on to own one of the best restaurants in Minneapolis. I called Ernie at his hotel and went up to his suite. There were a lot of people there, including Barton. I said hello to him, but spent most of my time with Fliegel. I hadn't really seen him since."

The thrust of Barton's testimony referred back to that evening in Milwaukee in Fliegel's hotel suite. "The story he told in the jury room was all lies," Arcel declared in his memoir. "He claimed that I had approached him to help me with any boxing problems I had. What on earth could a man who wrote for a small newspaper in Minnesota do to help anyone in New York with the problems that existed there at that time? I refuted all his accusations and bald-face lies and added that if he were under oath, he had committed perjury. I was questioned for two harrowing days for no rhyme or reason. The jury exonerated me of all charges, and to this day I have no idea what prompted Barton to bring that terrible incident about." (On another occasion he speculated that Barton's principal motive in leveling accusations against him was careerism, that at the urging of Minnesota senator Hubert Humphrey, the newsman had sought to make himself more visible as an anti-corruption candidate for appointment to a Federal Commission on boxing.[9] It was also curious that Barton never referred to his allegations or testimony in his lengthy memoir *My Lifetime in Sports*, which otherwise included railings against James Norris and corruption in the boxing business.[10])

What Arcel did not touch on in his memoir was that his grand jury appearance didn't concern merely Barton's allegations but also what exactly had transpired during his meeting with the Managers Guild for the Ellington Agency, and the more answers that were offered about this episode by the trainer and other interested parties, the smellier the fish on the ice. About the only thing everyone agreed on was that money, somewhere between thirteen and seventeen thousand dollars, had changed hands.

As far as Arcel was concerned, there had been nothing wrong in making "donations" to the guild for its cooperation in providing fighters for his TV bouts; they were the equivalent of normal performance fees. Dan Parker thought there was plenty wrong with it, the *New York Daily Mirror* columnist accusing the guild of shaking down Arcel at the rate of $500 a month, and with little guarantee of supplying fighters for the ABC show if Norris didn't want them as competitive headliners.[11] Then there was the explanation of the money tendered by Honest Bill Daly, the expert on Carbo lead pipes and whose title as "treasurer" of the International Boxing Guild brought to mind that of the "recording secretary" played by Tony Galento in *On the Waterfront*. After months of eluding subpoenas from both Federal and New York authorities to testify on the activities of the Guild, Daly sat down with *Sports Illustrated* in April 1956 to offer his version of the transaction with Arcel. Asked whether the money had been extorted, as charged by Parker, Daly called the *Mirror* columnist a "phony" and went on:

> When he got his TV deal, Ray said he'd like to help out his pals with a welfare fund for the Guild. From time to time he offered to give money to the Guild, but the Guild attorney said that wouldn't be right. Well, I opened up a magazine to be a voice for fight managers. Then we went out and hustled ads like any other magazine, and if a guy like Ray was doin' good, we sold him a bill of goods that if he was doin' good, he should take ads. We gave him full-page ads, we did, and he was only new. He was competin' with the IBC. We told him every manager and boxin' writer would get a free copy. At that time he

was havin' difficulty getting talent, and you have to let people know you're in business.... Arcel could afford to pay more for the ads than most people.

Asked if he had any opinion on the attack against Arcel in Boston, Daly said he "couldn't even offer an idea of what caused it." What he didn't like, though, were insinuations that Carbo had been behind the thuggery. "I know him 26 years. He's nothin' but a gentleman."[12]

Although Arcel could never hear Daly's name without holding his nose ("He was a *momzer*; I always wanted to wash my hands around him"), his account to the grand jury did little to undercut the tale of the magazine as a vehicle for his "donations" to the guild. More generally, his testimony played back his past public statements about the Boston attack (he had no idea who had been behind it) and his involvement with managers who had gangland connections (if they had been licensed by the State Commission, who was he to question their honesty?). Even without his cooperation, however, Norris, Carbo, and their associates all closed out the decade in far more miserable shape than when entering it. In rapid order, the New York branch of the International Boxing Guild was outlawed; Norris was forced to step down as head of the IBC in favor of Truman Gibson; Hogan secured a two-year misdemeanor conviction against Carbo for his undeclared managing and matchmaking activities; and the IBC was enjoined from continuing its exclusive contract practices. Not everybody went along with those marching orders, of course. Gibson, for one, was little more than a puppet for both Norris and Carbo, the latter pulling strings from a cell in Rikers Island. But then a second wave of indictments came, under new Attorney General Robert Kennedy in the early 1960s, and this time Carbo walked into prison never to walk out again. Gibson, given a suspended sentence for his involvement in a grocery list of intimidations, extortions, and briberies, contributed the bold lettering to the indictments by acknowledging that the IBC had been in bed for years with the underworld so as to "maintain a free flow of fighters without interference, without strikes, without sudden illnesses, without sudden postponements."[13]

In the meantime, Ray Arcel was sharpening his knowledge of the foundry business in New Brunswick, New Jersey, following Kessler's advice to "run it the way you run a training camp." Didn't he miss boxing? "I did and I didn't. I can walk away from something and forget about it."

23

Panama Hats

In November 1994, Genaro Hernandez gave up his super feather-weight title to fight Oscar De La Hoya for the lightweight crown. In the sixth round of their match, De La Hoya unleashed a roundhouse left that compounded the nose break Hernandez had secretly suffered during a training sparring session. Rather than return for the seventh round, Hernandez had his handlers throw in the towel, telling reporters after-ward: "It's better to say '*no mas*' than not to say another word ever again."[1] There wasn't a fight fan in the world who didn't grasp the reference to the abrupt *no mas* withdrawal of Roberto Duran in his November 1980 lightweight title bout against Sugar Ray Leonard. Nobody was closer to that "no more" than Arcel, and this after years of his own no more to boxing.

As he customarily told the story, Arcel was perfectly content working for Meehanite and taking in an occasional fight with his wife Steve, when he received a call in February 1972 from Carlos Eleta. The two men had known each other since 1944, when Eleta had sent a couple of Panaman-ian boxers up to New York to hone their skills. Arcel had found them enough sparring work between lessons at Stillman's to polish them enough to send them back to Panama City after about a year, and there Eleta had managed them as successful club fighters. What the Panaman-ian promoter wanted now was for Arcel to do the traveling, specifically to fly down to the Canal Zone to take a look at Alfonso (Peppermint) Frazer, slated to fight the Argentinean Nicolino Locche for the world junior welterweight title. Eleta had personally put up the $100,000 plus expenses needed to get Locche to Panama and had become anxious that his investment in local boy Frazer might backfire.

After protesting that he hadn't been in the game for years, Arcel gave in to Eleta's pleadings, calculating that he had amassed enough vacation time for a two-to-three-week trip and knowing that nobody was more sympathetic to the ring bug than Harry Kessler. When the trainer and Steve arrived in Panama, it was two weeks before the scheduled March 10, 1972, bout. "There wasn't that much time for me to be useful to Carlos, so the first thing I did on the very day we arrived was to get to know Frazer, both as a person and as a fighter. He spoke English fluently and cooperated with me all the way down the line. But I also noticed right away that while two weeks wasn't very much time for me, it was far too much for Peppermint. He was already reaching a peak, and the first thing I did was cut down on his boxing."

The second problem was Locche, known in his native country as "*El Intocable* [The Untouchable]."

> Arcel: I really knew nothing about him and I had to get a look at him, but he was training in a private gym that was closed off to just about everybody except those in his camp. That's where some luck came in. When I agreed to go to Panama, I told Eleta I didn't want to talk about money, just as long as I could get around in a place I didn't know at all. He assigned me a private chauffeur who was called Chiclet because he was always chewing that gum. My luck was that when Chiclet wasn't driving me around, he was driving Locche and his entourage. It was thanks to that driver that I managed to get into the gym. "Dress like an ordinary Panamanian," he told me. "Casual clothes, sunglasses, and a hat. They won't look at you twice if they think you're part of the local scene." Chiclet also stayed with me when we arrived, telling the guy at the door that we were friends. I couldn't believe it, but we had no trouble getting in.

Arcel told Jerry Izenberg what he saw in Locche, and it wasn't good news for Frazer. "Right away I know our man Peppermint has a problem. This Locche is excellent. He is a good mechanic, but I get a feeling there's something more there. Then I see it. He is backing away and the sparring partner is moving in. Now Locche misses a left hand and leans back and he's on the ropes and I can't figure out what the hell he's trying to do. The kid moves to him and then I really see it for the first time — the real rope-a-dope. He grabs his kid, pulls him in, spins him around. Now their positions are reversed, and he's beating the hell out of the kid."[2]

Satisfied that he had seen enough for forearming Frazer, Arcel only belatedly realized that he himself had been under surveillance:

> I tried not to show that I noticed this guy watching me, but then finally he approached me and asked me in English if I was Panamanian. I told him I was in Panama on vacation, had heard about the champion, and wanted to see him for myself. He didn't buy it, especially the vacation part, even though that

happened to be literally true. Then he comes out with it: He's recognized me from Stillman's in New York where he often went as a reporter for an Argentinean newspaper when there was somebody from his country fighting in the States. He asked me if I was going to be in Frazer's corner. I told him no one had asked me to do that, which was also literally true. I could see he was upset, and I got out of there before anybody else came up with questions.

Depending on the version offered to Izenberg or that contained in his memoir, Arcel immediately went back to Eleta and Frazer and outlined a plan for thwarting Locche's tactic, or just shared it with the manager on the day of the fight so as not to tip their hand to the reporters and local boxing types who circulated in their gym much more freely than was permitted at the Argentinean's training site. However it was doled out, the advice to Frazer was: "You walk out there in the center of the ring when the bell rings and you throw the biggest right hand you ever threw in your life. I don't even care if it lands, just so he knows you got one. Then he'll feint and slide back to the ropes. Just remember: You're the one on home ground, you're the local hero. There'll be 20,000 Panamanians cheering you on. When he goes to the ropes, you step back to the center of the ring and laugh at him. Now those 20,000 Panamanians will have seen you throw that right hand. They'll know you came to fight. So don't follow him. Make him come off the ropes. If he doesn't, 20,000 Panamanians will do it for you."

The tactic worked, and Frazer won a unanimous 15-round decision at Panama City's Gimnasio Nuevo Panama. With the victory secured, Arcel packed to return to his job in New Brunswick. When Eleta opened his checkbook to pay the fee Arcel had refused to take up front, the trainer declined again, saying that he felt more than compensated by the satisfaction of knowing he "still had it" where tutoring boxers was concerned. But Eleta didn't let it go at that. A couple of weeks later he was calling New York to ask Arcel to help train Roberto Duran for a June lightweight title fight against Ken Buchanan in Madison Square Garden. "Carlos just didn't get it," Arcel mock-complained in his memoir. "I had a full-time job. I was running a whole division for Meehanite, where we blended alloys for foundry use. I couldn't just keep coming and going."

Arcel had already seen Duran, but not in the ring. In September 1971 he was told he could see "another Benny Valgar" if he went to see the same Ken Buchanan taking on Ismael Laguna at Madison Square Garden. He went reluctantly, in that period wanting to stay as far away as possible from the Garden, Norris, and such Norris associates as Honest Bill Daly. He and Steve watched Buchanan decision Laguna, but hardly to the point of evoking comparisons with one of his childhood heroes. "I saw a good boxer," as he put it later, "but I didn't see any Benny Valgar."[3] What he also didn't see was Duran polishing off Benny Huertas in a preliminary bout just as he and Steve took their seats. But Duran had seen them, and the fighter climbed out of the ring to go down to them. "He walked right up to me and kissed me on the cheek," Steve Arcel recalled. "Then later on I saw him all dressed up with this little woolen hat on his head. It was such an incredible contrast — from warrior in the ring to innocent looking boy."[4]

Arcel always had suspicions about the Duran kiss, not putting it past the skilled manipulator Eleta to have orchestrated it. One way or the other, though, he didn't need to be reminded who Duran was when the manager asked for his help. Still, there was his job for Kessler. The compromise solution was that the day-to-day conditioning would be handled by another ring veteran, Freddie Brown, at the Concord Hotel in the Catskills, while the tactical overseer, Arcel, spent every Saturday, Sunday, and Monday at the camp. Nestor Quinones, Duran's trainer from Panama, was also on the scene but in a markedly reduced role. It was a setup that Duran came to depend on for much of his career. As Eleta told a *Sports Illustrated* interviewer in 1978: "Our trouble is that the trainers [Duran] has in Panama can't handle him, they can't control him. And he knows that is not good for him. Only Brown and Arcel can control him. That is why before every fight he calls me and says, 'Where are they? I need them. Please call and get them for me.'"[5]

If Arcel was important to Duran, the converse was equally true. Over a 20-year period that included the most traumatic event of his ring career, the trainer made clear his admiration of the Panamanian, ranking him to within a hair of Benny Leonard. ("If they were ever in the ring together, I'd give it to Benny, but it would be close.") Izenberg went so far as to call Duran "Ray's Pygmalion."[6] The fastest way for a sportswriter to bring out the trainer's testiness was to suggest that he had made Duran the champion he would become in four different divisions, along the way earning distinction as the only fighter ever to win bouts in five different decades. As Arcel told Ronald K. Fried in *Corner Men*, "Nobody had to teach Duran how to fight. The first day I saw him working out down in Panama while I was down there for Frazer, I told everybody around him, 'Don't change his style. Leave him alone. I don't want any-body to ever tell him what to do. Let him fight.'"[7] On another occasion Arcel commented that Duran "might know more about fighting than I do. I rank him with Sugar Ray Robinson and Harry Greb — naturals who never had to be taught a thing about how to box."[8]

Duran came from one of the worst slums in Panama, Chorrillo in the San Felipe district of Panama City. With the area known popularly as "*La Casa de Piedra*" (The House of Stone), it was near inevitable that his early victories won him the nickname of "*Las Manos de Piedra*" (The Hands of Stone). From his first triumph in Colon City in 1968, he had been on a 28-fight consecutive winning streak, gaining increasing noto-riety for dropping opponents in the first or second round. His good looks also made him box office, making it even easier for Eleta to get North American attention for him. But Arcel also had causes for worry. One was that, with the exception of a couple of bouts in Mexico and the Huertas fight, Duran had mostly fought in Panama and wouldn't have been the first local hero to have a delayed and negative reaction to Madi-son Square Garden. Another was a tendency to showboat — a source of repeated warnings at the training camp. "We needed Quinones or some-body else to translate because Roberto didn't speak English and Freddie and I didn't have Spanish. Sometimes I had real doubts we were getting through. But I kept telling him that he was fighting for a championship and that meant he had to commit himself to hard fighting for three min-utes every round. There could be no rest, no breaks to wave back to the crowd when they cheered him, the way he did in Panama. I said to him, 'Roberto, up here they don't know anybody named Duran. Most of the crowd will probably be for Buchanan. You've got to go out there, establish yourself right away like you do at home, hurt him early. You can knock him out as fast as anybody else.'"

And then there was the matter of jabbing. Nobody stressed the importance of jabbing more than Arcel, and nobody considered it less important than Duran in training for the Buchanan fight. Finally exas-perated one day by his pupil's resistance, Arcel asked Brown to get into the ring with the Panamanian and told the boxer to throw a punch at his co-trainer, then in his late sixties. When Duran finally grasped that Arcel was serious, he let loose, only to have Brown slap him up and down on the face three times before any blow could be landed. The mortified Duran ran off, cursing the heavens and the trainers below them. "If he doesn't come back tomorrow, we haven't got much," Arcel told Brown. "If he does, we have a fighter."

Duran went back the next day and began concentrating on jabbing techniques. As Frazer had in Panama City, he followed instructions to victory. But it didn't go off quite as smoothly as it had in the Locche bout. Already edgy about his New York surroundings, Duran had to sit through an elaborate pre-fight ceremony that featured Panamanians in native dress and then bagpipers celebrating Buchanan. Once the first round bell sounded he was in full charge in the middle of the ring, but Buchanan, sensing his dire predicament against Duran's right hand, resorted to every trick that had ever won a fighter a decision on a foul. "He even went so far as to put his head outside the ropes to make believe Duran was fouling him," Arcel would recall. As the bell rang to end the 13th round, Duran got in another shot to which the staggering Buchanan responded, and the two of them went at it for a good 20 seconds off the clock. Finally, Buchanan crouched low and grabbed his groin, complaining he had been hit with a low blow. Buchanan's manager, Gil Clancy, didn't agree—he protested that the blow had come not from a Duran punch but from his knee. But when referee Johnny Lo Bianco ruled that there were still insufficient grounds for disqualification, and when Buchanan couldn't come out of his physical misery, Duran was awarded a TKO decision. Afterwards, Arcel said he held nothing against Clancy for trying to "steal" the fight, at the same time noting that Buchanan had to be hospitalized for the severe beating he had taken in the face, not in the midsection (above or below his waistband). But even some of the trainer's oldest newspaper cronies had doubts. Izenberg noted that the post-bell shot delivered by Duran in the 13th round was the third time in the fight he had done that.[9] Red Smith of the *New York Times* observed caustically that Lo Bianco had had little choice in ruling out a foul because "anything short of pulling a knife is regarded indulgently" in the boxing world.[10]

As far as Eleta was concerned, however, Arcel had delivered for him twice in a row. That was also the way the Panamanian regime of General Omar Torrijos felt, and it awarded the trainer the medallion of the Order of Vasco Nunez de Balboa for meritorious service to the country; the only other sports figures to have received that honor at the time were soccer great Pele and the Panama-born baseball Hall of Famer Rod Carew. Eleta was hardly going to let Arcel stick to foundry work, espe-

Carlos Eleta, Roberto Duran's manager, congratulates Arcel for receiving the Medal of Balboa in Panama. The wives of the two men look on.

cially not with Duran insisting on him and Brown as his regular corner men. Arcel agreed on condition they work as they had for the Buchanan fight, with him checking in with Brown every night by phone and limiting his own presence at the training camp to weekends. He also insisted that Eleta pay only Brown ("I was making enough money at Meehanite; I didn't need it"). As open to those conditions as Eleta was, he was equally deaf to demands from Buchanan's camp that a rematch be arranged. Instead, he had Duran fight a couple of times in Panama City, then returned him to New York for a non-title bout in November against Esteban De Jesus. There was little question that the snub of Buchanan stemmed from the foul claims and postures in the June fight.

But with De Jesus, Eleta also outsmarted himself. Arcel was the first to notice the coming problem a few days before the November fight. "It was unusually cold. I remember I had to wear an overcoat around. Coming out of the gymnasium one day, just walking to the car, I took my coat off and gave it to Duran. He couldn't take the cold at all. And sure enough, the next day he's sneezing and all blocked up. Carlos and I wanted to call the fight off. But he said no. 'I'm okay, I'm okay, I fight,' he kept saying."

Eleta and Arcel made the mistake of listening. In the first round Duran made his customary charge-and-swing, but De Jesus deftly countered and floored the champion with a left. Although the fight went the prescribed 10 rounds to a decision, Arcel saw that opening exchange as the key moment. "Roberto came up fighting, but the effects from the cold weakened him, and he never found a rhythm against De Jesus." The loss, the first in Duran's professional career, carried the consolation prize of alerting Eleta never to agree again to a fight in a cold climate. And indeed, Duran's next 10 bouts (all victories) were staged in warm, when not tropical, places. When it finally came time for De Jesus again, this time in March 1974 and with the title on the line, it too was held in Panama City.

If Eleta had been worried about his standing in Panama before the Frazer-Locche fight, events before the rematch with De Jesus showed how far he had come. A few nights before the bout he received a call at home warning him that the De Jesus camp was working on postponing the fight because of an alleged cut in the boxer's mouth. The maneuver followed weeks of failed attempts by De Jesus's handlers to get a bigger slice of the gate. Eleta immediately called the Panamanian Boxing Commission and requested that a doctor be sent to examine De Jesus. More telling, even as the examination was being conducted, officials from the Torrijos regime ordered the airport closed just in case the De Jesus party sought to flee the country. The airport was reopened again only after the Commission doctor found nothing serious in De Jesus's mouth and ordered the fight to proceed. "I don't know who Carlos called to get all that done," Arcel said afterward, "but he had a lot of the right friends in high places."

But all the well-placed connections seemed to have added up only to further embarrassment when De Jesus started off the rematch by again decking Duran in the first round with a counterpunch. Once back on his feet, though, Duran followed Arcel's orders to shelve the right hand that his Puerto Rican opponent was anticipating. "That's all he'll be looking for, I told him. And I know you're angry, and want to get even for New York. You want to take him out as fast as you can. But don't do

it. Stick with him, stay in close, until I give you the word." The word
came in the eleventh round, and De Jesus went down and didn't get up
again.

Duran met De Jesus a third time at Caesar's Palace in Las Vegas in
January 1978 with both the WBC and WBA titles on the line. This time
Arcel adopted yet another strategy — having Duran box and make De
Jesus the aggressor ("You could do anything with Roberto because he
wasn't just a puncher, he was also a great boxer"). When De Jesus finally
got tired in the twelfth round of waiting for the outsize swing that wasn't
going to come, he opened up enough for Duran to send him to the
canvas for another knockout.

The two wins over De Jesus were part of an amazing string of 41
straight victories by Duran, all the fights held in warm places such as
Miami or San Juan or in the spring and summer months of temperate
climates. If there was any smudge on Duran's luster in the 1970s, it was
following his 14th-round knockout of Ray Lampkin in Panama City in
March 1975. The bout ended with Lampkin hitting his head hard on
the canvas, but that didn't slow down TV interviewers rabid to get com-
ments from the successful title-holder. Later, there was divided opinion
about whether the interpreter on the global hookup had added his own
interpretation of a Duran remark or had simply mistranslated it, but the
champion's response to a question about having a rematch with Lampkin
came out as "Yes, I will kill him." With the Oregon contender still being
put on a stretcher for emergency transportation to the hospital in the
background, the reply painted Duran as a savage in the media around
the world. A typical reaction came from Jim Murray of the *Los Angeles
Times*. Shifting away from his regular habit of comparing Duran to the
first jungle animal that occurred to him, Murray affected little surprise
at the fighter's reputed comment because "manslaughter sells."[11] What
was not reported, according to Arcel, was that Duran, in fact, went to
the hospital every day of Lampkin's stay and said prayers at his bedside,
while also denying the "kill" remark attributed to him. Lampkin recovered without long-lasting injuries, fighting seven more times (with five
victories) before retiring.

Shortly after the third De Jesus fight in Las Vegas, Duran announced
his own retirement of sorts — from the lightweight division, where he
reigned as champion from 1972 to 1979. Moving on up to a welterweight
division more suitable to his added pounds, he went through eight adver-

saries quickly, scoring either a unanimous decision, a TKO, or a knock-out. This set him up for a title fight against Sugar Ray Leonard at Montreal's Olympic Stadium on June 20, 1980. Arcel could have been forgiven for a twinge at having Leonard across the ring from him. The sleek, handsome African American from North Carolina, who had turned professional after winning every amateur title in existence, including a gold medal at the 1976 Olympics, represented the biggest investment by the ABC television network in boxing since Arcel's own *Saturday Night Fights* 25 years earlier. ABC's marketing of Leonard, bolstered by the ballyhooing of broadcaster Howard Cossell, was so conspicuous that the boxer was often referred to as a media creation.

The ABC connection wasn't the only flashback Arcel had in the run-up to the bout. About three weeks into training at Grossinger's in the Catskills, Duran complained of a pain in his lower back. Rather than take the fighter to a local doctor, where gossip was apt to start and get back to the press, Arcel whisked him down to Jewish Memorial in Washington Heights, where an acquaintance served as head of the medical staff. Extensive tests found nothing but a cold that had settled in Duran's back, but the whole purpose of the hush-hush trip to Manhattan was defeated when hospital employees recognized Duran and got the word out soon enough to city press rooms. For the remainder of the training period at Grossinger's, Arcel and Brown had to beat off questions about Duran's condition and why he seemed to be on a reduced conditioning schedule. Things got even trickier in Montreal.

On the Monday preceding the Friday bout, Duran and Leonard went through their requisite physicals at a Montreal hospital. Later that day, in an eerie replay of Barney Ross's troubles with the doctor in Buffalo, Arcel received a phone call from the local Commission saying that Duran had a suspected heart condition and couldn't be cleared for the fight without further testing the following morning. Once again Eleta called in his contacts in Panama, getting no less than General Torrijos himself to send his plane to Montreal with the country's leading cardiac specialist aboard. With only the Panamanian doctor allowed in the examining room as an observer, Canadian physicians put Duran through five hours of tests, finally concluding that he had no heart problem that would prevent the fight.

What Duran did have after the lengthy hospital session, however, was an exhaustion problem. Arcel: "Naturally, we were relieved about the report, but there was still the training schedule and dealing with any psychological damage the heart scare had caused. We had little choice but to let Roberto rest completely that Tuesday and concentrate the last of his workouts on Wednesday and Thursday. We couldn't have done it without his temperament. He responded miraculously the last two days."

But that same temperament almost preempted the fight at the weigh-in. "Roberto and Leonard didn't like each other. Roberto had great contempt for all of Leonard's theatrics. He was ready to fight the guy at the weigh-in. It wasn't the usual farce you saw at weigh-ins. We really had to restrain him." Leonard's trainer, Angelo Dundee, was of the same view, even accusing Duran of harassment against his fighter on Montreal's streets. Dundee told Dave Anderson in *In the Corner*: "Duran abused Ray, and Ray couldn't handle it. Duran would see Ray walking with his wife in the street in Montreal and he'd yell, 'I keel your husband, I keel your husband!'"[12] Calculated or not, the abuse aimed at Leonard prompted him to abandon his usual cool boxing style during the fight with disastrous consequences.

Also striking during the run-up to the Montreal fight was Arcel's accentuated think-positive campaign, and this long before the false alarm over Duran's heart. Although he never addressed the issue directly, it was as though he deemed it necessary to step up the rhetoric in an attempt to counterbalance the enormous publicity machinery set in motion by ABC on behalf of its Great Black Hope. In an interview with William Nack of *Sports Illustrated*, Arcel all but wrote off Leonard as a serious match for Duran, declaring in part: "Leonard is an excellent boxer. He's a master craftsman. He can do anything, but we don't know one thing. Can he stand up under the body-battering that he's going to get from Duran in the early rounds? If Duran hurts you and you're backing up on the ropes, I'm telling you, he don't let you alone. He sticks to you like plaster. He's that vicious. And he has the unique ability to get stronger as the fight goes along."[13] Still earlier than that, after the press conference originally announcing the fight, according to what Vic Ziegel reported in *Inside Sports*, Arcel thought it necessary to give Duran immediate positive reinforcement by telling him, "You won the title right there. The other guy was full of crap. He's scared. As soon as he goes back to his room, he's going to the bathroom."[14]

In short, with or without the hasty conclusions of cardiologists, there was an edginess in the Duran camp from the outset. And it didn't ease when Carlos Padilla was announced as the referee for the bout. Brown had only recently had a run-in with Padilla when one of his fighters, Vito Antuofermo, had lost his middleweight title to Alan Minter. As Brown had seen it, Minter's victory had come in considerable part because of Padilla's haste in breaking up in-fighting — a tactic also important to Duran. Arcel didn't hesitate to go public with that concern, telling whoever wanted to listen that "the one thing I fear and dread is if the referee doesn't let Duran fight inside. Duran won't be able to fight his fight."[15] Whether that and remarks like it scalded Padilla, or the two trainers decided to bring their anxiety directly to its source, Arcel and Brown had a lengthy conversation with the arbiter just before the fight began. Afterward, Arcel revealed only that they had reminded Padilla that "you've got to let these boys fight ... the whole world is watching you."

It was only fitting that the weather be another source of agitation for the Duran camp. Arcel: "Olympic Stadium was this monstrous outdoor place, and rain was predicted for the entire afternoon and evening of the fight. But Panamanians also had this superstition that if you put a Rosary in a glass of water and stick it under the bed, the rain will stop. From what we heard later, people all over Panama did just that. At first, it didn't seem to work because even the preliminary bouts that night were fought in a heavy mist. The fans coming into the stadium were given big black plastic bags for protection. But just as the main event was about to start, the rain stopped. Everybody in Panama who stuck that Rosary and glass of water under the bed claimed it was because of their ritual."

After all the uncertainties that there would even be a fight, it started well for Duran when a second-round right almost dropped Leonard for the evening. In retrospect, that was the start of something good, but Arcel and Brown were still too jittery to take anything for granted. "I kept fearing he would come back to the corner and say he was tired," Arcel admitted. "Then what would we do? Take a chance on his heart?"

That proved unnecessary. Showing little wear from all that he had been through with his back and the medical tests, Duran won a unanimous 15-round decision. There was little doubt that Leonard had all but insured that verdict by abandoning his usual lithe style to go toe-to-toe with an opponent who liked nothing better. If there were celebrations in the Latin communities of Canada and the United States, there was pandemonium in Panama, where businesses had closed early and the streets had been deserted while the country had sat in front of TV sets. For hours after the verdict had been announced, the streets of Panama City, Colon, and other cities were improvised festivals. Somewhat obscured amid all the revelry was the screeching Duran had unloaded on Leonard even after the final bell.

What followed were very long days for Roberto Duran and very long nights for Ray Arcel.

24

No More

To make sure the guests of honor were on hand for the celebrations in Panama, Torrijos again dispatched a government plane, this time to New York to pick up Duran, Arcel, and Brown with their wives, Duran's small son, and promoter Don King. The sight of the plane making its approach sent thousands of cheering Panamanians running over the tarmac of Panama City airport, forcing it to stay in the air an extra half-hour while police cleared a landing area. From that point on it was Roberto Duran Day, with tens of thousands lining the streets for a motorcade from the airport to the presidential palace. Steve Arcel's most vivid memory of the day was how Duran had entrusted to her the bling he usually wore for fear that grasping fans would snatch some of it, and how she had to hold her bag with a death grip in the carnival atmosphere. "On the ride to the palace," she recalled, "the bodyguard running alongside our jeep also handed me his watch, saying he was afraid of losing it. Before all the ceremonies were over, I ended up holding a Walkie-Talkie for somebody."[1]

The festivities went on for days. The state television network left little air time for anything but reruns of the fight. Duran appeared everywhere, from the balcony of the presidential palace to neighborhood cantinas. At one point he also appeared on a busy street with a lion he had raised as a pet from birth, causing panic and the hurried arrival of heavily armed police. Once the police recognized the lion walker, they were content to have both of them get into a van for transportation back to the boxer's fenced-in estate.

Arcel called it a "welcome relief" when, after non-stop lunches and dinners, he flew back to New York. Just as after the Frazer-Locche fight, though, little time passed before Eleta came calling, now about Duran's scheduled November rematch with Leonard in New Orleans.

Having retired from Meehanite, Arcel was more than up for it — and
had to be. When he and Eleta walked into a West Side restaurant
where they were to meet Duran, he was astonished by what greeted him.
"Duran was with a group of friends. He had blown up to a good 200
pounds from all the partying and celebrating! Right then and there I
knew I had to get this roly poly up to camp to start bringing down his
weight."

In fact, Arcel should have been the last one surprised since Duran's
weight was a constant topic of discussion among boxing pundits. Writing
in the *New York Times* on one occasion, Red Smith ventured that "if we
add up all the flesh Roberto has shed in the last seven years, simple arith-
metic shows that if it weren't for Ray and Freddie, he would weigh 718
pounds." Arcel's own explanation for the poundage was Duran's childhood. "As a kid, he didn't have what-not to eat," he told Smith. "His
family was broken up and he literally slept in the streets. Sometimes he
would swim to the Canal Zone to pick mangoes to eat, but once he
stuffed his pockets and shirt with all the fruit he could, he almost
drowned swimming back."[2]

Whether or not that was just another of the fairy tales that flourished
around Duran as he became successful, the "roly poly" had to be dealt
with. Once again the training plan involved Freddie Brown, but with a
little more chill in the air between the trainers. According to Jerry Izenberg, the trouble had started the previous year when Izenberg had written
an article describing Brown's looks as being like "an aerial view of the
Burma Road." As Izenberg later explained, 'Let's just say Freddie never
reminded anybody of Robert Redford, and I didn't think that was a state
secret. But the night of the dinner held by the Boxing Writers Association
for honoring various people, Freddie's daughter came up to me and
started in about how dare I insult her father, stuff like that. I didn't think
much of it because both the daughter and the wife were among the most
unpleasant people I've ever met." And the connection to Arcel? "Well,
it so happened he was being honored that night as the Trainer of the
Year, the second time the BWA had named him. And once Brown's
daughter got through with me for what I had written, she started in on
how Ray was always being honored because he had all these newspapermen as friends and Freddie was always being ignored even though Freddie
worked with the fighters longer in terms of time. She didn't want to hear
about how Freddie was basically conditioning the fighters and Ray was

the tactician. It just wasn't fair that Arcel was getting credit and her father wasn't getting it."[3]

Not even Izenberg believed there had been scenes between the trainers, though. "That wasn't their way. But if you're at home and hearing it from these two women all the time about how Ray Arcel was taking credit for what you had done, it certainly didn't do much for their relationship. And sure enough, after the second Duran-Leonard fight, they went separate ways."[4]

But first there was that bout in New Orleans, plus another in Las Vegas. For his own October heavyweight fight against Muhammad Ali in Nevada, Larry Holmes had asked that Arcel be in his corner. But feeling more of a commitment to Eleta, Arcel promoted Brown to Holmes (all three had already worked together a couple of years earlier) while he went off to Grossinger's with Duran. Arcel's one request to Brown was that he get in touch with him as soon as the Holmes-Ali bout was over because "we were both going to have to work hard for the Leonard match."

Back up in the Catskills, Arcel found that getting the pounds off Duran was easy compared to other problems. "The guy was really amazing when it came to weight. Sometimes it seemed like he added pounds just by taking a deep breath, but then he could take them off again practically by exhaling. What was harder was trying to cut down his time with the hangers-on who were always with him. They absolutely idolized him, and if he so much as had a thought about breaking his diet, they would have been right there with the food. Some of them slept in hallways right outside his room. It didn't help that it was September when we really got down to work, and that's not a warm time in the mountains."

Only too aware of Duran's aversion to cold weather, Arcel kept his eye on the calendar as he got the fighter to sweat off 20 pounds. But then, with Holmes's successful title defense against Ali on October 2, Brown was free to accompany Duran down to Miami for the rest of his conditioning. "Freddie knew to concentrate on the weight problem, and it was much easier to slim down in a warm climate like Miami. Like me, the main problem he had was keeping an eye on the crowd Roberto attracted around him. That's always a tricky one for a trainer. On the one hand, you don't want these people undoing at night what you've accomplished during the day. But you also can't forget that some of them the fighter has known all his life. Maybe he's come to depend on them. You can't just go in and say, 'Get rid of this guy and get rid of that one.' You could end up losing the boxer's trust. It's a tightrope, you have to walk it, and that's all there is to it."

In the end, the two trainers succeeded in reducing Duran's weight to the same 146 pounds that Leonard registered at the weigh-in. The drastic loss was comparable to anything Arcel had accomplished with Charlie Phil Rosenberg; the complaints about it would come later. The only serious issue in the final days of camp was preventing Duran from peaking too soon and dealing with his pouts when he wasn't allowed to spar as much as he wanted. But if he could be snippy about his training regime, he was all shears when it came to Leonard. At the weigh-in the two were twins in glares and insults that were anything but witty. Well before the bell for the opening round there was expectation of far worse ugliness than there had been in Montreal. Only Arcel claimed otherwise. Even afterward he depicted Duran as "nonchalant" and "normal" before the action at the Louisiana Superdome. The "normal" was more credible than the "nonchalant," but only as in "Duran normal."

From the opening bell Leonard showed that he wasn't going to repeat his Montreal mistake with the flat-footed slugging that played to Duran's strength. Moreover, the challenger's agile weaving and rapid volleying served to make Duran look sluggish even when he wasn't actually hit. In the fifth round, Arcel would say later, he sensed something amiss but was unable — then or subsequently — to put his finger on what it was.

Through the first six rounds Leonard appeared to be not only ahead on points but to be building momentum. Then in the seventh round he began openly mocking Duran and his manhood so audibly that Cossell scolded on the air that "this is not what Ray Leonard should be doing."[5] The taunting reached a climax when Leonard seemed to wind up for a bolo punch with his right, then snap a left directly into the hesitant Duran's face. At the end of the round Duran waved his arm in disgust as he returned to his corner. But there was also little doubt that he was behind on the cards of the judges.

With the eighth round came the onset of 30 years of allegations, denials, conjectures, and contradictions over what took place before the eyes of millions of people around the world. Leonard picked up where he had left off, accompanying every weave with more taunting. At exactly 2:44 into the round Duran backed away and muttered to referee Octavio

Meyran. What he was revealed later as having said was "*No quiero pelear con el payaso* (I don't want to fight with this clown)." When the astounded Meyran asked if he was sure, Duran mouthed the infamous "*No mas, no mas!*" and went off to his corner, creating a stunned silence throughout the Superdome, at least for a few seconds before the eruption of an angry roar. The fight was formally recorded as an eighth-round TKO for Leonard. At the time he had been leading on all three cards, 68–66, 68–66, and 67–66.[6]

For the rest of his life Arcel had to answer "What happened in New Orleans?" more than any other question. His answers were a patchwork of bafflement, distaste, sorrow, and assertion of belief in Duran as one of the greatest fighters in boxing history. What he tried to avoid (echoes of Barney Ross after the Marcel Cerdan fight) was Duran's own charge on one occasion that he had been "over-trained," had lost too much weight too fast, and had been "allowed" to eat too much after the weigh-in, causing severe stomach cramps while he was in the ring.[7] (Duran did not mention his objections to being slowed down by Arcel and Brown in his final days of training; on the other hand, he did indicate the fifth round, the juncture at which Arcel had noticed something "wrong," as the point when his stomach had begun getting the best of him.) Only years later, in interviews with such journalists as Izenberg and Ira Berkow of the *New York Times*, did he take on the eating part of the Duran allegations, and with a skeptical tone that said he didn't accept it for a second. "After the weigh-in I asked the chef at the Hyatt Regency Hotel to prepare a thermos of broth. [Duran] drank a small cup of the broth and I drank the rest. He preferred drinking tea. Later, he ate a steak, that's all, for his pre-fight meal. He ate his own steak and finished Carlos Eleta's steak. The only thing I didn't like is that he drank a glass of orange juice and he gulped it instead of sipping it. Maybe that gave him the cramps."[8]

Eleta didn't have patience even for that unlikely possibility. "He didn't quit because of stomach cramps," the manager snapped to a reporter. "He quit because he was embarrassed."[9] As for what exactly he was embarrassed about, the implication was that it was the trash talk Leonard had unleashed on him, especially the insults questioning his manhood. That factor might or might not have been included in the tersest explanation of all for the abrupt withdrawal: Leonard's boast that "I made him quit."[10]

The New Orleans bout demolished Duran's standing in his native country. His product and charity endorsements vanished from television and magazines as quickly as technically possible. The national hero of newspaper editorials became a national punching bag. But that was Panama. What Louisiana Commission officials wanted to know, and right away, was what had happened and why. For a combination of circumstances, much of the explaining fell on Arcel's shoulders.

On one point Arcel remained firm for years: That he personally never asked Duran what had led him to quit the fight. The first time he didn't ask was in the dressing room immediately afterward, and with the artless explanation of "I didn't think it was my business." Elaborating with Dave Anderson in *In the Corner* years later, Arcel contended, "I've never talked to Duran about why he quit. Never asked him for an explanation. I know him well enough to let bygones be bygones. I learned a long time ago that speech is silver, that silence is golden. The secret of being a trainer is to know and understand the individual you're working with. Know when to say something. Know when to be quiet."[11] One unasked question, of course, was how deep his understanding of Duran could have been if he had been so caught off guard by what had taken place in the Superdome. A second might have been how much that understanding relied on a passive, if not altogether submissive, role vis-a-vis its object outside of ring tactics in the strictest sense.

While Brown and the camp doctor took Duran to a local hospital for treatment of his facial cuts and for whatever else he said was ailing him (nothing serious turned up), Arcel went with Eleta to an impromptu Commission hearing on the fight. It was the setting for the posture he would assume over and over in future years — the same one heard after his beating in Boston and the attempted suicide of his daughter in New York — that some events were "beyond explanation."

"Emile Bruno was running the hearing," recalled Arcel. "We'd been close friends since 1923, when he had been a trainer. At one point, when all these Commission members were vilifying Duran, I asked for permission to speak. 'Commissioner Bruno,' I told him, 'this was one of the greatest crowd pleasers we ever had in boxing. Whatever happened to him in this ring tonight, no one can explain, not even Duran himself. You and I have trained many fighters in the past, and some of the reactions of these men can never be explained. Duran has given the public many thrills by his great performances, and he became a victim of himself.'"

Bruno wasn't impressed and ordered the fight purse held up pending a more thorough investigation. But he immediately had to switch gears when Eleta informed him that under the terms of the fight a Letter of Credit had been sent to his bank in Panama and released for payment the moment the boxers had stepped into the ring. Whatever the Byzantine motives behind that arrangement, Bruno had no recourse against it and had to settle for levying a fine of $7500 against Duran. Eleta wrote out a check on the spot, and that was just about the end of official action on the Superdome fiasco.

It was hardly the end for either Arcel or Duran, however. Izenberg accompanied Arcel back to his hotel that evening and described him as "looking like a heart attack." At one point the trainer branded Duran's *no mas* as "unforgivable"[12] (a word he would also use in his 1983 interview with Elli Wohlgelernter), but otherwise ventured only that Duran "had had enough of [Leonard's] theatrics and clowning." Later on he made the singular admission — not volunteered in the wake of earlier family and professional crises — that after leaving Izenberg and reaching his hotel room he "broke down and cried." He was aware of the abnormality of his reaction, too. "It takes an awful lot to make me cry," he told Wohlgelernter. "In the course of my life I've had tragedies. I had a young wife who died of cancer; she suffered for two years. My sister-in-law died of cancer. My brother died with cancer. I couldn't cry. With Duran, though, I cried."[13] In his memoir he added, "The whole situation was more than I could take.... It was a bitter disappointment. Duran was not a quitter, and I don't think he himself could ever explain what had happened to him.... It took me a long time to get over it, if I ever did."

There were plenty of people ready to make sure he didn't. The very night of the fight, shortly after falling asleep, he was reawakened by a call from somebody he described as "a guy I knew in New York." What he heard in his ear was: "I have to admire your gall. I've known you for many, many years. I never thought you'd get mixed up in a fix." Given the blatancy of Duran's withdrawal, a fix was, in fact, one of the least circulated theories about what had taken place. Still, the accusation, even from a single acquaintance, was another thorn Arcel wrapped within his depression, to the point that he told several people that he was through with boxing for good. "Some of my friends in the newspaper field wouldn't leave me alone for weeks," he recalled for Fried. "They thought I knew something. I said to them, 'What do I know? What you saw, I saw. I know as much about it as you do.'" When the follow-up question was why he hadn't at least felt it necessary to ask Duran what had gone on, the answer was some version of the silence-is-golden bromide. His baldest statement to that effect was "I didn't want to antagonize him."[14] Here and there, though, he did let it be known that he didn't buy Duran's stomach cramps tale. Speaking with Harvey Araton in the *New York Daily News* on December 6, 1989, for instance, he offered: "I think what it came down to was that the other kid had a fight plan to antagonize Duran, and he just couldn't take it. Maybe it was Angelo Dundee [*ed: Leonard's trainer*] who authored it, I don't know, but we hadn't prepared him for that. We thought Leonard would fight a basic fight, none of the clowning stuff. It was a mistake. Duran didn't like Leonard from the start, and he snapped when he thought he was being embarrassed. It was like a guy who has never done anything wrong in his whole life committing a crime. He made a mistake. He knew it, too."[15]

25

The Final Rounds

Despite his declared intention after New Orleans of easing into his ninth decade without worrying anymore about who made weight and who didn't, Arcel turned up one more time for Duran.

After a nine-month layoff, the Panamanian took tentative steps toward rehabilitation in the eyes of his countrymen by scoring unanimous decisions in non-title bouts against Nino Gonzalez in Cleveland and Luigi Minchillo in Las Vegas in August and September of 1981, respectively. But clear as the victories were, they were also low on the galvanizing scale and kept the scars from New Orleans acutely visible. What was needed was more drama. Don King came to the rescue with a match-up against Wilfredo Benitez for the junior middleweight title in Las Vegas on January 30, 1982. The box office angle was the return of the prodigal Duran against the Puerto Rican who held the record for being the youngest fighter ever to win a title, Benitez having been only 17 when he took the WBA junior welterweight crown in 1976. Arcel, who had watched the Gonzalez and Minchillo fights as just another fan, was once again asked by Eleta to come on board. According to the trainer, he agreed because of Duran's "need for redemption." But the practicalities of preparing for the redemption were anything but practical. No trainer has ever supervised from a greater distance.

In light of Duran's standing as first a proud and then a disgraced emblem of Panama, Eleta and the Torrijos regime had their ideas about the best way to prepare for recouping national honor. The most original one was that Duran should do his training on Coiba, the largest island (194 square miles) in Central America, and whose development was largely limited to a penal colony that for decades generated horror stories of brutalized and murdered inmates. Within the remote, Devil's Island–like location there was a hierarchy of imprisonment: buildings with unbarred windows for the general population, escape deterrence left to the ever-present sharks around the island; and a maximum security facility for those deemed "especially dangerous" (mostly political prisoners). For almost two months Duran, his Panamanian trainers, and sparring partners were quartered in the four rooms of an administration building dubbed the "Torrijos Suite" because the General had once stayed there during an inspection tour. Although the living conditions were passable for anyone wanting to live in a penal colony, the training facilities were not. To remedy this, King contributed $25,000 to the government for converting an abandoned theater into a gymnasium. Supplies were brought every few days from Panama City by long-time Duran associate and interpreter Luis Henriquez, and the cooking was done by a Chinese inmate who happened to come from Duran's San Felipe district. Prisoners from the general population were allowed to watch the workouts as recreation.

All of this Arcel heard about long distance from Eleta and Henriquez, with the actual training left to the Panamanians on Coiba. The reports left him with some misgivings, and his first look at Duran with Henriquez and the trainers in Las Vegas two weeks before the bout confirmed that his apprehensions were well-founded. But when he warned them that they had so over-trained Duran he had become "stale," and that they needed to cut back on his workload at once, the trainers blew up, noting that they were the ones who had done all the serious conditioning on Coiba while Arcel had been in his Lexington Avenue apartment. Arcel backed down. "Since they had been in charge of his training up to that point, I had to accept their judgment so as not to create any dissension that would upset Duran. But I never changed my opinion — he had been over-trained."

The fight — a drowsy 15-round affair that was awarded to Benitez unanimously — didn't contradict Arcel's assessment. In language similar to that following Benny Leonard's last comeback appearance, Arcel allowed as how Duran "showed some of his early form in the opening rounds" and had done "as well as he could have under the circumstances," but that he should have taken his overall performance as reason for retiring once and for all. When Eleta made the same case to Duran, he was shown the door after all their years together. It was under completely different management that Duran, always in need of cash to support his extravagant life style, kept coming back after paying lip service to retirement. In 1983–84 he reigned as the junior middleweight champion, then in 1989 as the middleweight titlist. The new crowns didn't impress Arcel all that much. As far as he was concerned, there was the great lightweight champion of the 1970s and then there was all the rest. Duran finally retired in January 2002 at the age of 50, and only then largely because of injuries suffered in a car crash.

Arcel's association with Duran overshadowed the work he was doing

The long-retired Arcel takes a look at former charge Duran in the gym.

around the same time with Larry Holmes. He first seconded the heavy-weight in a March 1978 battle against Ernie Shavers that Holmes won by unanimous decision, putting him directly in line for a WBC title fight against Ken Norton three months later. When Holmes won that bout on a split decision, he might have been more surprised than any-body. Arcel: "Larry had it all in the ring, and I compared him a lot with Jack Sharkey. The one thing he seemed low on was self-confidence. I always had to give him a kick to make him realize how good he was. I think some of that came from the fact that Don King kept him around for so long as Muhammad Ali's sparring partner. He was looked at for so long as just the warm-up guy, he never really developed that sense of pride and confidence and feeling of belonging that a fighter needs. I always had to keep telling him, 'You're going to be long retired before people realize what a great fighter you are.' I guess I was also thinking that it would take that long for him to realize it, too."

Although Holmes was always keen to have Arcel backing him, not everybody around him was. In 1979, Richie Giachetti began breathing heavily when King insisted that both Arcel and Brown flank him in train-ing Holmes for a return match with Shavers, with the title on the line. As Giachetti told Dave Anderson:

> I said, "What do we need them for?" Don said, "You got to have names." ...
> Ray arrived a few days before the fight. So when we had our meeting, I told him and Freddie what I wanted Larry to do. Stick and move. Lateral movement. In and out. Don't clinch. Stay away from Ernie's big hand. As soon as I said that, Ray said, "No, you're wrong." I said, "What do you mean, no?" Ray said, "Larry's got to hate Shavers more." I said, "When we go into the ring, Larry would beat up his own mother if he had to." Ray said, "He's not talking bad about Shavers," and then he said, "I think Larry should go to the body more." I said, "Go to the body, huh? Well, Mr. Arcel, I have high respect for you, but if you go to the body, Mr. Arcel, what do you give away?" He said, "Your head." But now he got mad and said, "What do you think, that I don't know boxing? I've been in boxing seventy years." I said, "Mr. Arcel, what does Ernie Shavers do better than anybody else in boxing?" He got mad again and said, "Don't you think I know? He's the best puncher there is." I said, "Case closed. The meeting's over. I don't want to hear anything more out of you guys." I couldn't say anything about that to the newspapermen at the time because it would have been sour grapes. Ray Arcel is a great name.... I had to keep my mouth shut. I had to be humble.[1]

According to Jerry Izenberg, Giachetti had a lot to be humble about. "He always blamed King for bringing in Ray and Freddie, but I was the one who got that ball rolling. I'd watched Holmes fighting under Gia-chetti, and it was pretty clear that he had been getting through without a convincing jab. Getting through well, mind you, but still riding for a fall if he couldn't work on that part of his game. When I suggested to Ray he take a look at Holmes, he didn't want to hear about it at first. Nobody was more sensitive than Ray about stealing another trainer's fighter. But one day I brought Larry around to Ray's apartment, and he couldn't do anything about it. One thing led to another, and in the space of one afternoon Ray taught him 23 ways to use a jab, including how to deliberately miss with it. It was after that tutorial that Holmes went to King about Ray."[2]

Whatever the feelings his trainers had for one another, Holmes came out with a TKO victory in the eleventh round over Shavers — lengthening a string that would reach 48 straight wins from the start of his ring career in 1973. But Izenberg and Arcel weren't the only ones who had doubts about the Giachetti approach. So did Eddie Futch, whose training career intersected with Joe Frazier, Ken Norton, Michael Spinks, and just about every other significant heavyweight in the last part of the 20th century, and who would help set the stage for Arcel's swan song at the ring post. When Futch got his first look at Holmes training for the Shavers title fight, he told Anderson, "I didn't like it. He wasn't boxing his sparring partners, he was fighting them, slugging it out.... I told him, 'You're in great shape, Larry, but you're working wrong. Fighting your sparring partners isn't the way to get ready for Shavers.' He said, 'I can do that with these guys, but I don't intend to fight Shavers that way. I intend to box Shavers.' I said, 'But at some point in the fight you're going to do subconsciously what you're practicing here. If you do that with Shavers, you could be in trouble.' ... And Larry did just what I warned him he would do. He got knocked down by a right hand."[3]

At first, particularly in light of the victory over Shavers, Futch's observations were merely academic criticism. But when Holmes, who had his own whims where trainers were concerned, had a falling out with Giachetti some time later, it was to Futch he turned. And that made it easier when, once again, Arcel was brought in to back up the chief trainer, this time at Holmes's explicit request. "Unlike the last time at the Holmes camp, Eddie welcomed me. We'd been friends for many years and shared similar ideas about boxing. He really extended himself, and made what could have been an awkward situation a very rewarding experience. And we never had trouble communicating with Larry. He was gracious from start to finish, and I don't think we ever gave him crossed signals." The key to having two such high-powered trainers working side by side was Arcel's sense of correctness. "Whatever suggestions I had," he told Wohlgelernter, "I'd whisper them to Eddie before we went up into the corner between rounds. He could take them or not. He was the boss."[4]

Asked why he had asked for Arcel's help, Holmes told Ronald Fried: "It was the experience he had being around the fighters — all the great fighters, and training them — Roberto Duran — watching them work, getting to know them, liking them, and I wanted someone that knows boxing to talk boxing."[5] Although he didn't emphasize the word "talk," that was very much on his mind since, in conversations with friends, Holmes complained that, for all his ring expertise, Futch mumbled to the point of inaudibility, leaving the boxer often unsure of what he had been told. He would point to this problem a couple of years later in justifying his return to Giachetti.

What all the musical trainers were getting themselves into, meanwhile, was a fight shaping up as one of the ugliest in years, and only incidentally because of the fighters. Eight decades after Jack London had been looking around for a Great White Hope, the theme of Gerry Cooney's challenge to Holmes was exactly the same. As Arcel put it, "There were terrible racial tensions stirred up in the name of selling the fight. It was a very nasty situation. It was a throwback to experiences I'd had 50 years before, and I was amazed nothing had really changed in all that time."

Nobody was more responsible for pumping up the tensions than King, who led Holmes and Cooney from city to city for a series of press conferences aimed at underlining a color battle. At his drollest, Holmes could admit that "give me eight black guys in the ring and I make ten dollars. Give me Gerry Cooney and I make $10 million."[6] But when he wasn't cut off at the media meetings for ridiculing the thrust of the promotion, he also emphasized that when "I look at Gerry Cooney, I don't see a white man, a black man, or a Spaniard. I just see some guy trying to take my head off."[7] That wasn't the desired motif, though, not with sports books reporting unprecedented action one way or the other, Hollywood stars such as Sylvester Stallone falling over themselves to get photographed with Cooney, and *Time* magazine putting the challenger on the cover with "Rocky," with some editorial drooling about the social significance of the June 11, 1982, bout at Caesar's Palace (it had originally been slated for March but put off because of Cooney back problems).[8]

For all of Arcel's deference to Futch, there was one snag in the training that reflected his outlook more than that of the chief trainer: weight. Holmes was just as obsessed with pounds as Arcel was, despite Futch's regularly expressed alarm that he should have been concentrating on other things during his training. As the corner man told Anderson:

> He had a fixation about it, and he was lucky it didn't cost him ... with Cooney....
> He was up around 219, 221 until the last week, then I brought him down to
> 217. I figured that with two days of rest, he would weigh 218, 219, a good
> weight for him. He worked well at that weight. And it was hot, it was June in
> Vegas, so two days before the fight I knocked off the roadwork. The fight was
> Friday, but I told him not to run Wednesday morning and Thursday morning.
> But on Wednesday morning he got up and ran anyway in all that heat. He
> wanted his weight to be 213. At the weigh-in on Thursday, when Larry was
> called to get up on the scales, he kept his running suit on. Right away that told
> me he had run and didn't want me to know about it. Sure enough, he weighed
> 212½ with his running suit on. His real weight was probably 210, 211. Too
> light, much too light.[9]

But Futch didn't raise the subject. "There was nothing I could do about it at that point except try to compensate for it during the fight itself. I told him, 'Stay in the center of the ring as much as possible and use that good jab. Look for your shot. Stay off the ropes and out of the corners. This kid's got a good left hook, especially to the body.' ...I didn't want Larry hit in the body with shots that would take his legs away from him."[10]

Arcel accented the positive, helped by all the idle time Cooney had accumulated for more than a year, while Holmes had been fighting regularly. "It wasn't much of a secret that Cooney's trainer Victor Vallee liked only sure things and convinced his manager Dennis Rappaport that it was better to wait for an easy mark than take on somebody who might prove to be difficult. That had added up to a long wait before the Holmes fight. I pointed that out to Larry, reminding him that even Primo Carnera, who also depended on easy opponents, at least had fought a good 80 times before going for the title. To me, Cooney was absolutely inexperienced."[11]

The planned strategies and historical reassurances might have been sufficient for an orthodox match, but there was little that was orthodox about the Holmes-Cooney encounter. By the time the fight got started,

Caesar's Palace was more armory than arena. Police uniforms were to be seen everywhere, and the ones that weren't to be seen were on sniper duty at strategic elevated positions around the ring. The publicity campaign ignited by King and enthusiastically endorsed by Rappaport had been so successful that both white supremacist and black power groups put in an appearance, toting their rhetoric along with them. Given the hysteria whipped up around the bout, what took place in the ring was hardly surprising.[11]

By Arcel's count, Cooney fouled Holmes eight times; worse, the referee did nothing to stop it. "It was the most racially promoted fight I ever remember," he told Anderson. "I always had great respect for Mills Lane as a referee, but the night of that fight Mills became an Irishman." He added in his memoir: "In all his previous fights Cooney had never landed a foul punch. In this fight he immediately started to use foul tactics.... One time his low blow landed on Larry's cup. You could tell it was deliberate. At one point even Lane had to give Larry a five-minute rest and warn Cooney."[12]

As obvious as some of the fouls were, Futch was more concerned with Holmes wearing down from his secret weight loss. To that end his strategy for all the early rounds was to jab and move and box, not get into a slugging swap that would run him down. Holmes held up, and after a tenth-round blow that staggered Cooney, Futch smelled the finish line. "Before the twelfth round I said, 'Now go out and get him.' I knew Cooney didn't have much left, but I still didn't want Larry to get into a punch-out because he was already down too low. With that heat sapping his weight and strength I didn't want Cooney to be able to come on and catch him at a disadvantage."[13]

The bout ended in the thirteenth round when Vallee came to the aid of his beaten fighter by throwing in the towel. For Holmes it was the 40th of his 48 straight wins. For Arcel it was the last of hundreds of wins.

26

After the Ring

Ray Arcel was 83 years old when he put the Holmes-Cooney fight behind him. As a trainer, as a TV producer, as a promoter, and as a company representative, he had seen hundreds of American cities and a few European ones. What he had rarely done, though, was to travel without an agenda — without the fighter who had to be accompanied to an appointment in the ring, without the telecast plans that had to be nailed down locally, without the merchandise that had to be bought or sold. Now, though, through Spain, England, France, Italy, and Israel, at regular intervals through the 1980s, his only agenda was his own curiosity. "It was the quality in him that attracted me from the first time I met him in San Francisco," his wife Steve recalled. "He was curious about everything. Even when we went to Israel, it wasn't like he thought he was on some religious pilgrimage. He just wanted to *know* about Jerusalem and Masada and the other things we saw. It wasn't *his* Jerusalem, not in the way a lot of religious people think about it. He might have observed the High Holy Days, but he wasn't what I would call fervent. For Ray, Jerusalem was in the world, so he should have known about it."[1]

To illustrate her point, Steve said that while they were at the Wailing Wall a fire broke out and the fire department had to be called. "But it took them forever to get in there with their hoses and equipment because somebody pointed out they weren't all wearing yamulkas and they couldn't go any further until they were. Some of the people around us thought that was proper, but Ray and I thought it was funny as hell."

Even in Israel, though, he wasn't just another tourist. "We were in a market in Jericho, and suddenly one of the merchants looks at him and goes T-E-L-E-V-I-S-I-O-N T-E-L-E-V-I-S-I-O-N! D-U-R-A-N D-U-R-A-N! Before we knew it, there was this small crowd of people around us. They recognized him from the Duran fights and started waving papers for autographs. Ray was terribly moved, and he stood there for I-don't-know-how-long signing his name and getting his picture taken."

What he was moved by in a different way was a bullfight in Spain. Steve Arcel: "Spain to me had always meant Goya and flamenco and bullfights, so I thought we had to take it all in. I really wanted to see a bullfight when we were in Andalusia. Ray didn't act all that enthusiastic, but he didn't say no and we went to the Puerto Banus Marbella. All the spectacle at the beginning was breath-taking, but the closer it got to the moment of truth, the more uncomfortable I became. Ray wasn't just uncomfortable, he was outraged! For him it was nothing but brutality, and he had tears in his eyes when the bull was killed. As far as he was concerned, what we had paid to see was nothing more than senseless violence."

A trip more to his liking was to London, where he appeared as the surprise guest of surprise guests in a *This Is Your Life* episode devoted to Jackie Berg. Both on camera and off, Berg made it clear that Arcel's appearance was the highlight of the show for him. "All the old stories came out," according to Steve Arcel, "or at least the ones Jackie wanted his wife and daughter to hear."

When he wasn't abroad, Arcel was displaying more of that curiosity in going to the theater, museums, and photo galleries in Manhattan. "One night, we went to see this musical about the songs of Jacques Brel," Izenberg remembered. "And as we're sitting there taking it in, I look over at Ray and see how absorbed he is in it all, and it occurs to me that there probably wasn't another boxing trainer in the world who would have been sitting there for that show. Trainers and Jacques Brel just didn't mix!"[2]

Aside from Izenberg, Arcel's most frequent contacts through his retirement years were *Daily News* cartoonist Bill Gallo and writer Bill Heinz, whom the Arcels visited several times at his Vermont home. Both made liberal use of the Arcel lore in their writings. When even Izenberg had heard some of the old stories once too often, he organized little afternoon trips:

> There was this one time in particular that I got him to come along to see the heavyweight Ray Mercer working out. He was retired, out of the game for years, but even then he was very scrupulous about making sure it was all right

with Mercer's trainer, that nobody got the impression he was there to poach on the guy's fighter. No problem. We meet Mercer, Ray wishes him luck. Then he notices Al Cole, the cruiserweight, working out on the heavy bag. He watches for a few minutes, then politely goes over to Cole and introduces himself. Cole has heard of him, of course, but maybe only vaguely. Then Ray says, "Would you mind if I suggest something?" Cole says no. You could see it coming because where Arcel was concerned, it was always about the jab. There's this little girl standing there, Cole's niece, and Ray turns to her and says, "Could you do me a favor? Could you tell your uncle to buy a long floor mirror and every morning, first thing he does when he gets up, could you tell him to stand in front of that mirror and throw 500 jabs?"

Arcel's own reward for the day came when the boxer indicated that the trainer's name was much more familiar to him than the length of his history. "'How old do you think I am,' Ray asked Cole. And Cole acts a little nervous, but finally comes out and guesses 'in your sixties.' Ray loved it, absolutely loved it, when he could shock the guy by saying, 'You're 20 years off.'"[3]

For those who did know that he had been in the game for sixty-five years and had trained an estimated two thousand fighters in that

With wife Stephanie at the 1986 Boxing Writers Dinner.

time, there were more logical acknowledgements. In 1982, *Ring* magazine elected him to its Hall of Fame. Nine years later he would collect another plaque from the International Boxing Hall of Fame. At least as important as either of those honors, however, was the opening of the Ray Arcel Medical Center, a diagnostic clinic in the Times Square area operated by Ring 8 of the Veteran Boxers Association chapter for New York and New Jersey. Although the clinic itself could not provide therapies, it offered full examinations free of charge and recommended next steps. For Arcel, the center was making the best of a horrible situation that had been allowed to fester far too long. "We know the clinic is just a drop in the bucket. Years ago, insurance should have been provided for boxers by promoters and state commissions. Some sort of pension plan should have been in place for boxers when they were retired, including health benefits. But there's too much political control in boxing, and it's always been in one direction. There are no unions like there are in baseball. The boxer has absolutely no financial protection, and the people who run the sport have always acted like that's the normal way of things, so why bother changing them?"

Arcel's own first noticeable physical problem was with his hearing. Already in his 1983 interview for the American Jewish Committee, Elli Wohlgelernter was forced to repeat several questions for understanding. But if he began losing his hearing, according to Izenberg, he never lost the *look*—glacial disapproval that required no subtitles. "I first saw it with Steve. She had a way of using salty language that he didn't think was right for a woman. He seldom had to say anything when she let loose with some four-letter word, just glance over at her. I know how uncomfortable that can feel because one day he was coming to visit and I drove down to the train station to pick him up. Let's say that since I'd seen him last I'd let myself go a little, about 20 pounds worth of letting go. He comes down from the train and before we even say hello, he throws me the look. I got rid of that weight real fast."[4]

In 1988, Arcel was diagnosed with leukemia. It wasn't long before the man who prided himself on sprinting with his boxers and walking five miles back and forth with his wife to attend a gallery opening was restricted to a wheelchair. He still carried on for years, very conscious of his role in boxing and more than willing to take up Steve's suggestion for a memoir recapitulating the major moments in his career. Then, after on-and-off periods of battling his cancer, usually at Beth Israel Hospital, he was admitted to the facility's hospice in early 1994. Steve recalled denying the significance of that step to herself until she asked Arcel's doctor one day when she would be able to take him home and received the sharply enunciated reply of "You won't *be* taking him home." Death came the first week of March, at the age of 94. A paid memorial notice in the *New York Times* declared: "Deceased 3/7/94. My beloved husband and best friend. You gave new meaning to the word humanity, and you live forever in my heart. Stephanie."[5]

Arcel's ashes were buried in an estate known as Vagabond Farm, not too far from Frenchtown, Pennsylvania, in Bucks County. "It was a long story why there," Steve said. "When I had been much younger, I loved a poem by Don Blanding called 'Vagabond House.' '*When I have a house as I sometimes may/I'll suit my fancy in every way....*' Anyway, I got to know this couple who were very well off. He was one of the first people to use containers in shipping. A real tycoon. And they heard so much from me about 'Vagabond House' that when they bought this huge tract of land in Pennsylvania, they decided to call it Vagabond Farm. Ray and I went there quite a lot, and he really loved it. So that seemed like the ideal place for burying his ashes."

The Central Park bench Stephanie bought to honor her late husband.

But not the ideal place for planting trees. "The idea was to have a tree marking the spot, but it never grew. So I thought of something else."

What Steve Arcel thought of was to pay the Central Park Conservatory for a Fifth Avenue bench dedicated to her late husband. And there the bench sits today at 61st Street, only a low wall away from where Arcel jogged with hundreds of fighters up and down, up and down.

Epilogue

Much of the Ray Arcel story, as he recounted it, had an historicist tinge: His career had to have evolved the way it had simply because it had. In coming under the World War I–period influences of Benny Valgar, Dai Dollings, and Doc Bagley, he had fused teenage drive with precocious accomplishment, and that was that. Alternatives, such as the doctor his father had wanted him to be, had never been seriously contemplated, either when they might have been seen in a practical way or in an adult melancholy of missed opportunities. Regrets were always too late, not to say irrelevant to what had taken place. Tough times made monkeys eat red peppers.

But those early influences in Billy Grupp's gym also meant committing from the youngest plausible age to the "code," that unwritten constitution that regulates all enterprises with as many dark rooms as lighted ones. Professional boxing, whether back before the Walker Law or in the age of capital letters in the cable TV alphabet, came with a skyscraper's complement of both kinds of rooms. The faster managers, trainers, and fighters accepted that, the sooner they were allowed at least to dream about the big time. Ray Arcel accepted that floor plan as much as anybody else. It could hardly have disoriented somebody who as a teenager had run Christmas deliveries for corrupt political boss Jimmy Hines and who, like most street kids, liked believing in his own street canniness.

But turning a blind eye to the manipulative and the sordid was not what singled out Arcel, not even when, as with the assault in Boston, it had jeopardized his own life. More telling was how he spent much of his career trying to ignore the suspicious and outrageous while massaging thousands and thousands of muscles and preaching brain over brawn — and then balancing all that with a sense of personal rectitude that won

193

admiration from just about anybody exposed to him for more than a
break between rounds. No doubt some of the praise was self-serving —

writers who would have
had to examine their own
investigative thorough-
ness and satisfaction with
glib one-liners if they
questioned too much the
representative of the insti-
tution they wanted to be
exceptional. But that was
secondary to Arcel's belief
in himself and to the rigor
with which he insisted
that his sense of morality
was defined not by box-
ing as such but by the
fighters in his charge.
There was no denying
the contradictions, even
self-delusions, in such a
posture, particularly for
somebody hailed by those
closest to him for his
curiosity in so many mat-
ters outside the ring. But

Arcel at home in his final year.

it was what he needed in order to get on with it all.

What he got on with, of course, was an amazing record training
one champion after another in one weight division after another. None
of this was without cost, even within his private notions of priorities.
Not only were there his family estrangements and discomfits, but also
what he couldn't help but consider a betrayal by a fighter he considered
his son of sons. Ray Arcel hurt a lot; it just wasn't for others to know it.
That was part of the code, too, and it was his as much as that of the profession that has never celebrated choice.

Arcel as Medic

In response to a question from *Look* magazine, Arcel displayed the contents of the bag he carried around while seconding fighters. In the magazine's issue of September 23, 1941, he revealed the contents as:

1. Sangasan for arresting nasal haemorrhages.
2. Hemostatic, a blood-clotting agent.
3. Iodine.
4. Venom solution for clotting blood without caking.
5. Monsell's solution, a last resort blood coagulant that cakes and must be cut off a wound.
6. Hydrogen peroxide antiseptic.
7. Adrenalin chloride for stopping bleeding.
8. Extra-strength ammonia for backing up smelling salts.
9. Aromatic spirits of ammonia, administered with water as a stimulant or for settling a queasy stomach.
10. Smelling salts capsules.
11. Rosin, for fighter's shoes.
12. Collodion, for coating a wound.
13. Monsell's powder, a variation on Monsell's solution, used in a paste form mixed with adrenalin chloride.

Arcelisms

Whether speaking with his fighters or with newspaper people, Arcel was given to passing along aphorisms, bromides, or mere clichés that he counted on for summing up his attitude toward a given situation. Among those most repeated over the years were:

- Hard times make monkeys eat red peppers.
- To rest is to rust.
- No one has a contract with God.
- Don't confuse kindness with weakness.
- Boxing is brain over brawn.
- Never overestimate yourself or underestimate the other guy.
- For money you get honey.
- If you can learn to win, you can learn to lose.
- A quitter never wins and a winner never quits.
- Don't be a district attorney [on being asked too many questions].
- When you lose your head, you lose the best part of your body.
- You are what you eat.
- Chew but don't swallow.

Another mantra was saved for one of his fighters in danger of losing a bout. From Abe Goldstein to Larry Holmes, he sent his charges back to the center of the ring with the incredulous "Are you going to let him take away your championship?"

Chapter Notes

Chapter 1

1. Among those who have incorporated this Liebling observation into their discussion of Arcel is Ronald Fried in his book *Corner Men: Great Boxing Trainers* (New York: Four Walls Eight Windows, 1991), p. 56.
2. Interview with author.
3. Interview with author.
4. Interview with author.

Chapter 2

1. Mike McCormick, *Terre Haute: Queen City of the Wabash* (Charleston SC: Arcadia, 2005), p. 63.
2. Nick Salvatore, *Eugene V. Debs: Citizen and Socialist* (Urbana: University of Illinois Press, 2007).
3. McCormick, p. 69.
4. Author's interview with local historian Mike McCormick.
5. On October 11, 1983, Arcel sat down with interviewer Elli Wohlgelernter for the first of two long audio-taped interviews (10 cassette sides adding up to several hours) as part of a series on "Jews in Sports" being gathered by the American Jewish Committee (AJC). The second session was held on November 8, 1983. Although the material largely reiterated the stories and attitudes Arcel had shared with newspaper columnists over the years, it also contained nuances, sometimes merely vocal, not always evident in the frequently paraphrased accounts that appeared in print. Moreover, thanks to Wohlgelertner's insistence, Arcel elaborated on some personal and family episodes that he had managed to sidestep elsewhere. Subsequent references to the AJC are to these two lengthy interviews.
6. AJC interview with Wohlgelernter.
7. Ibid.
8. Interview with author.
9. Author interviews with family members, see note 1, chapter10 below.
10. Author interviews with Stanley Teitel, principal of Stuyvesant High School, and Henry Greenberg, director of the school's alumni association.

Chapter 3

1. Kenneth T. Jackson, *The Encyclopedia of New York City* (New Haven: Yale University Press, 1995), p. 1059.
2. John Jarrett, *Champ in the Corner: The Ray Arcel Story* (Stroud: Stadia, 2007), p. 15.
3. AJC interview with Wohlgelernter.
4. Ibid. (also paraphrased in his memoir).
5. Ibid. (also paraphrased in his memoir).
6. Fried, p. xvi.
7. Dave Anderson, *In the Corner: Great Boxing Trainers Talk About Their Art* (New York: William Morrow, 1991), p. 150.

Chapter 4

1. "T.A. Gillespie Company Shell Loading Plant Explosion," Wikipedia.com.
2. AJC interview with Wohlgelernter.
3. Jordan Sprechman, *This Day in New York Sports* (Champaign, IL: Sports Museum Press, 1998), p. 60.
4. AJC interview with Wohlgelernter, in his memoir, and in Fried and Anderson, among other places.
5. Budd Schulberg, *The Harder They Fall* (New York: Random House), 1947, p. 36.
6. Fried, p. 37.
7. Ibid., p. 38.
8. Ibid., p. 39.
9. Anderson, p. 174.
10. Fried, p. 38.

Chapter 6

1. In his memoir Arcel admits to never being completely on top of the name game where Genaro was concerned.
2. Hyman R. Segal, *They Called Him Champ* (New York: Citadel, 1959), p. 149.
3. AJC interview.
4. Segal, p. 101.
5. Although his memoir provides the most details about this clash with Rosenberg, Arcel told parts of the story to many columnists, including Jerry Izenberg in the New York *Post*, August 31, 1982.
6. Segal, pp. 84–87.
7. AJC interview with Wohlgelernter.

Chapter 7

1. "Stephen T. McDonald," BoxRec Boxing Encyclopedia.
2. John Tebbel, *The Media in America* (New York: Mentor Books, 1974), p. 392.
3. John Tebbel, "Curiosities and Calamities of the Big Tunney-Dempsey Scrap," *Literary Digest*, October 8, 1927, p. 63.

Chapter 8

1. Jarrett, p. 74.
2. *New York Times*, February 26, 1920.
3. *New York Journal-American*, February 24, 1945.
4. Ibid.

Chapter 9

1. Cited by Fried (p. 202) who says the paper, found among Bimstein's possessions after his death, could not be identified.
2. Attributed by Fried (p. 191) to Harold Conrad, but with no indication whether it was conversational or printed remark.
3. John Harding with Jack Berg, *Jack "Kid" Berg: The Whitechapel Windmill* (London: Robson Books, 1987), pp. 40–43.
4. Ibid., p. 20.
5. Ibid., p. 101.
6. *The Ring*, June 1929.
7. Berg biography, Wikipedia.
8. Harding, p. 130.
9. Ibid., p. 153.

Chapter 10

1. Interview with author.
2. AJC interview with Wohlgelernter.
3. Interview with author.
4. Interview with author.
5. Anderson, p. 147.
6. AJC interview with Wohlgelernter.
7. Ibid.
8. Ibid.
9. Interview with author.
10. Interview with author.
11. Interview with author.

Chapter 11

1. Paul R. Kavleff, *The Purple Gang: Organized Crime in Detroit, 1910–1945* (Fort Lee, NJ: Barricade Books, 2000).
2. BoxRec Boxing Encyclopedia.
3. *Time*, October 5, 1925.
4. *The Ring*, November 1931.
5. *Jews in Sports.org/profile*.
6. AJC interview with Wohlgelernter.
7. *The Ring*, November 1932.
8. *New York Sun*, October 6, 1932.
9. Bud Greenspan, "It Was as a Ref That Unbeaten Champ Benny Leonard Met His End in the Ring," *Sports Illustrated*, May 31, 1976.

Chapter 12

1. Allen Bodner, *When Boxing Was a Jewish Sport* (Westport, CT: Praeger, 1997, p. 113.
2. Ibid., p. 112.

Chapter 13

1. Ross himself recounted much of his life in *No Man Stands Alone* (Philadelphia: Lippincott, 1957). In 2006, Douglas Century published a full-scale biography covering the boxer's entire life entitled simply *Barney Ross* (New York: Shocken).
2. Arcel goes into detail in his memoir about his relationship with Yarosz, as does Jarrett, pp. 94–98.
3. Jarrett, p. 129.
4. Ibid.

Chapter 14

1. Fried, p. 190.
2. *New York Daily News*, September 15, 1985.
3. Fried, p. 190.
4. Ibid., p. 211.
5. *New York Journal American*, June 20, 1948.
6. BoxRec Boxing Encyclopedia.
7. Fried, p. 211.
8. Most of the Galento lore has been collected in Joseph Monninger, *Two Ton: One Fight, One Night, Tony Galento v. Joe Louis* (Hanover, NH: Steerforth, 2006).
9. *New York Journal-American*, June 20, 1948.
10. AJC interview with Wohlgelernter.
11. Ibid.

Chapter 15

1. Anderson, p. 128.
2. W.C. Heinz, "It Was Like a Light Bulb Busted in Your Brain," *TV Guide*, November 19, 1988.
3. *The Ring*, April 1940.
4. New York *World Telegram*, January 10, 1942.
5. AJC interview with Wohlgelernter.
6. Budd Schulberg, *Ringside: A Treasury of Boxing Reportage* (Chicago: Ivan B. Dee, 2006), p. 266.
7. *New York Journal-American*, July 2, 1946.
8. *New York Post*, August 30, 1989.

Chapter 16

1. AJC interview with Wohlgelernter.
2. Ibid.
3. AJC interview with Wohlgelernter.

4. Interview with author.
5. AJC interview with Wohlgelernter.
6. AJC interview with Wohlgelernter.

Chapter 17

1. BoxRec Boxing Encyclopedia.
2. Ibid.
3. Ibid.
4. Fried, p. 330.
5. As recorded by Bill Gallo in the New York *Daily News*, November 6, 1988.

Chapter 18

1. Jeffrey T. Sammons, *Beyond the Ring: The Role of Boxing in American Society* (Urbana: University of Illinois Press, 1988), p. 37.
2. Sammons, p. 44.
3. Ibid., p. 46.
4. Ibid., p. 98.
5. *New Orleans Times-Picayune*, June 21, 1936.
6. Anderson, p. 130.
7. AJC interview with Wohlgelernter.
8. Ibid.

Chapter 19

1. IMDb.com biography and Ephraim Katz, *The Film Encyclopedia* (New York: Thomas Y. Crowell, 1979).
2. Fried, p. 82.
3. *New York Times,* March 25, 1942.
4. There are numerous accounts of Louis's tax troubles throughout boxing literature. One of the most concise is in Sammons, p. 239.
5. AJC interview with Wohlgelernter.
6. Ibid.
7. *Detroit News*, February 1, 1945.
8. *New York Daily News*, February 24, 1946.
9. AJC interview with Wohlgelernter.

Chapter 20

1. AJC interview with Wohlgelernter.
2. *Boxing and Wrestling*, April 1960.
3. AJC interview with Wohlgelernter.
4. *New York Post*, February 1, 1952.

Chapter 21

1. AJC interview with Wohlgelernter.
2. Jarrett, p. 197.

3. Ibid., p. 198.
4. Ibid., p. 199.
5. Ibid.
6. Sammons, p. 149.
7. AJC interview with Wohlgelernter.
8. *The Ring*, March 1953.
9. Jarrett, p. 201.
10. Anderson, p. 137.
11. *New York Daily Mirror*, October 2, 1953.
12. AJC interview with Wohlgelernter.
13. Ibid.
14. Sammons, p. 171.
15. AJC interview with Wohlgelernter.
16. Fried, p. xxv.

Chapter 22

1. AJC interview with Wohlgelernter.
2. Ibid.
3. *New York Daily News*, March 8, 1951.
4. Interview with author.
5. *Purchasing Week*, August 10, 1954.
6. Harry Kessler, *The Millionaire Referee* (St. Louis: Harkess, 1982), p. 242.
7. Kessler, p. 243.
8. Sammons, pp. 156–176.
9. AJC interview with Wohlgelernter.
10. George A. Barton, *A Lifetime in Sports* (Minneapolis: The Olympic Press, 1957).
11. *New York Daily Mirror*, October 2, 1953.
12. *Sports Illustrated*, April 2, 1956.
13. Sammons, p. 173.

Chapter 23

1. *New York Times*, June 7, 2011.
2. Interview with author.
3. AJC interview with Wohlgelernter (among other places).
4. Interview with author.
5. *Sports Illustrated*, January 30, 1978.
6. Interview with author.
7. Fried, p. 61.
8. AJC interview with Wohlgelernter.
9. Interview with author.
10. *New York Times*, June 27, 1972.
11. Los Angeles *Times*, December 5, 1989.
12. Anderson, p. 81.
13. Fried, p. 99.
14. *Inside Sports*, June 30, 1980.
15. He admitted as much in his AJC interview with Wohlgelernter.

Chapter 24

1. Interview with author.
2. *New York Times*, June 21, 1979.
3. Interview with author.
4. Interview with author.
5. Cosell's blurt was widely commented upon at the time, and may now be heard on YouTube transmissions of the bout.
6. Every sports section in the country carried extended coverage of the fight on November 26, 1980.
7. Fried (p. 284) cites the "cramps" excuse as one of the major reasons for the falling out between Arcel and Brown, with the latter claiming that he was the one who came up with the story and who felt betrayed when Arcel and Eleta, among others, dismissed it publicly.
8. Izenberg in the New York *Post* on November 25, 1980, Berkow in the *New York Times* on April 13, 1987.
9. *Sports Illustrated*, December 8, 1980.
10. See note 6, this chapter.
11. Anderson, p. 142.
12. Interview with author.
13. Jarrett, p. 212.
14. AJC interview with Wohlgerlenter.
15. New York *Daily News*, December 6, 1989.

Chapter 25

1. Anderson, p. 266.
2. Interview with author
3. Anderson, p. 251.
4. AJC interview with Wohlgelernter.
5. Fried, p. 106.
6. Unsourced Wikiquote.
7. Unsourced Wikiquote.
8. The weekly's June 14, 1982, cover coupled the Las Vegas fight against Holmes with Stallone's popularity, running the headline "Boxing Scores One-Two Punch at the Box Office."
9. Anderson, pp. 251–252.
10. Ibid, p. 252.
11. *New York Daily News*, June 11, 1982, and June 12, 1982.
12. Anderson, p. 142.
13. Ibid., p. 252.

Chapter 26

1. Interview with author.
2. Interview with author.
3. Interview with author.
4. Interview with author.
5. *New York Times*, March 7, 1994.

Bibliography

Anderson, Dave. *In the Corner: Great Boxing Trainers Talk About Their Art*. New York: William Morrow, 1991.

Barton, George A. *My Lifetime in Sports*. Minneapolis: The Olympic Press, 1957.

Bodner, Allen. *When Boxing Was a Jewish Sport*. Westport, CT: Praeger, 1997.

Brenner, Teddy. *Only the Ring Was Square*. Englewood Cliffs, NJ: Prentice-Hall, 1981.

Century, Douglas. *Barney Ross*. New York: Shocken, 2006.

Fried, Ronald K. *Corner Men: Great Boxing Trainers*. New York: Four Walls Eight Windows, 1991.

Gipe, George. *The Great American Sports Book*. Garden City, NY: Doubleday, 1978.

Gorn, Elliott J. *The Manly Art: Bare-Knuckle Prize Fighting in America*. Ithaca: Cornell University Press, 1986.

Harding, John, with Jack Berg. *Jack "Kid" Berg: The Whitechapel Windmill*. London: Robson Books, 1987.

Heinz, W.C., ed. *The Fireside Book of Boxing*. New York: Simon & Schuster, 1961.

Jackson, Kenneth T., ed. *The Encyclopedia of New York City*. New Haven: Yale University Press, 1995.

Jarrett, John. *Champ in the Corner: The Ray Arcel Story*. Stroud: Stadia, 2007.

Katz, Ephraim. *The Film Encyclopedia*. New York: Thomas Y. Crowell, 1979.

Kavleff, Paul R. *The Purple Gang: Organized Crime in Detroit, 1910–1945*. Fort Lee, NJ: Barricade Books, 2000.

Kessler, Harry, as told to Alma Kessler and Robert Suhosky. *The Millionaire Referee*. St. Louis: Harkness, 1982.

Liebling, A.J. *The Sweet Science*. New York: Simon & Schuster, 1986.

McCormick, Mike. *Terre Haute: Queen City of the Wabash*. Charleston, SC: Arcadia, 2005.

Monninger, Joseph. *Two Ton: One Fight, One Night, Tony Galento v. Joe Louis*. Hanover, NH: Steerforth, 2006.

Rader, Benjamin G. *American Sports: From the Age of Folk Games to the Age of Spectators*. Englewood Cliffs, NJ: Prentice-Hall, 1983.

Ross, Barney. *No Man Stands Alone*. Philadelphia: Lippincott, 1957.

Ross, Ron. *Bummy Davis Vs. Murder, Inc.: The Rise and Fall of the Jewish Mafia and an Ill-Fated Prizefighter*. New York: St. Martin's, 2003.

Rotella, Carlo. *Cut Time*. Boston: Houghton Mifflin, 2003.

Salvatore, Nick. *Eugene V. Debs: Citizen and Socialist*. Urbana: University of Illinois Press, 2007.

Sammons, Jeffrey T. *Beyond the Ring: The Role of Boxing in American Society*. Urbana: University of Illinois Press, 1988.

Schulberg, Budd. *The Harder They Fall*. New York: Random House, 1947.

_____. *Ringside: A Treasury of Boxing Reportage*. Chicago: Ivan R. Dee, 2006.

Segal, Hyman R. *They Called Him Champ: The Story of Champ Segal and His Fabulous Era*. New York: The Citadel Press, 1959.

Sprechman, Jordan. *This Day in New York Sports*, Champaign, IL: Sports Museum Press, 1998.

Tebbel, John. *The Media in America*. New York: Mentor Books, 1974.

Interviews

Arcel, Stephanie. Various dates.

Bloch, Clement. September 14, 2008.

Bloch, Jill. June 5, 2008.

Clancy, Gil. September 14, 2009.

Gallo, Bill. October 13, 2008.

Grossberg, Henry. February 24, 2011.

Izenberg, Jerry. August 20, 2009, and July 6, 2011.

Kessler, Fran. August 23, 2010, and March 15, 2011.

Libero, Lila. May 30, 2008.

McCormick, Mike. June 13, 2007, and February 18, 2009.

Molloy, Susan. May 21, 2008, and February 18, 2011.

Teitel, Stanley. February 20, 2011.

Turtletaub, Saul. August 17, 2008.

Index